ALBERTA
THE PIONEER YEARS

TO KNOW TO UNDERSTAND TO PARTICIPATE
THE CANADIAN HERITAGE IS YOUR HERITAGE

**ALBERTA HERITAGE
LEARNING RESOURCES
PROJECT**

A Project of Alberta Education
Funded
By
The Alberta Heritage Savings Trust Fund
and
Dedicated to the Students
of Alberta
by the
Government of Alberta
1979

We acknowledge the co-operation
of the publishers and authors in
including their works in the Alberta Heritage collection.

MEMBERS OF THE SELECTION COMMITTEE

William F. Lockhart/*Managing Editor, Alberta Education*
Leslie L. Aitken/*Alberta Education*
Louis Burke/*Lethbridge Separate School District*
Heather-Belle Dowling/*County of Strathcona Municipal Library*
Shirley I. Paustian/*Edmonton Public School District*
Hilda Ross/*Freelancer and Instructor of Creative Writing*
John N. White/*East Smoky School Division*

David Shaw & Associates Ltd./*Project Cover Design*

ALBERTA

THE PIONEER YEARS

HAROLD FRYER

Our generation passeth away, and another generation cometh;
But the earth abideth forever.

Ecclesiastes 1-4

STAGECOACH

STAGECOACH PUBLISHING CO. LTD.
P.O. Box 3399, Langley, B.C. V3A 4R7

Typesetting, layout and design by
Mainland Graphics Ltd., Langley, B.C.

Canadian Cataloguing in Publication Data

Fryer, Harold, 1923-
    Alberta

    Bibliography: p.
    ISBN 0-88983-012-6 bd.
    ISBN 0-88983-014-2 pa.

    1. Frontier and pioneer life - Alberta.
2. Alberta - History. 3. Alberta -
Biography. I. Title.
FC 3661.F79   971.23   C77-002217-0
F1076

Contents

This book is dedicated to the trailblazers and
pioneers who contributed so greatly to make this
province the finest in the country.

ALBERTA

THE PIONEER YEARS

In just over a century, Alberta has blossomed from "North West Territory" to booming, industrialized province. Where, but a few years ago, only the Indian, buffalo and fur trader roamed the land, modern cities and communities have appeared, muskeg and rivers have been tamed by gravel and steel, and paved highways form a commercial lifeline where only the ubiquitous Red River cart had dared.

But not everything has changed. For Alberta is yet a frontier province, its people pioneers of the twentieth century. As such, it is natural for them to show an appreciation for those who ushered the province into the atomic age.

Some of these pioneers have won immortality. Kootenai Brown, the amazing soldier, prospector, buffalo hunter, wolfer, and murderer, founded a national park and is so honored. Jerry Potts, the "dead shot and plainsman without parallel" who contributed so greatly to the establishing of the North West Mounted Police, is remembered as Canada's own Davy Crockett. The Mounties and their westward march to do battle with the evil whisky traders is standard reading for Canadian students.

But so many have not been remembered; or if they have, only to the point of being mentioned in old records. This is a tragedy of no small magnitude, and in this volume the author has attempted to shed new life on many of these overlooked heroes and heroines of Alberta's past. Ma Brainard's fabulous food was known around the world. Who remembers her today? Who has heard of her?

There are so many others: Sam Livingston was not only Calgary's first citizen but one of its most colorful. Single-handedly, Martin Nordegg defied the experts and founded a coal-mining industry and town. He was courageous, far-sighted and a generous and respected employer who suffered as an enemy alien during the First World War. The Canadian government recognized his loyalty to his new land by granting him unlimited freedom and would have permitted him to take out citizenship. Yet Nordegg waited until after Armistice to become a Canadian citizen, as he thought that to have done so during the war would have been the easy way.

Alex Monkman discovered the mountain pass that today bears his name. Despite the valiant effort of Peace River residents prior to the Second World War, no highway yet follows this route through the Rockies to British Columbia. But someday Monkman's dream will be fulfilled.

Then there was General Thomas Bland Strange, commander-in-chief of the Alberta Field Force during the Riel Rebellion. General Middleton not only won all the glory but $20,000 and a medal. Strange and his men received little more than a pat on the back for their efforts.

Alberta has known tragedy. There was the great Frank slide disaster, when Turtle Mountain collapsed and 90 million tons of rock buried the mining town. Tragedy struck again when the Hillcrest Mine disaster claimed 189 lives. Almost as dramatic were the days of Prohibition, when the province's "blue-coated Mounties" assumed the duties of the senior force and made Alberta a no-man's-land for lawbreakers. And Prohibition gave birth to its own heroes, villains and legends.

In short, Alberta has known every kind of adventure in its history. The days of the nomadic Indian tribes and of the great buffalo herds may be gone. But they most certainly should not be forgotten. *ALBERTA — The Pioneer Years* goes a long way towards seeing that this does not happen.

KOOTENAI BROWN
FRONTIERSMAN

*Pony Express rider, Indian fighter, wolfer, whisky trader,
big game guide, murderer — and founder of a park: this was the
amazing John George "Kootenai" Brown.*

TO write about Kootenai Brown is to give a pretty fair synopsis of the early days of the West. Prospector, buffalo hunter, mail carrier with the Pony Express, squaw man, Indian fighter, wolfer, whisky trader, Rocky Mountain Ranger, big game guide, scout and packer for the NWMP, forest ranger, park guardian—he was all those and a few more—including soldier and murderer. Furthermore, he lost none of his color in his later years when he wore a wide brimmed western hat over his shoulder-length, snow-white hair, bushy white moustache and fringed buckskin jacket and trousers that draped his gaunt frame. Only his clipped English accent belied any misconception that he was born and raised on the western prairie.

Who, then, was this walking enigma—this Old World-educated character who in his younger days was a wanton killer of wildlife when he travelled with a gang of wolfers on the prairies—this man who became a conservationist and helped found Waterton Lakes National Park?

Though dozens of stories have been written about his early years, most of them lacking in accuracy, thanks to Professor William Rodney in his book *Kootenai Brown*, much of the chaff has been winnowed from the wheat and we now have a clear picture. John George Brown was born in County Clare, Ireland, on September 13, 1839, the son of an Irish mother and an English father, James Montague Brown. Thanks to a strong-willed grandmother, John was accepted into the British Army and received his commission at the Military College at Sandhurst in 1858. Though some imaginative writers have given John Brown an Oxford and Cambridge education, there is no record of this. He did, however, obtain a better than average education from private tutors and his determined grandmother. There are stories of Brown serving with a Guards Regiment in Queen Victoria's Court,

but William Rodney has also shot this theory full of holes. He did not, as many have claimed, get posted to India for becoming too familiar with some of the good Queen's ladies-in-waiting.

He did, however, get posted to India in late 1858 in time to take part in the Indian Mutiny. Again there are stories of his many escapades while in India, including one that has him being given an elephant by a grateful Rajah for some outstanding favor. Another claims he was forced to flee to South America on a freight ship after quarrelling with and killing a fellow officer. Colorful reading, indeed, but not so, claims William Rodney. In fact there seems little evidence that John Brown's career in India was anything but run-of-the-mill. The mutiny was almost over when his regiment reached Calcutta and in 1860 he returned home to England. After a year in England, he sold his commission, left the army and embarked on a sailing ship for the goldfields of British Columbia and a completely new way of life.

Brown's travelling companion was Arthur Wellesley Vowell, a man destined to become, among other things, British Columbia's Gold Commissioner. Brown and Vowell were stranded for more than a week in Panama when the ship that was to take them to San Francisco failed to show. Consequently, they were broke when they reached San Francisco and had to work on the docks to raise passage for Victoria. There they had to work again to raise a grubstake for the Cariboo goldfields. As Brown later wrote: "Chopping poles in the vicinity kept me afloat during my stay of one winter...."

Brown, Vowell and the 5,000 or so hopefuls who headed into the Cariboo in 1863 to find their fortunes were doomed to disappointment. Although prospecting proved a poor venture, Brown stuck it out for two years, made $3,000 one winter by trapping, but lost it the following summer in a shaky

mining deal. In 1864 he had no more to show for his efforts than a host of yarns that probably grew better over the years through countless tellings.

"I had no money when I went into the Cariboo and none when I came out in 1864," he claimed. "But I had a little fortune for awhile in between… When I left Williams Creek I had 50 cents in my pocket; my clothes were in rags; I had no shirt and no socks, but I had a good pair of boots. When I got to Boston Bar, a little village on the Fraser River, I still had 50 cents in my pocket."

He was not broke for long. Upriver from Boston Bar is a 25-mile-long stretch of wild water. Brown made $6 a day and board working on boats on this length of the Fraser, but it was brutal work. Often when the rivermen could no longer track the boat—that is, haul it upriver by rope—they had to unload and carry the cargo upstream on their backs. The packers needed the strength of a horse, the agility of mountain goats and the tenacity of English bull-dogs. It was not the life for John Brown. When word came of a gold strike at Wild Horse Creek (now Fort Steele) in the East Kootenay, he was off to seek his fortune there.

Brown's luck at Wild Horse Creek as a prospector proved no better than it had in the Cariboo. Consequently, when he was offered a job as a police constable, he took it. His main claim to fame as a law enforcement officer came when he arrested Joseph Conklin, William Kirby and Ozias Harvey on a charge of passing several thousand dollars worth of bogus gold dust. He felt pretty proud of himself but quit the police force a month later when he received a reduction in pay.

He had another fling at prospecting when he staked a claim with four other miners. When they found "it was not panning out very well" they sold out to a company of Chinese for $500 and a horse, which Brown won in a bet.

"Having disposed of our holdings on the creek,"

wrote Brown, "the five of us packed through Kootenai Pass and soon after started for Edmonton, where we heard they were mining for gold on the Saskatchewan River. We had no clear idea where Edmonton was and there was no one to tell us."

Not surprisingly, they never reached their destination—at least not as a group. Quite possibly, though, somewhere along the route between Wild Horse Creek and where they emerged from the mountains in the Kootenai Lakes (now Waterton) district, the group had dealings with the Indian tribe from which Kootenai Brown derived his nickname. Since they started with only one horse and arrived in what is now Alberta with five, quite likely they got the other four from the Kootenai Indians.

When the group emerged from the mountains, they climbed a low ridge. According to Brown, "The prairies as far as we could see…was one living mass of buffalo. Thousands of head there were, far thicker than ever cattle grazed the bunch grass of the foothills."

As soon as Brown and his companions left the Rocky Mountains they were in the hunting grounds of the fierce Blackfoot tribes. These hostile warriors had allowed very few white men to enter their territory and Kootenai had been warned to be constantly alert for trouble. However, it was not until they had crossed some 250 miles of the plains to Seven Persons Creek, southwest of modern Medicine Hat, that they were attacked.

"We were traveling in a north-easterly direction, believing we were on our way to the goldfields of

"Kootenai" Brown's cabin, Waterton Lakes, October 10, 1883. Seated: A. Stavely Hill (left), and "Kootenai" Brown.

Edmonton," Brown remembered. "At a clump of cottonwoods we stopped to eat. As we were eating we were surprised by a flight of arrows and we knew our first 'war party' had begun. We thought our time had come. The Indians had no firearms but they were all young bucks—a war party out for anything they could get… If the Indians had had guns they would have killed us all."

The white men killed two of the Indians and the others decided to look for easier victims elsewhere. But before the fight was over Kootenai got an arrow in the back. It penetrated so near a kidney that it would have been fatal had his companions not been able to remove the arrow and patch him up with bandages and turpentine. Being young and tough, in a week he had fully recuperated.

Twenty years later while a scout with the Rocky Mountain Rangers during the Northwest Rebellion, Kootenai revisited the area of the fight. He located the skulls of the two warriors killed there, plus five bullets imbedded in the cottonwoods nearby.

Shortly after their narrow escape the five men split up, three heading to where they thought Fort Edmonton should be and Kootenai and another man nicknamed "Goldtooth" following the South Saskatchewan River to wherever it would take them. Since Goldtooth had lost his horse during the Indian raid, he built a boat of buffalo hide stretched over a wooden frame in which he floated down the river, while Kootenai followed along the bank. They soon lost track of one another, but both eventually ended up at a Metis settlement at Duck Lake in what is now Saskatchewan, where they spent the winter. Brown must have been very impressed with the carefree halfbreed plainsmen, for he later joined them as a buffalo hunter and even married a Metis girl. But more of that later. As it was, he and Goldtooth left the Metis settlement early in the spring and travelled to Fort Garry (Winnipeg) by sleigh.

In Manitoba Brown got his first taste of trading by buying furs from the Cree and Chippewa Indians between Portage La Prairie and the White Mud River during the winter of 1866-67. It was not a period of which he was proud in later years. John Gibbons, the man he worked for, used whisky to induce the Indians to trade. Almost invariably the Indians' furs would be traded away before their thirst for booze was satisfied.

When their furs ran out in the middle of one big spree, some of the bolder members of one group of Indians from Minnesota tried to steal some whisky to keep the party going. An American named Jim Clewett, who also worked for Gibbons, caught them in the act and a shooting battle ensued. Clewett and an Indian were killed and another American named Billy Sammon was badly wounded. Likely Brown and a man named O'Lone would also have been killed had not Brown and Gibbons been able to hold off the angry Indians—some 28 of them—while O'Lone slipped out to a nearby Metis settlement for help.

It was an incident that Kootenai regretted in later years, though it probably did not bother him too much at the time. However, after another season with Gibbons, he lost interest in the fur trade. In April of 1868 he headed south to the Dakota Territory and signed on with Major Ruffee's Mail Company at Fort Stevenson at a salary of $50 a month. His job was to carry the United States Mail from Fort Stevenson through the heart of the Sioux Indian Territory to Fort Benton, Montana.

"There were station keepers every 50 or 60 miles," Brown recalled. "They ran a bigger risk than we did although they weren't paid any more. Most of the station keepers were eventually killed and the company lost hundreds of horses, killed and stolen by the Indians. Their enormous losses finally led the company to bankruptcy and they still owe me $400 today."

An ordinary man might have given up mail carrying after Brown's experience, but Kootenai was no ordinary man. When Ruffee's company failed, the U.S. Army took over the mail route and Kootenai hired on with them. On May 15, 1868, he and a Sioux halfbreed named Joe Martin took the place of two riders, Charley MacDonald and Joe Hamlin, who had been killed by the Sioux somewhere between Forts Stevenson and Totten.

Brown and Martin almost met the same fate. On their first trip they were captured by a Sioux war party led by none other than the soon-to-be famous (or infamous) Chief Sitting Bull who, in 1876 wiped out General George Custer and his 7th Cavalry at the Battle of the Little Big Horn. It was fortunate for Brown that his partner was part Sioux, otherwise both their scalps might have adorned some Sioux warriors' belts. He and Martin were taken to the Sioux camp where they were stripped, but not too well guarded as Martin had convinced the warriors that both he and Brown were part Sioux. They escaped during the night and made their way on foot back to Fort Stevenson, where they arrived mosquito-bitten and bloody-footed the following afternoon.

"There was a bastion on the fort and one of the sentries saw us coming," Kootenai remembered. "He reported to the sergeant of the guard and he in turn to the officer of the day that two Indians were approaching the fort bare naked. The guard was sent out to capture us but when the sergeant saw who we were he ran out to meet us with, 'What's up? What's up?' I replied, 'Oh, nothing much. The Sioux have your mail, horses and our clothes and came mighty near getting us. We walked in from Strawberry Lake.'"

For five months after his narrow escape Kootenai took on a storekeeping job. Then, in November, he was back to carrying the mail. This time he took on the added responsibility of supervising the building of five shelters at approximately 45-mile intervals between Forts Stevenson and Totten. Most of the carriers were Canadian Metis who used dogs to haul the mail during the winter months. The dangers were not nearly so great then, for the Sioux had signed a treaty during the summer. But no treaty could be signed with the weather. Blizzards were frequent on the Dakota plains and in March, 1869, a fierce one caught Kootenai and four companions —Shank, Bittner, Richer and Voyles—on the trail 15 miles from Totten. When they lost the trail the five built a snow shelter and stayed in it overnight. Next day, however, the storm was just as intense and the men decided to head for better shelter, leaving their sleighs behind. On the way they became separated. Brown and Richer struggled back to the sleighs where they waited out the storm. The others were not as lucky. The bodies of Shank and Bittner were eventually located, but Voyles' was never found.

Even after that experience, Brown stayed with the Pony Express until 1874, during which time he met and married a pretty Metis girl, Olive Lyonnais, of French-Canadian and Indian stock. But by then the Dakota Territory was becoming crowded; at least by Kootenai Brown's standards. Settlers were flocking in and it was becoming too tame for him. On June 9, 1874, he packed up his wife and a new baby daughter and headed back to the Canadian prairies to yet another way of life. For the next couple of years he roamed the plains, following the buffalo with a camp of Canadian halfbreeds.

"The half-breed hunting camp was an institution all its own and a law unto itself," Kootenai wrote of his experience with the Metis buffalo hunters. "They lived in tents in the winter and put up log cabins wherever winter overtook them." Exact location of their hunting territory is hard to pin-point as there were no boundary markers then, but roughly it covered the southeastern part of Alberta and the southwestern sector of Saskatchewan.

It was a carefree life. The Metis were a happy, fun-loving people. Every evening when they were not hunting they would gather at someone's tent or cabin for a party or a dance. But the hunts were all business and highly organized. Scouts rode out to locate a big buffalo herd—sometimes a hundred or more miles from camp. Then the whole camp would move and re-locate nearer the big herd. Each hunter had at least two "buffalo runners," fast horses that could outrun the buffalo, while each camp had as many as 4,000 horses—tough cayuses that never saw grain but rustled for themselves summer and winter.

On the hunt the horsemen walked their ponies slowly towards the buffalo in an extended line. Usually the buffalo went on quietly grazing until the hunters were quite close, at which time the buffalo would break into a trot. At a signal from the hunt leader the riders closed up, then at the command, "Equa! Equa!" ("Now! Now!") they spurred their mounts to a full gallop.

"It was some experience," Kootenai remembered. "Dust flying, horns clashing, buffalo bellowing, men yelling, and all going at top speed."

Men with the best buffalo runners usually made the most kills. Each hunter was responsible for butchering and skinning his kills, after which his wife and children came out with a pony hitched to a two-wheeled cart to haul in the meat. No meat was wasted in a Metis camp. What could not be eaten fresh was either dried or made into pemmican. Father Albert Lacombe, the beloved Roman Catholic priest who spent over 60 years with the Metis and Indians in what is now Alberta, taught them that waste was sin. Apparently, though, the Blackfoot tribes did not share the Metis doctrine. "They were the wasters," Brown claimed. "They killed for the joy of killing, taking only hides and tongues and leaving the rest to rot." With white hunters to the south killing only for the hides, the buffalo were soon on the point of extinction.

Brown, however, believed it inevitable that the buffalo had to go. "We couldn't have settlers and buffalo," he said. "I have heard it said, too, that the United States government offered a reward for killing buffalo. They believed that they could not conquer the Sioux Indians as long as the buffalo roamed the prairies. I am sorry as a lover of sport…(and) as a humanitarian that they are gone, but they had to go."

In 1876-77 came a period that Kootenai later regretted. It was an incongruous time for a man who later became a conservationist. The buffalo were becoming scarce so, to make a living, he joined a band of wolfers—white men who killed wolves by poison. Wolf hides were worth $2.50 each and thousands of the wily animals then roamed the plains. A bottle of strychnine costing perhaps $6.00 was enough to poison a large buffalo carcass.

"It was a common thing to get 20 wolves the first morning after the poison had been put out," Brown remembered. One of his partners, Bill Martin, claimed he got 125 wolves in a week, all within 200 yards of a poisoned carcass.

Wolfers were a hated group—despised by whites and Indians alike. Perhaps, then, it was inevitable that the trade would lead Brown into trouble. It came in the spring of 1877 at Fort Stewart, Montana, on the Missouri River. After a drinking spree he quarrelled with a man named Louis Ell. Apparently Ell tried to cheat Kootenai out of the proceeds from some pelts they had sold. Whatever the facts of the matter, the argument led to a fight. Kootenai, whose temper was always short, stabbed Ell to death.

Many writers claim that after the fight Kootenai gathered his wife and children—two girls now—and fled to Canada with the sheriff in hot pursuit. Not quite true, claims William Rodney in his book, *Kootenai Brown*. Kootenai tried to escape, true enough, but was captured by Sheriff Rowe of Fort

Benton and brought back for trial.

While awaiting trial Kootenai had time to ponder his crime and on July 23, 1877, he tried to commit suicide by stabbing himself in the chest. Fortunately he did not succeed. Later he was acquitted by a Territorial Grand Jury at a trial held in Helena in November. "The most beautiful words in the English language are 'Not guilty,'" Brown told a friend many years later. It was about the only thing anyone ever heard him say about a period he wanted to forget, but never could.

Following the trial Brown gathered his family and moved to what is now Waterton Lakes National Park, where he built a cabin beside the Kootenai (now Waterton) Lakes. The wild grandeur of the area had haunted him from the day in 1865 when he and his friends emerged from the Kootenai Pass on their way to Edmonton from Wild Horse Creek. While contemplating his life in the Fort Benton jail, he had determined, if acquitted, to return to the lakes to live out the rest of his life.

Though a lonely place for Olive, who was used to the conviviality of Metis hunting camps, for Kootenai it was ideal. Here he could hunt and fish and do as he pleased, beholden to no man. Nor was earning a living a problem. Game abounded and lakes and streams teemed with fish. If he needed flour, sugar, tea or other staples, he simply sold a wagonload of fish. "I used to sell fish at Macleod," he recalled. "We caught them in the Waterton Lakes and fished both winter and summer. I have seen me get $75 for my load of fish and we thought that a big price in those days."

Fort Macleod was a bustling town that owed its origin to the North West Mounted Police but, despite its location in southern Alberta, it was primarily an American outpost. Fort Benton merchants I.G. Baker, T.C. Powers and Murphy Neeland were Macleod's biggest businessmen. Bullwhackers profanely urging long strings of oxen along the Whoop-up Trail from Fort Benton brought in most of the merchandise and until the arrival of CPR in 1883, all outgoing mail bore American stamps.

On one of his trips to Fort Macleod, Kootenai was introduced to H.A. (Fred) Kanouse who was also squatted on land near Kootenai Lakes. The two became friends and decided to go into partnership, starting a store on what later became Brown's first homestead. "Fred and I had a stock valued at $4,000 and our customers were Indians, mostly Kootenais, Nez Perces and Flatheads from the Flathead Reservation in Montana," Brown recalled.

The Indians were great gamblers and Brown and Kanouse often won back the goods they had just sold. "I was a foot racer and a good shot and in competitions with them on the track and with the rifle I could always beat them," Kootenai boasted. "We had two good horses and in horse racing we also got the best of them. In fact we beat them at every turn."

I.G. Baker (above) and the Conrad brothers were rulers of the American Fur trade in Alberta. Charles Conrad served as guide for the North West Mounted Police, who were unaware of his position as I.G. Baker's manager in Alberta, and operator of Robber's Roost.

The Indians grew angrier as time passed and perhaps it was fortunate that the American government finally stopped their Indians from coming into Canada to trade. Otherwise, Brown and Kanouse might well have had a full-blown war on their hands. As it was, trade slackened and Brown sold out to Kanouse, who moved the business to Fort Macleod. By then Brown had established himself as a big game, fishing and tourist guide. He was attracting all the work he could handle and no longer needed to live dangerously, pitting his wits against several tribes of Indians.

Also by then, Brown was well known to ex-Mounted Policeman C.E.D. Wood and E.T. Saunders, who had recently started the Fort Macleod *Gazette.* Items in their paper like the following, which appeared in the spring of 1883, did much to help Brown's guiding business: "Mr. Brown of Kootenai Lakes brought to town on Saturday a trout weighing 30 pounds… Some people may think this is a fishy story, but we have seen the trout and can vouch for its truth."

With the CPR slowly stretching westward, in 1883 Kootenai began getting assignments to guide some prominent people, including the Earl of Latham. Stavely Hill of the Oxley Ranch who accompanied Lord Latham wrote of Brown: "He was a wild Indian looking fellow, in a slouch hat and curiously constructed garments… He had seen service in the British Army but with his long hair and moccasins had not much of the European remaining in his appearance…" Brown was proud of his "wild Indian" appearance and undoubtedly impressed Lord Latham more than if he had turned out on the shores of Kootenai Lakes dressed in tuxedo and top hat.

For the next couple of years Kootenai continued to get good coverage from the Fort Macleod *Gazette*. The November 14, 1888, issue contained an item alluding to the unseasonably warm weather: "J.G. Brown from Kootenai Lakes was in town last week. Mr. Brown informs us that he rode from the lakes to Macleod, a distance of 50 miles, and that he was uncomfortably warm while trotting along…" Next March 21, the *Gazette* reported: "J.G. Brown, who came to town yesterday, nearly lost a horse by drowning in the Kootenai River…"

These mundane accounts told of the rather quiet life Kootenai was then leading. Strangely, there is no mention of the death of his lovely Olive, who passed away sometime between 1883 and '85. According to Marie Rose Smith, who met Kootenai after 1885 and later wrote several articles about him which the Glenbow-Alberta Institute has preserved, Olive never recuperated from giving birth to a son, Leo, and died while Kootenai was on a hunting trip.

Kootenai was away on another extended hunting trip in 1885 when Major L. Crozier of the North West Mounted Police, leading a contingent of Mounties and civilian volunteers, tangled with Gabriel Dumont and his Metis army at Duck Lake,

Saskatchewan, and the North West Rebellion began. Fort Macleod, Fort Calgary and most other settlements in southern Alberta were in the midst of some 4,000 Blackfoot, Blood, Peigan and Stoney Indians. If they went on the warpath all the whites in the area could be wiped out. Consequently, John Stewart, a former officer with the Princess Louise Dragoon Guards, offered to raise four troops of Rocky Mountain Rangers to patrol the area. The Canadian Army agreed with the idea and when Kootenai Brown returned from his hunt he volunteered. He was accepted along with 114 other plainsmen who were able to ride hard and shoot straight.

The Rangers, with their Western sombreros, buckskin shirts, Cartridge belts and knives, leather chaps and Mexican spurs, were a colorful group. All sat their horses with the ease of long practice. Kootenai, able to speak many Indian dialects fluently, became a scout. The Rangers patrolled a vast area between the Red Deer River on the north and the American border on the south. Had they been called on to fight, they undoubtedly would have given a good account of themselves. However, only one patrol exchanged shots with hostile Indians, who immediately turned tail for the Montana border.

Brown's services lasted 77 days for which he received $118.50 in cash and $80.00 in scrip, which he exchanged for 320 acres of land next to his original homestead. While with the Rangers somewhere near modern Medicine Hat Kootenai

Group at John George "Kootenai" Brown's house, Waterton Park, 1910. "Kootenai" Brown, second right front, Mrs. Brown, extreme right rear.

met an Indian woman, who later became his wife. Some writers have claimed that she was a beautiful princess, daughter of a high ranking chief. In reality she was neither, but she was a faithful companion to Brown, a fine cook and a meticulous housekeeper.

"Oftimes the Browns traveled in the mountains with pack horses," Marie Rose Smith wrote of Kootenai and Isabella. "He was an excellent shot and energetic at keeping the pot full. Mrs. Brown was splendid at tanning hides and curing meat. She also was a good shot herself, bringing in many prairie chickens, partridges and ducks."

It was an idyllic life, one that they could have enjoyed for the rest of their days. Unfortunately, fish and game gradually grew scarcer and Kootenai had to look for another means of earning a living. As it happened, the NWMP began pasturing some of their horses along the nearby Belly River. Kootenai approached them for a job and was immediately hired.

He continued to work for the Mounted Police off and on for 10 years, sometimes as a guide, sometimes as a trainer for their horses. During this period he began fighting to have his beloved Kootenai Lakes area set aside as a national park. Game was growing ever scarcer and if action was not taken he knew that in a few years it would be too late to save species such as the Rocky Mountain Big Horn sheep, grizzlies and mountain goat. His friends—John Herron who became a Liberal-Conservative Member of Parliament for the Fort Macleod riding, C.E.D. Wood of the Macleod *Gazette*, and F.W. Godsal, a rancher in the Cowley district—shared his feelings. Godsal contacted William Pearce, Superintendent of Mines, who was stationed at Calgary. Finally, on May 30, 1895, after a flood of letters from Pearce and others, the federal government set aside a small tract of land as a forest reserve.

Meanwhile, Kootenai had to find ways to make a living. He had known for years of the oil seepages along Blakiston (now Cameron) Creek and had used the black liquid to grease his wagon. When oil companies began exploring the area around 1890 he teamed with William Aldridge, a Mormon farmer from Cardston, to exploit the seepages. Aldridge and his son Oliver devised a means of collecting the oil in barrels which was then sold to the farmers settling around Cardston for $1 a gallon. Aldridge and Brown were probably the only ones who did make a little money from the oil as, due to poor roads and primitive drilling equipment, the boom went bust, although some companies kept trying for the bonanza for many years.

It was not until January of 1901 that Brown's fight for a federal park paid off monetarily, when he was appointed fishery officer for the reserve at a salary of $50 a year. Meanwhile, he kept fighting for a national park. He did not get his wish then, but in 1908, through his friends, F.W. Godsal and John Herron, he became game guardian of the Kootenay Reserve, an Alberta government appointment. The next step—a big one—came in March of 1910 when the federal forestry appointed him forest ranger in charge of the Kootenay Forest Reserve. At the age of 71 he started a new career in the Civil Service of Canada.

Kootenai attacked his new job with an enthusiasm that belied his years. To get through the mountain of paperwork faster he asked for—and got—a typewriter which he mastered through hard work. At the same time he began trying to persuade his superior, Howard Douglas, Commissioner of Parks, to have the Kootenay Forest Reserve enlarged and made into a national park adjoining Glacier National Park in Montana. With pressure coming from Brown, Douglas, Herron and Godsal, the Federal Government finally yielded and, in 1911, Kootenay Forest Reserve became a park. But, by some strange reasoning, it was reduced in size from 54 square miles to 13½ square miles. As a further insult, its name was changed from Kootenay to that of the lakes in the main valley. These lakes were named for Charles Waterton, an 18th century English naturalist, by Lieutenant Thomas Blakiston who discovered them in 1858 while with the Palliser Expedition.

Though his territory shrank when it became a national park, Kootenai's workload did not. As acting superintendent he was responsible for rangers, road builders, trail cutters and other staff. His advancing years did not keep him from driving himself and his staff and trying to turn the park into a first-class tourist attraction. In 1914 his dream of a park and game preserve joined to Glacier National Park finally became a reality, when the federal government enlarged Waterton to 423 square miles. The park then required a full superintendent but Kootenai did not get the job. "Ranger Brown cannot exercise proper supervision over the extended area due to extreme age," Chief Superintendent C.B. Hervey advised his superiors after visiting the park and Brown's assistant, Robert Cooper, got the job in his place.

After the demotion—and undoubtedly because of it—notations of failing health began to appear more often in Brown's well-kept diary. In the spring of 1916, after a serious bout of illness, he made his will and bequeathed all his possessions to his faithful Isabella. On July 18 he passed quietly into his final sleep.

But his dream of a great park lives on. In 1932 it became Glacier-Waterton International Peace Park by consent of the Canadian and United States governments; a vast game reserve and mountain playground where the people of two nations intermingle in ever-increasing numbers to admire nature's magnificent wonderland. In it Kootenai Brown lies buried between his two wives in a specially marked grave.

He must be very pleased. ●

Major-General Thomas Bland Strange, 1871.

General Strange's
ALBERTA FIELD FORCE

Although it has largely been overlooked by historians, General Thomas Strange's Alberta Field Force played a substantial role in the quelling of the 1885 North West Rebellion. When the shooting stopped, General Middleton received $20,000 and a medal. General Strange got little more than a pat on the back.

PROBABLY the Alberta Field Force has never gained the recognition it deserved. It was overshadowed by the work of General Frederick Middleton's troops who engaged Louis Riel's Metis and Indians at Fish Creek, Batoche and other points in Saskatchewan and quelled the 1885 North West Rebellion. But they did not do it alone. The Alberta Field Force led by General Thomas Bland Strange also did its part. It was called on to do a job. It did it and then was largely forgotten. This is not a story intended to undo an injustice but merely a chapter to help tell some of the part the men led by General Strange played in helping to put down the North West Rebellion.

Much has been written about the rebellion—of how Louis Riel either rightly or wrongly led an uprising of Metis and Indians against the Canadian government to try to acquire for his people rights that were being swept aside as white settlers moved into the West. Many now agree that he was not asking too much in wanting a voice for his people in government and the right to choose land where they wished. Most now agree that the Indians were being shabbily treated and deprived of many of the rights promised in the treaties of a decade before. The government in Ottawa was slow to respond to request for more food for the Indians, who, with the buffalo gone, were literally starving. In some cases

Rocky Mountain Rangers in formation, 1885, with J.G. "Kootenai" Brown, chief scout, in the lead.

unfeeling Indian agents had actually been selling food that the Indians should have gotten, thus adding to their misery.

No wonder, then, that when the government failed to respond to a petition sent by Louis Riel and his lieutenants, the Metis, led by fiery Gabriel Dumont, decided to take matters into their own hands. Dumont began taking white prisoners and on March 25 seized Hillyard Mitchell's store at Duck Lake. The next day Dumont's men defeated a force of NWMP and civilian volunteers led by Major L.N.F. Crozier, who came from Fort Carlton to Duck Lake to restore peace. And the North West Rebellion was on!

Even before the Duck Lake battle, the Canadian Militia under Lieutenant-General F.D. Middleton was ordered to mobilize and head west to be ready to quell an uprising. At the same time, Major-General Thomas Bland Strange, veteran officer of both the British and Canadian armies, who had retired in 1881 to become manager of the Military Colonization Company's ranch near Gleichen, beside the Blackfoot Reserve, received a telegram from Ottawa asking him to form an Alberta Field Force and to stand by to help Middleton's troops if needed.

After exchanging telegrams with General Middleton, who had moved west to Fort Qu'Appelle, General Strange headed for Calgary on the newly-built Canadian Pacific Railway during the latter part of March. Fearing that an uprising would begin any

day, Commissioner A.G. Irvine of the NWMP had been ordered from headquarters in Regina to the Fort Carlton-Battleford-Prince Albert area with every man who could be spared from southern Saskatchewan and Alberta. Consequently, Calgary had been left with only a half a dozen policemen. Literally surrounded by Stoney, Sarcee, Blood and Blackfoot Indians, the place was almost in a state of panic, and there was considerable opposition to having its men enlisted for anything but home defence. Nevertheless, General Strange began putting his Field Force together, getting Major James Walker to organize a Calgary Home Guard.

General Strange had no trouble enlisting cowboys, men with no military training but used to taking orders and eminently skilled in riding and shooting. These men formed the Alberta Mounted Rifles, commanded by Major J. Hatton, a former militia officer, who enlisted Sergeants Dunn and Lauder of the NWMP as his lieutenants. Inspector Sam Steele of the NWMP was called in from policing the B.C. section of the CPR, given the rank of Major and asked to form a unit Strange named "Steele's Scouts." Major Stewart raised an outfit called the Rocky Mountain Rangers, who were stationed at Fort Macleod and Lethbridge. Their job was to patrol the ranch country north of the Montana border and repel any possible Indian attack.

To fill out the Force the 65th Carabiniers Mount Royal under Colonel J.A. Ouimet, the 92nd Winnipeg Light Infantry under Lieutenant-Colonel W.

Osborne Smith and the 7th Voltigeurs de Quebec under Lieutenant-Colonel P. Amyot arrived from the East. Even before all his troops arrived, Gen. Strange got word of the Duck Lake battle and later of the April 2 massacre at Frog Lake. There was need for haste as the Indians north of the North Saskatchewan River and in the Battle River area were making threats if not actually on the warpath, but Strange could not start north until April 20, for it took that long to get his force together. By then he had been joined by Major A. Bowen Perry of the NWMP, who brought 20 men and a nine-pound cannon from Fort Macleod to form the Force's artillery. But, by April 20, they were ready to roll. General Strange selected his son, Lieutenant E. Bland Strange as his Aide-de-Camp and artillery officer, while Surgeon-Major Pennefather was Medical Officer and Canon John MacKay and the Reverend John McDougall acted as Chaplains and scouts. Five days before the northward trek began, Lieutenant Coryell led a troop of 15 of Steele's Scouts north to reconnoiter the route and enlist any settlers he found for a Home Guard to secure the Red Deer River Crossing.

The Alberta Field Force marched in three echelons, General Strange leading the first. Sam Steele with 60 men, and 2, 5, 6 and 7 Companies of the 65th Carabiniers formed the General's group. They made good time, crossed the Red Deer River with no trouble and arrived in Edmonton on May 1.

The next group was not as lucky. By April 23, when Major Perry led his group north to the Red Deer River, they found it to be swollen by the spring thaw. The party consisting of 20 NWMP with the field gun and 1, 3, 5, and 8 Companies of the 65th, almost lost the cannon while crossing the Red Deer when the raft carrying it broke loose. Only by luck and hard riding did Major Perry overtake the raft three miles downstream and grab a rope as it floated past. By then the riverbanks had steepened and the cannon had to be hoisted up by hand. The trail north of the river was soft and muddy and the weary group did not reach Edmonton till a week later.

At the Red Deer River Crossing Major Perry had assigned Lieutenant Normandeau and 20 men of Number 8 Company of the 65th to erect a fort in case hostile Indians should try to cut army communication lines. Normandeau took over John McLellan's year-old hotel, reinforced it, installed loopholes and bastions and dug a moat. His men dubbed it Fort Normandeau and a replica of it now stands on the spot, on the south side of the river just south of the city of Red Deer. Captains Ostell and Ethier of the 65th were likewise assigned the task of erecting forts at the Battle River Crossing (Ponoka) and on Sam Lucas' Government Farm near Pipestone Creek (Wetaskiwin). None of the forts fired a shot in anger and all were abandoned after the North West Rebellion ended.

Lieutenant-Colonel W. Osborne Smith led the third contingent from Calgary. His outfit consisted of four companies of the Winnipeg Light Infantry, some of the Alberta Mounted Rifles and a considerable number of transport vehicles. The group had been delayed awaiting the arrival of saddles for the Alberta Mounted Rifles. Lieutenant Dunn and some of the AMR were assigned the task of patrolling the Calgary-Edmonton Trail. The rest of the men arrived in Edmonton on May 10.

Five days before, the first of the Field Force, men of the 5th and 6th Companies of the 65th led by Steele's Scouts, had already started east, following a trail north of the Saskatchewan River toward Fort Pitt. They were hoping to intercept Chief Big Bear's rebels and the warriors who had instigated the massacre at Frog Lake.

Three days later, May 8, Companies 3 and 4 of the 65th followed, but it was not until May 16 that General Strange and staff, Major Perry and his gun crew and the Winnipeg Light Infantry started toward Fort Pitt. They chose to travel by river, using a large barge measuring 100 by 25 feet, a ferry that had been in use at Clover Bar, a scow of undetermined size and a 'gunboat' made from a scow and armed with the field gun mounted on a platform. As 'armor' the scow employed sacks of flour, beef, pork and other supplies piled so that the men could fire from behind a protective wall. Men of the 65th named the gunboat the *Big Bear*, probably as a reminder that the Cree chief was the reason for their journey. General Strange decided to make the trip in stages, with Fort Victoria, 70 or so miles downstream from Edmonton the first leg of the journey. Dozens of freighters followed the Force, keeping to the trail on the north side of the river.

At Fort Victoria General Strange supervised the formation of a Home Guard in case Chief Pakan and his Crees should take to the warpath. When the trek resumed, the Winnipeg Light Infantry changed places with the 65th Carabiniers, manning the flotilla while the Winnipeggers took to the trail with Steele's Scouts in the lead.

They had been alerted to look out for Plains Cree Chief Big Bear's warriors who could be roaming to the west of Fort Pitt. Consequently, when someone, probably accidently, fired a shot, the men were so jittery that they got into a heated battle with some poplar trees and reportedly won hands down. Men of the 65th scampered ashore, reconnoitered the area, but found nothing. The Force reached Fort Pitt on May 24 and found Big Bear's people had put it to the torch. Lieutenant Coryell had led a detachment to Frog Lake, where they buried the nine men murdered by Big Bear's renegades after Canon John MacKay read the funeral service.

To fill in some of the gaps, particularly as to why the Alberta Field Force followed the route it did: Before leaving Calgary word came in that all the white men at the trading post at Frog Lake, located some 20 miles north of the Saskatchewan River and

Steele's Scouts, near Frenchman's Butte, Sask., in May, 1885. Sketch by T. Bland Strange.

just west of the present Alberta-Saskatchewan border, had been murdered, the white women taken prisoner and the settlement put to the torch. The report was not quite factual, for two white men, W.B. Cameron and James Simpson, both Hudson's Bay Company employees, were spared. They were taken prisoner along with the two white women, Mrs. John Gowanlock and Mrs. John Delaney, and the Metis men, women and children of Frog Lake, as well as all the civilian population of Fort Pitt. General Strange's orders were to overtake Big Bear and his warriors and try to free the prisoners.

The nine men at Frog Lake might not have died had Corporal R.B. Sleigh and his six-man detachment of Mounted Police been allowed to stay. But when Chief Big Bear's warriors, led by War Chief Wandering Spirit (they actually were uninvited guests at the Frog Lake Reserve), began making threats and issuing ultimatums after hearing of Gabriel Dumont's defeat of the Mounted Police and Prince Albert Volunteers at Duck Lake, Thomas Quinn, John Gowanlock, Father Fafard and other leading men at Frog Lake decided to send the police away. Six policemen, they reasoned, would not be enough to put down a revolt if it started. And keeping them at Frog Lake might only aggravate the Indians to revolt. Thus, on April 1, Corporal Sleigh led his little platoon quietly out of the village toward Fort Pitt, taking most of the powder and shot from both the HBC and George Dill's stores with them.

The following day, April 2, Wandering Spirit instigated a massacre in which two Catholic priests and seven other men were killed. After a week of looting and burning the stores, Big Bear's Plains Crees, accompanied by Wood Crees from the Frog Lake Reserve and Chippewyans from Cold Lake, headed for Fort Pitt to rout the NWMP detachment there.

Inspector Frances J. Dickens, son of the famous novelist Charles Dickens, was in charge of the NWMP detachment at Fort Pitt. He was not entirely unprepared to repel an attack and would have done so had the situation warranted it. When word came through that Dumont had defeated Crozier at Duck Lake, Dickens set about reinforcing Fort Pitt, tearing down the outlying shacks as a precaution against fire and fortifying the five main buildings by barricading doors and windows and cutting loopholes in the walls. Quite a number of civilians had come in from outlying areas for protection and Dickens had sent a messenger to Battleford asking for 50 reinforcements. These never arrived for the simple reason that the courier was captured by Riel's people. But, with his own men reinforced by the civilians, Dickens could have put up quite a fight. This he was prepared to do when, on April 3, Henry Quinn, a nephew of the Frog Lake Indian agent, Thomas Quinn, brought the news of the hostilities at Frog Lake. Henry Quinn had started from Frog Lake early the morning of April 2, had heard the shooting

(Top) Scow used to transport infantry on Saskatchewan River, Alberta, in May of 1885. It consisted of a narrow platform with protective barrels of salt pork and beef and sacks of flour. Loop holes were formed by intervals between packs and holes cut in gunwale. (Center) Sectional drawing of horse-boat. This unwieldly craft later sank on Saskatchewan River at Fort Victoria. (Bottom) The gunboat Big Bear on Saskatchewan River. The scow had a platform on which gun was lashed. Barrels of salt pork, beef and flour were arranged along the sides as protection.

and guessed its meaning.

Eleven days later Big Bear's warriors appeared on the hill overlooking Fort Pitt and demanded that Inspector Dickens surrender. This he refused to do, but he did allow W.J. McLean, head factor for the HBC for the district, to go and have a talk with Big Bear. Unfortunately, just as McLean was in a deep discussion with the Indians, three scouts that Dickens had sent to reconnoiter the area north and west of the fort inadvertently rode into the Indian camp. Pandemonium broke loose as NWMP Constables David Cowan and Clarence Loasby, and Henry Quinn, who had been signed on as a Special Constable, spurred their horses in an effort to reach the safety of the fort. Only Loasby made it and he was badly wounded. Cowan was shot through the heart as he tried to run when his horse was shot from under him. Quinn escaped but could not get to the fort and was captured the following day.

Thinking that the intrusion by the police scouts had been planned, War Chief Wandering Spirit took Factor McLean prisoner and forced him to send a note to his wife at the fort, demanding that Dickens surrender all the civilians and abandon the fort. When the civilians decided to surrender to Big Bear, Dickens decided that there was no longer any reason to try to hold the post. He and his men boarded a scow built for just such an eventuality and headed downriver towards Battleford. In a diary found on the body of Corporal Sleigh after he was killed May 2 at the Battle of Cut Knife Hill on Chief Poundmaker's Reserve was the following terse account of the evacuation:

"April 14—Everybody in good spirits. Indians on hill 800 yards from fort; 250 Indians armed and mounted. Big Bear sent letter down; everybody to evacuate fort and give up arms...

"April 15—Hudson's Bay employees—28 in number—gave themselves up to Big Bear. Impossible to hold fort now so had to retire gracefully...."

As soon as the police left, the Indians took over the fort, looting and drinking and eventually putting the place to the torch. They then moved to the northeast, hoping to join up with Poundmaker. Some 5 miles from Fort Pitt, Wandering Spirit decided to hold a Thirst Dance in order to inflame his young men to fight if and when government troops should appear. They were in the midst of their ritual—a dance in which young men endure torture and go without food or drink, sometimes for days, to prove their masculinity—when the whole camp was thrown into confusion by a lookout who began shouting and pointing towards Fort Pitt. On a knoll in the distance could be seen the smoke of cookfires of what was obviously a military camp. It was the smoke from the cookfires of Steele's Scouts, the advance guard of the Alberta Field Force. By the next night, May 25, General Strange and most of his men were also camped on the hill overlooking the smoldering ruins of Fort Pitt.

Steele's Scouts had been reconnoitering the area around Fort Pitt and had found the body of Constable Cowan, his heart cut from his chest and impaled on a stick stuck in the ground. They buried him as a party led by Lieutenant Coryell had buried the nine men killed at Frog Lake. The following day Steele led his men to the east, following the trail on the north side of the Saskatchewan River. He was looking for a place to camp when, suddenly, a bullet whizzed past his head and an Indian sprang from the tall grass. Fortunately for the Scouts, they had anticipated just such an ambush and in the shoot-out that ensued, one of the Indians died and the rest of the small band fled to the east. They warned Big Bear that the white soldiers were following his trail.

About 12 miles northeast of Fort Pitt was a high, cone-shaped hill known as Frenchman's Butte. It was there that Big Bear decided to dig in and put up a fight. After getting word from Steele of the skirmish with the Cree war party, General Strange led his men toward that hill. In his book *Gunner Jingo's Jubilee*, an interesting story of his colorful life, General Strange wrote:

"On the morning of May 28, the force roused without the sound of bugle and after a scanty breakfast, at daybreak moved toward Frenchman's Butte. The advance was led by Major Steele's Scouts, dismounted, flanking each side of the Trail. Next came the main body consisting of 300 men of the Winnipeg Light Infantry and Quebec Voltigeurs, while the nine-pound gun under Lieutenant Strange brought up the rear.

"Suddenly we came to a comparatively open space, to which trails converged from every direction. It was the encampment where the braves held their last Sun Dance (Sun Dance to the Blackfoot tribes, Thirst Dance to the Crees)...

"I was riding with the advanced scouts when we came upon a campfire, still alight, with an abandoned dough-cake still in the ashes... Streamers of red and white calico—the spoils of Fort Pitt—hung from the branches of a tree on the opposite side of a bare glacis slope. The valley, about 500 yards wide, was intersected by a sluggish creek, widening into a swamp, and fringed here and there with willows...

"The crest of the hill was thickly wooded and the field glasses revealed what seemed to be a long line of rifle pits along the edge...

"The field gun was ordered to open fire from the edge of the descent, which drew a heavy response. I deployed the small force at my disposal and ordered Major Steele's Mounted Police and scouts to extend to the left, dismount and descend the hill to a fringe of willows and brush along the edge of the creek.

"The Voltigeurs under Colonel Hughes and Major Prevost went down the hill on the double and extended along the creek on the right of the dismounted cavalry. The Winnipeg Light Infantry, under Major Thibadeau, took what cover they could in the willow bushes along the edge of the swamp. Two companies of the Winnipeg Battalion, under Colonel Osborne Smith, were held in support on the hill, while Major Hatton's Alberta Mounted Rifles were dismounted and ordered to cover the flank, where the woods were the thickest.

"No sooner had my men extended when the whole line of rifle pits opened fire from the opposite summit for about a mile. But the fire was without effect, for the range was long... Lieutenant Strange got the exact range—600 yards—of the pits with a few cannon shells. He then tried shrapnel, evidently without much effect, as the fire from the pits did not slacken...."

When the infantry could not cross the swamp at the bottom of the hill without exposing themselves to heavy fire, and Steele reported that he could not outflank the enemy without extending his line too far, General Strange decided to withdraw. His men had only a day's rations with them and were very short of ammunition. Also in the back of his mind was the picture of what had happened to General George Custer and his 7th U.S. Cavalry when they ran into a larger force led by Chief Sitting Bull of the Sioux at the Battle of the Little Big Horn nine years before. Moreover, General Middleton's troops had suffered fairly high casualties fighting Riel's Metis and Poundmaker's Crees at Duck Lake, Fish Creek and Cut Knife Hill in Saskatchewan. General Strange expected reinforcements would be coming up the Saskatchewan from Battleford by riverboat momentarily. Therefore, it seemed wise to pull back and fight another day.

Pulling back was not as simple as it sounds. The Force was under heavy rifle fire from the crest of Frenchman's Butte and Constable McRae of Steele's Scouts and Privates Lemai and Marcotte of the 7th Voltigeurs were wounded, Lemai in full view of the Crees. Strange told a Voltigeur officer to take a stretcher party and bring in Lemai, but instead got the insubordinate answer: "General, I've been shot at quite enough today, and I'm damned if I'm going out there again!"

Instead of angering the General, the answer made him laugh. "Okay," he thought, "I'll bring the man in myself." He gave his son orders to give covering fire with the cannon, organized a stretcher party consisting of himself, Dr. Pare, Father Prevost, the battalion chaplain, and two stretcher bearers, and set out to bring the wounded man in.

"We found the man well to the front in an exposed position," General Strange wrote, "and I must confess some impatience, which the good priest did not seem to share, during the confession of sin. I suggested to the brave padre the desirability of lumping the details, which he did, and placing the wounded men under Dr. Pare's direction, on a stretcher, the party moved up the hill, I bringing up the rear with the man's rifle. The fire grew hotter as we ascended; the rear man dropped his end of the stretcher and I took his place. Thus, General Jingo met his retribution by having to carry his wounded off his last battlefield.

"The Force returned to Fort Pitt, to remain for some days awaiting the arrival of provisions; and thus ended the Battle of Frenchman's Butte."

A week later at Fort Pitt the wail of a steam whistle heralded the arrival of the sternwheeler *Northcote*, bringing provisions, reinforcements and General Middleton from Battleford. Some of Big Bear's prisoners had been turned loose that morning, and they too heard the steam whistle as they tramped wearily towards Fort Pitt. Later that night, General Strange's private cook treated ex-prisoners, the Reverend Charles Quinney and his wife, W.B. Cameron, Henry Quinn, F. Dufresne and a number of Metis women and children, to a feast such as they had only dreamed about since being taken prisoner two months before.

The next morning Steele with 63 mounted men headed out after the Indians, who were now fleeing, and caught up to them a couple of days later. Advance scouts ran into an ambush the first day out and Scout J. Fisk was wounded. Steele then knew the main body was not far away and overtook them as they attempted to flee across an arm of Loon Lake in Saskatchewan on the morning of the third day. In the ensuing battle at least six Crees were killed, including Chief Cut Arm, a good friend to the prisoners who had been under his care. Two of Steele's Scouts were also wounded, including Sergeant Major William Fury, who had been with Steele in British Columbia, policing the CPR.

Ironically, while the battle was in progress, Factor McLean had twice sent a messenger to contact Steele on behalf of the prisoners. Unfortunately, the messenger was wounded and forced to turn back. Since Steele's force was too small to overpower the Cree war party, the prisoners, though not well guarded, could not get away. They were finally released after a long tramp to the north of the Beaver River. They were a bedraggled looking group when they finally ran into a party of General Middleton's troops at Loon Lake. They had been given no food and survived the long march by eating what few rabbits and birds they could shoot on the way with the single shotgun lent them by the Wood Crees.

After the battle at Loon Lake, the Indian war party split up, the Chippewyans heading back to their reserve at Cold Lake, the Wood Crees going north beyond the Beaver River, and the Plains Crees, led by Big Bear, to the northeast. General Middleton, who was now in command of the combined force, decided to follow Steele's Scouts with his infantry soldiers. He ordered General Strange to head northwest to the Beaver River to cut off Big Bear should he head that way. Strange left Fort Pitt on June 6, taking W.B. Cameron along as guide. He found no Indians at the Chippewyan Reserve near Cold Lake but, by the amount of loot from Fort Pitt scattered

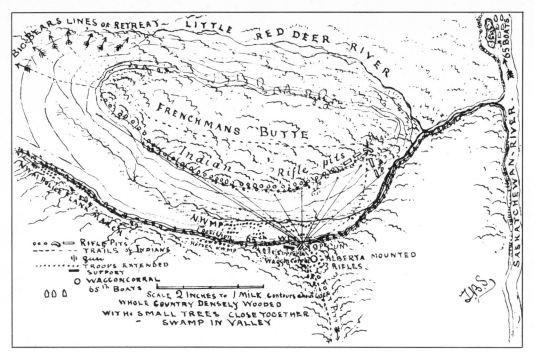

Map of emplacements at Battle of Frenchman's Butte, Saskatchewan, in May of 1885. The battle between Alberta Field Force, under General T.B. Strange's command, and Cree Indians, under Big Bear and Wandering Spirit, war chief.

around, he knew they were not far off. On the evening of June 9, Father LeGoff, their priest, brought them in to surrender. They pleaded innocent of any charges of wrongdoing at Frog Lake and Fort Pitt, claiming that Chief Wandering Spirit had forced them to participate in the looting. Cameron, however, had seen some of the Chippewyans participate voluntarily. The ringleaders were arrested, while the others were disarmed and released.

While General Strange was chasing the Chippewyans, the Wood Crees had decided to give themselves up. Though the Frog Lake Massacre had occurred on their reserve, it had been Big Bear's Plains Crees led by Wandering Spirit who had instigated the murders. Big Bear's people, who had no reserve of their own, had been visiting their cousins at Frog Lake as unwelcome guests. Most of the Wood Crees wanted no part of the massacre but had participated because of fear of reprisals by Wandering Spirit's angry warriors: Ironically, Wandering Spirit followed the Wood Crees north from Loon Lake for he, in turn, feared reprisals by his own people for exciting them to take up arms against the whites. He accompanied the Wood Crees back to Fort Pitt after their surrender, then tried to commit suicide by stabbing himself in the chest. Unfortunately for him, his aim was bad and he lived to stand trial and hang for his crimes.

After the Loon Lake battle, Big Bear headed east, hoping to escape to the United States. He did not make it. On July 2 he was captured at Fort Carlton by Sergeant Smart and Constables Colebrook, Sullivan and Nichols of the NWMP. Since W.B. Cameron and others testified that Big Bear had tried to prevent the murders at Frog Lake, he was given only three years in prison and served two.

Even before Big Bear was captured, the North

West Rebellion was over, Louis Riel's troops having surrendered after being beaten by General Middleton's force at Batoche, before Middleton came to join Strange at Fort Pitt. Since there was no longer any need for the Alberta Field Force, it was quickly disbanded. The 7th Voltigeurs, 65th Carabiniers and Winnipeg Rifles started for home, travelling the first leg down the North Saskatchewan River by steamer. Steele's Scouts, the Alberta Mounted Rifles and the rest of the Alberta Field Force headed for Edmonton and Calgary where they obtained their discharge.

There was one other unit of the Alberta Field Force not already mentioned. This was the St. Albert Mounted Rifles commanded by Captain Sam Cunningham. Consisting of some 60 men in all, they wore no uniforms and were armed with Snider rifles, while the rest of the force were armed with Winchesters. Before coming down to Fort Pitt to join the rest of the Force, Captain Cunningham had led his men on patrols in and around the trading post of Lac La Biche. They returned to Edmonton with the others and were demobilized.

The disbanding of the Alberta Field Force was quick and final. It had been formed for one purpose—to protect the settlers and help put down the rebellion. It had done its job well and, without fuss or feathers, broke up.

General Strange returned to his ranch near Gleichen and later retired in England, where he died at an old age. He undoubtedly did not get the recognition he should have for his part in quelling the rebellion. While General Middleton received a $20,000 award and a medal, General Strange got little more than a pat on the back. However, most who have written about him speak of him with more affection than they do of General Middleton and, perhaps, that is all the reward he would have wanted. ●

The trail's origins have been lost in history. The Indians used it for centuries, then the white settlers. With the coming of the CPR, the Calgary-Edmonton Trail became Alberta's most important transportation link.

The Calgary - Edmonton Trail

SOME claim that the old trail dates back to antiquity— that it was the route followed by the first Indians as they crossed the narrow channel of water from Siberia to Alaska, then slowly migrated down the length of the North American Continent to Mexico. As Hugh Dempsey, in the Autumn 1959 issue of the *Alberta Historical Review*, quoted an aged Peigan Indian named Running Wolf:

"There is a well known trail we call the Old North Trail. It runs north and south along the Rocky Mountains. No one knows how long it has been used by the Indians. My father told me it originated in the migrations of a great tribe of Indians from the distant north to the south; and all the tribes have, ever since, continued to follow in their tracks. In many places the white man's roads and towns have obliterated the old trail. It forked where the city of Calgary now stands. The right fork ran north into the Barren Lands as far as people live. The main

A stagecoach on the Calgary-Edmonton trail. Note the unusual passenger "compartment," which faces to the rear and is covered only by a canopy. (Passengers sat on the sides, facing each other). This was the ultimate in air-conditioned comfort — hot in summer and cold in winter! Shock absorbers had not been invented either.

trail ran south along the eastern side of the Rockies, at a uniform distance from the mountains.... It extended south into the country inhabited by a people with dark skins and long hair falling over their faces (Mexico?)"

If the Calgary-Edmonton Trail (Edmonton-Calgary Trail as it is known from the north end) is that old, it was not heavily travelled until fairly recent times. Explorer-trader David Thompson made the first recorded mention of it in 1800. He travelled the northern portion of it south from Fort Edmonton until he reached a point somewhere near Ponoka, then headed west to Rocky Mountain House. Thompson called the trail the "Wolf's Track," which probably was the Indian name for the route. Indians of the Blackfoot tribes often followed the trail, or one farther to the east through Tail Creek, when heading to Fort Edmonton to trade. And the McDougalls, Reverend John and his trader brother Dave, followed it south from Edmonton to Lone Pine, near modern Bowden, then switched off in a south-westerly direction when, in 1873, they headed out to establish a mission for the Stoney Indians at Morley. Some of the early free traders like Sam Livingston, when he was living in the Victoria and Edmonton area, occasionally took the trail through

Tail Creek, Blackfoot Crossing, Fort Whoop-Up and on down to Fort Benton to trade, rather than taking the long trip to Fort Garry (Winnipeg). But the Calgary-Edmonton Trail itself did not come into being until 1875 when the North West Mounted Police arrived to build Fort Calgary and the Reverend John McDougall opened a fork of his trail straight south from Lone Pine to the new police post on the Bow River.

From then on as Calgary began to grow with the coming of the I.G. Baker and Hudson's Bay Company stores, the trail gradually grew busier. It now extended south through Fort Macleod all the way to Fort Benton, Montana, the terminus of steam navigation on the Missouri River, from where great bull-trains pulling tandem wagons moved freight north. Only the first 50 miles or so north of Calgary lent themselves to the heavy freight wagons, so between Calgary and Edmonton most freight went by the ubiquitous Red River cart, much better suited to navigate the mudholes and soft black loam of this stretch. After the Canadian Pacific Railway arrived in Calgary in 1883, the trail became busier than ever and extended north of Edmonton to Athabasca Landing, which became the southern terminus for river transportation on the Athabasca-

Mackenzie River system, moving freight all the way to the Arctic Ocean.

With the coming of the CPR, the Calgary-Edmonton Trail became Alberta's most important transportation link. Freighters who had for years trailed their noisy Red River carts across 1,000 miles of prairie from Winnipeg over the Winnipeg-Fort Carlton-Edmonton Trail while bringing in trade goods now abandoned the old route for the new. Freight rates at Edmonton dropped from over 16 cents a pound for goods coming over the old route to three cents a pound coming over the Trail from Calgary. For the first time since Edmonton had been established as a trading post over eight decades before, it could expect mail with regularity instead of the once-in-a-while system it had known for so long.

The Trail retained its importance until 1891, when the Calgary & Edmonton Railway reached Edmonton and threw the old road into disuse. For the next 20 years, except for local traffic and for some of the settlers, who either did not have train fare or preferred to travel to their new homesteads by covered wagons loaded with household effects, the trail was largely abandoned. It lay dormant until motor cars began using it with some regularity in 1910. From that day to this, highway engineers have been hard pressed to build, rebuild and rebuild again, as they try to keep abreast of the ever increasing flow of traffic.

Even before the CPR reached Calgary in 1883, one-time buffalo hunter and trader Ad Macpherson joined Jim Coleman to form the first stage company on the trail. They named their company the Royal Stage Lines and on their initial run they left Edmonton on July 24 with Coleman handling the reins of the four-horse team. Heading south on the stage, which was really only a freight wagon with seats, Coleman took his two passengers, J. Herbert and Thomas Dunlop, to the end of the rails, 35 miles east of Calgary, arriving on July 30. There Herbert and Dunlop climbed aboard a CPR work train for the initial segment of their train ride to Medicine Hat, where they caught a passenger train for the east.

Obviously Macpherson and Coleman named their stage line in anticipation of obtaining the contract to carry the mail between Edmonton and Calgary. In this they were disappointed, for postal authorities chose to continue to send mail over the Winnipeg-Edmonton Trail for at least a couple of months after the rails reached Calgary. Moreover, mail destined for Calgary was put off the train at Medicine Hat and carried via Fort Macleod to Calgary by stage line. Things like this invariably straighten themselves out and the mail eventually went directly to Calgary by train. Moreover, when the contract to carry mail between Calgary and Edmonton was given, it went to the Royal Mail Stage Lines. But this was not the original company, two Calgary men, Leeson and Scott, having started a new company and adopted that name as

Macpherson and Coleman had by then gone out of business. Leeson and Scott made their initial stage run to Edmonton on June 12, 1884, nearly a year after the CPR arrived in Calgary. At last Edmonton could expect to get mail on a regular schedule.

Another stagecoach company, which began service on the trail in the summer of 1883, was operated by Donald McLeod, the man Art Belanger, in his book *The Calgary-Edmonton Trail*, calls the "Mr. Everything" of business. Donald McLeod, who came to Canada from his native Scotland in 1862 with the Hudson's Bay Company, had served in various posts throughout the West before settling in Edmonton in 1870. Since then he had tried his hand in most of the enterprises of the settlement, including real estate and lumbering. He had for a time been freighting from Winnipeg to Edmonton, but with the arrival of the rails at Calgary, decided to open a stage line, calling it the Edmonton and Calgary Stage. His inaugural run was on August 6, 1883, when he left Jasper House in Edmonton at nine in the morning. He advertised stops at Steamboat landing (Edmonton), Peace Hills (Wetaskiwin), Battle River (Ponoka), Red Deer River Crossing, Willow Creek (Olds) and Calgary. A one-way ticket between Edmonton and Calgary was a flat $25 — certainly no bargain considering the rough ride, as the accommodation was something less than luxurious and the open stages offered little protection from the elements. There were no discounts for passenger or luggage getting soaked in a rainstorm or river crossing or for delays due to the driver getting lost on the prairie in a fog, such as happened to driver Pete Campbell in February of 1888.

Campbell was heading north out of Calgary along Nose Creek when he ran into a dense fog that obliterated the trail. According to Hugh Dempsey, in an article on the Calgary-Edmonton Trail in the Autumn, 1959, *Alberta Historical Review*, "The trail was faint and the driver soon lost his way. After traveling aimlessly for about 10 miles, he stumbled across a deserted cabin in the Sharp Hills.

"Next morning the fog was still thick and the whole day was occupied in relocating the trail. At last, at nightfall, he sighted Dickson's stopping place (now the town of Airdrie) and was once again on the proper road...."

The fog finally cleared on the sixth day. By then Campbell was only 40 miles from Calgary. He had started out with a wagon but had to switch to a sleigh at Dickson's where he encountered deep snow. But Pete Campbell never did reach Edmonton on that trip for, at Brazeau's stopping place near present-day Leduc, he met a worried looking teamster who had been sent from Edmonton to meet him. The two men exchanged mail, passengers and freight and Campbell headed back to Calgary, taking some three weeks to complete his round trip. Actually there was not too much out of the ordinary about

A Calgary-Edmonton stagecoach crossing a mudhole, of which there were many in 1888 — but one of many hazards to pioneer travellers.

Campbell's journey, for most anything could happen on those trips and usually did.

All the stage drivers and freighters on the old trail were colorful and resourceful fellows, many of them Metis (Red River cart men) who had spent many years moving everything from pemmican to tobacco over the prairie trails. Men like the Laboucans, Selvais and Saloises of the old Duhamel settlement on the Battle River south of modern Camrose were in great demand as freighters. Other well-known names on the trail were Kelly, Breen, Burns, McDonald and Inkster. All had to face mud, mosquitoes, flooding streams and occasionally prairie fires in summer, and drifting snow and extreme cold in winter. Every now and then a freighter would head south on a good sleigh road, only to run into a gusty chinook on the southern end, possibly near Lone Pine, and have to exchange his sleigh for a wagon. Usually the trip took 10 days one way with a load of freight if the road and weather was good and a whole lot longer if it was not. Stopping houses, none of them luxury hotels, sometimes had ornery proprietors who charged exhorbitant prices. One man complained of paying 50 cents for a meal of bannock and butter, the equivalent of $5.00 today, and of being overcharged for feed and shelter for his horses as well. But most of the stopping houses were owned by one-time freighters who knew the needs of the travellers and did their best to provide adequate food and accommodation.

Some of these stopping places were: Dickson's, 18 miles from Calgary; Scarlett's 35 miles out; Lone Pine and Content's; and Bannerman's and McLellan's at the Red Deer River Crossing. North of the Crossing were such places as Barnett's, Anderson's, Lucas' Farm, Telford's and Brazeau's. In 1885, during the North West Rebellion when Major-General T. Bland Strange led the Alberta Field Force north from Calgary to help quell rebel Crees under Chief Big Bear, three of these stopping places were turned into armed forts by men of the 65th Montreal Rifles. These were R. McLellan's new hotel at the Red Deer River Crossing, which became Fort Normandeau (a replica stands there today); the Hudson's Bay Company post at the Battle River Crossing (near Ponoka) which was named Fort Ostell; and the Lucas' Farm House, which was dubbed Fort Ethier.

On the march north, which started from Calgary on April 20, General Strange learned that, besides Chief Big Bear's renegades, whom he later learned had murdered nine men at Frog Lake, other Indian bands were also on a looting spree, if not actually on the warpath—particularly in the Battle and Red Deer River areas. To make sure rambunctious Indians did not cut his communication lines, he left Lieutenant Normandeau and 20 men of the 65th Montreal Rifles to build a fort at the Red Deer River.

(Above) A more modern touch on the Calgary-Edmonton trail, the twin bridges at Blackfalds, 1912. (Right) Progress meant roads. Here a large crew grades a new road from Wetaskiwin to Hobbema in 1902. All work had to be done by man and horsepower.

Lieutenant Normandeau, to save time and expense, took over Robert McLellan's Hotel, built the year before, and had his men cut loopholes in the walls and build a palisade of 10-foot logs set in a two-foot trench around it. He reinforced the walls of the hotel with planks and clay, dug a well and erected three bastions, or lookout towers and prepared to repel any attack.

At the same time, Captain John Benjamin Ostell was doing essentially the same thing to the Hudson's Bay Company post at the Battle River and Captain L.J. Ethier was converting Indian Farm Instructor Sam Lucas' house near what is now Wetaskiwin into the fort that his men insisted on calling Fort Ethier. They were built as a show of force more than anything, for none were armed with anything more than men with rifles, none saw action, and all three were abandoned soon after the Rebellion was over.

On July 8, 1885, to replenish supplies depleted in the Edmonton area by the Rebellion, the I.G. Baker Company, which had stores in Calgary, Fort Macleod and other southern Alberta and Montana centers, started north from Calgary with the biggest freight convoy ever to travel the trail up to that time. Heavy freight wagons in tandems of three drawn by long strings of oxen carrying 630,000 pounds of cargo headed out. These outfits were a common sight on the Fort Benton, Macleod-Calgary Trail, where firm prairie soil made a good roadbed. But the freighters had so much trouble getting the heavy wagons through the northern end of the Calgary-Edmonton Trail that they vowed never again to try such a feat. Red River carts and single wagons were the only practical vehicles for the route.

Undoubtedly the worst hazard on the trail was the river crossing. During spring break-up and fall freeze-up, no one could travel the route. Men built ice bridges after freeze-up to strengthen the ice, but until a couple of heavy loads had gone over without breaking through, the first freighters crossing the rivers literally took their lives in their hands. The worst places were Nose Creek, Blackmud Creek, Pipestone, Big Stone and Wolf Creeks, and the Blindman River. The toll on horses and machinery was "something terrible," according to one freighter. He estimated that 50 horses died on the trail in 1888 alone.

In 1886 the government of the North West Territories gave its sanction to the trail when it sent out C.A. Biggar to survey the south end from Calgary to Red Deer River Crossing and G.P. Roy to lay out the north end. They left it pretty much as it had been except for changing approaches to some of the streams to make for easier crossing. Surveying did not help travel much, however. About the only "improvements" George Roy thought the trail needed was "a little ditching, a small culvert, a slight cut, or a few branches thrown on a soft spot." Nothing like keeping costs down to a bare minimum.

As it turned out, there was not at that time much reason to spend a lot of money on the trail. This was the beginning of the railway expansion era on the prairies and it seemed everyone wanted to get into the act. Edmonton, of course, was crying for a railway and indeed had expected to have the CPR

come through, only to lose it to Calgary when the federal government decided to use the shorter route. Therefore, when businessmen from both Calgary and Edmonton organized the Calgary and Edmonton Railway Company with a promise to push the line through, Edmonton, at least, welcomed the news with great anticipation. Construction crews started pushing the line north in 1890 and reached the Red Deer River by freeze-up that fall. The following spring they continued the line to Edmonton, although people in North Edmonton soon lost their enthusiasm for the line when they learned that the railway company was not planning to cross the North Saskatchewan River, but were making South Edmonton, or Strathcona, the end of the line. It turned out that the Calgary and Edmonton Railway Company had no intention of operating the line once it was built, but had only agreed to build it to obtain the land grant of 6,400 acres given to them by the Dominion Government for every mile of track laid down. Having obtained this, the company leased the line to the CPR then, in 1904, got out of railroading altogether by leasing the line to the CPR for a further 99 years. Strange and devious things might have happened, but at last Edmonton— South Edmonton at least—was on a railroad line.

With the railway completed, except for local traffic near towns that sprang up along the line—

towns like Airdrie, Olds, Innisfail, Red Deer, Lacombe, Wetaskiwin and Leduc— the old trail lay dormant for the next 15 years. Then, in 1906, it saw the beginning of the automobile age when G. Corriveau and his son drove over the road from Edmonton to Calgary. Surprisingly, it took them only 11½ hours — good time considering the condition of the trail. At one stage they reportedly hit a blazing 40 miles per hour. That was the start and, as more and more cars hit the trail, the Alberta Government decided to do its part and spent $600,000 to improve the route by bridging rivers, shaving hills and grading long stretches of muskeg sloughs.

Gradually the route improved from dirt road to gravel track to paved highway connecting the villages and towns along the way. That was the Black Route which became Highway 2, then 2A after a new Highway 2 was built starting in the 1950s, and which is still being improved today. Where 2A connects all the towns, Highway 2 bypasses all of them. Neither route deviates very far from the old trail the colorful freighters with their carts and wagons followed nearly 100 years ago.

Consequently, though it may be Highway 2 or 2A to engineers, to most Albertans it will remain what it has always been— the Calgary-Edmonton, or Edmonton-Calgary-Trail. ●

(Above) In 1922 trailblazing Alex Monkman discovered the pass which today bears his name. Twelve years later, tired of waiting for a railway or a highway to utilize the route, Peace River residents began construction of an all-volunteer roadway. This old photograph shows the sturdy Kinuseo bridge with its span of 112 feet which cost all of $80 in materials.

(Left) When the Monkman Pass Highway Association was promised financial aid by the Edmonton Chamber of Commerce if they could get a car over their roadway, Louis Stojan donated the 1927 Model-T Ford shown here. Sixty miles from its destination, the history-making Ford was abandoned upon the start of the war. In June of 1967, almost 30 years after, members of the Grande Prairie River Rats Association hauled it out of the bush for restoration.

TRAILBLAZER ALEX MONKMAN

*Alex Monkman found a fine low pass through the Rockies, but
all the Peace River country ever got out of it were promises of a
railroad and highway that never materialized.*

A mountain pass, a lake and a creek are named after him; had things turned out as planned, there would also be a highway bearing his name. For a trailblazer Alex Monkman certainly was. In 1899 he helped cut the first trail into the Grande Prairie area, a wagon path from Spirit River to Lake Saskatoon, where he built a post for the trading partners, Fletcher Bredin and James Cornwall. In 1922, while trapping in the mountains west of Beaverlodge, he discovered the pass that bears his name and the following year guided Murray Hill,

CNR reconnaissance engineer, showing him it was a logical route for a railroad from the Peace River Country to the Pacific Coast. The fact that the railway was never built, nor the Monkman Pass Highway that was started in 1937 ever finished, is no fault of his. He certainly showed the way and it seems inevitable that sooner or later a paved road will wend its way through the low Rocky Mountain pass named for early Peace River pioneer, Alex Monkman.

Fortunately (largely due to the efforts of W.D.

Albright, long time Superintendent of the Beaverlodge Experimental Farm), quite a lot is known about Alex Monkman's early life. He was born in the Red River Valley near Winnipeg in 1870 and moved with his parents to Prince Albert, Saskatchewan, when he was four years old. Alex remembered that his father did a little farming and hunted for buffalo every year until 1881 when the great beasts all but disappeared from the plains. Though young at the time, the memory of living in a buffalo skin tent while his father hunted the buffalo remained with Alex Monkman for the rest of his life.

"We lived in Prince Albert from 1874 until 1886," he told Albright in a 1933 interview. "I was there the time of the Riel Rebellion in 1885. Then I went to Montana. The reason for leaving Prince Albert was that the wages paid there at that time were only $15.00 a month. I met a man from Montana who told me wages there were $40 to $75 per month... In 1886 I got $75.00 per month for breaking horses and riding the range...."

It was the Klondike gold rush that brought Alex Monkman to the Peace River Country. After working for 11 years as a bronco-buster and miner in Montana, he drifted north to Edmonton, where he worked for lumberman John Walters, building and painting cutters and sleighs. Then, when the news of the gold strike in the Yukon turned the slow-growing town into a bustling gathering place for prospective gold miners from all over the United States and Canada, Monkman too caught the gold fever and joined the host of humanity heading north.

In the spring of 1898 he started out with a party of five, led by a Scotsman named William Lang, driving nine Red River carts and a wagon and following the trail to Fort Assiniboine and over the Swan Hills to Willow Point on the west end of Lesser Slave Lake. Unlike the gold-seekers who were determined to reach the Klondike or die in the attempt, Monkman was more concerned with finding a spot where he could make a decent living and more or less be his own boss. When he heard at the Lesser Slave Lake settlement that some of the prospectors were making $30 to $50 a day washing gold on the Wapiti and Smoky Rivers, he was tempted to have a look. At least he was until he hauled some freight between Lesser Slave Lake and Peace River Crossing for Twelve-Foot Davis, long-time trader whose name is practically synonymous with the Peace River Country. Davis was doubtful of the chances of anyone finding gold in paying quantities anywhere in the North. "Young man," he told Monkman, "you are crazy coming into this country looking for gold. I came through from the Cariboo 40 years ago. The trail I came over is all grown over now and doesn't lead to the Klondike, anyhow. You should have gone up the coast."

When Monkman could find no one who had hit paydirt on either the Smoky or the Wapiti River, he was still tempted to try for the Klondike. But when he got as far as Dunvegan, he met some of the fellows he had worked with in Montana, who told him they had turned back north of Fort St. John when they found the trail next to impossible. Monkman, too, decided to turn back. That decision became a lot easier when he met his future brother-in-law, Albert Tate, at Dunvegan. Tate was the manager of the local Hudson's Bay Company post and was in the process of moving the long established post and HBC headquarters for the Peace River Country to Lesser Slave Lake. Though there seems to be no record of it, it seems quite likely that Monkman helped Tate move to the new post.

Something about the Peace River Country obviously appealed to Monkman, for he decided to stay rather than return to Edmonton. That decision may not have been made until after he took a job freighting for a man named Anderson. Then, a month or so later, he met W. Fletcher Bredin and James Cornwall at their trading post at Slave Lake. Their enthusiasm for the country soon rubbed off on Monkman; particularly after they put him to work running dogs and buying fur for them the following winter, then, the next summer, sent him to the Grande Prairie district to choose a site for a trading post and to blaze a trail into the area from Spirit River. Monkman followed an old Indian trail from Spirit River and chose a spot for the new post where the trail forked near Lake Saskatoon. In an article based on his 1933 interview with the old trailblazer, entitled "Early Days in the Grande Prairie," W.D. Albright wrote:

"After picking a site for the post, Monkman went back by the Cadotte Lake pitching trail, being informed that it led through the narrowest belt of timber between two prairies, but the banks of the Burnt River which the trail crossed were found (to be) as high as the banks of the Smoky and all over could be seen the marks on the trees where Dave Sexsmith had recently brought through his Red River cart, the first wheeled vehicle to reach the Grande Prairie. After this Bredin and Cornwall had the trail cut over the Saddle Hills, which is practically the route of the present highway. The cutting was done by Cornwall, Monkman, Quick and Vellner."

Once the trail was chopped out, Monkman headed back to Lesser Slave Lake for a load of supplies, then returned to Lake Saskatoon where he built a house and set up his store. "By the time the house was finished it was Christmas time and the trappers were coming in and trade was good from the start," he remembered. If he still had any doubts about making the country his home, he dispelled them by July of 1900, when he journeyed to Edmonton to marry Louisa Ann Tate and brought her back to Lake Saskatoon.

That honeymoon trip into the Peace gave Mrs. Monkman a memorable introduction to northern adventure, for 1900 was an extremely wet year. The newlyweds travelled to Athabasca Landing from Edmonton with Fletcher Bredin, who was taking in a wagon load of freight. From Athabasca Landing they travelled up the river by York boats to Mirror Landing. That was one of the few years when the Lesser Slave River was high enough for navigation and they were able to continue by boat all the way up the Lesser Slave from the Athabasca River into Lesser Slave Lake and down the length of the lake to the settlement on Willow Point. The residents at the Willow Point settlement, however, did not consider the high water all that advantageous, for it had flooded the whole point and they had been forced to build sidewalks on stilts in order to get from one building to another. That fall everyone pulled up stakes and moved a mile or so farther west to where the village of Grouard is now located.

If Mrs. Monkman had not seen her share of adventure on the first leg of the journey, there was more to come. After bouncing across the rough and muddy trail between Grouard and Peace River Landing, they crossed the Peace River in a skiff with the disassembled wagon, the horses swimming along behind. That procedure was repeated at Dunvegan after another long bumpy ride on the north side of the river from Peace River Landing. Then came an experience Mrs. Monkman was not likely to forget. Monkman had plenty of help getting his outfit across the Peace and up the south bank after leaving Dunvegan, but from there on he needed extra freighters to take his trading outfit the rest of the way to Lake Saskatoon. Consequently, he had to leave Mrs. Monkman with the wagon while he went to Spirit River for help. It was a long, slow trip and he was not able to return until the following day. Mrs. Monkman spent a lonely sleepless night as what she thought was a bunch of grizzly bears roared their challenge to one another as to which one would have her for a late-night snack. As it turned out, the fighting grizzly bears had been mice — the quiet wilderness night and a vivid imagination having amplified their squeaky voices into the full-blown roar of angry grizzlies. Coyotes calling to each other and to the moon had also done little to alleviate her fears during her lonely vigil.

Until Bredin and Cornwall sold out to Revillon Freres in 1906, Alex Monkman remained in their employ and remembered the years as happy. During that span he and his brother-in-law, Albert Tate, did some prospecting during the summer months when the fur trade was at a standstill. They looked for iron and tungsten deposits along Naked Creek and the Wapiti River, but found no great ore bodies in either area. "But," said Monkman, "we were luckier than those who came after us, for when we were prospecting there was no land office to relieve us of filing fees. Mr. Tate sent samples to the assaying office but they proved of no value."

Alex Monkman obviously thought very highly of his employers, for he wrote: "I think Bredin and Cornwall deserve some credit for the settlement of Grande Prairie— more credit than the majority of people give them— and I think I may say I have done my 'little bit' toward this settlement. I was hired as a fur buyer and trader, having worked for them up to the 1st of June, 1906... While in the employ of Bredin and Cornwall I did a little farming on my own as early as 1903. As there was no other crop on the Grande Prairie at the time, I may safely say that I was the 'pioneer farmer' of the Grande Prairie, at least in a small way."

After leaving Bredin and Cornwall, Monkman took up ranching for awhile by buying up a herd of cattle that Jimmy McCreight had brought into the country from Calgary, over the old trail that led through Lac Ste. Anne, in 1903. He built up a herd, perhaps 150 head of horses and cattle, but finally had to give up ranching when homesteaders began filing in after 1908 and the amount of range land became restricted. He took up farming with the others and things went along fairly well until 1920 when high freight rates and low grain prices forced some of the homesteaders to abandon their farms. Alex Monkman, however, was a many-talented man and turned to trapping to supplement his farm income.

"In 1922," wrote E.C. Stacey in his book, *Monkman Pass Highway*, "there were nine trappers in the mountains southwest of Rio Grande, but only Monkman had enough supplies to push on for the entire winter. When he reached the Herrick River he found a spike of the 1904 Grand Trunk survey and quickly realized he had found the easiest and lowest pass and the most direct route from the Peace region (to the Pacific Coast). He reported his findings to the CPR and CNR and in 1933 he guided Murray Hill, reconnaissance engineer, through the Pass. Thus the finding and naming of the Monkman Pass."

Alex Monkman found a fine low pass through the Rockies, but all the Peace River Country got out of it were promises of a railroad and highway that never materialized. Finally by 1936 the people got tired of waiting. The CNR and CPR obviously had little intention of building a railway and the Alberta government flatly refused money for a highway at that time. The determined Peace River district residents began to build the highway themselves until the Second World War broke out and turned their efforts to more pressing issues.

They certainly made a good start on their highway. In October, 1936, South Peace citizens formed the Monkman Pass Highway Association, naming Alex Monkman honorary president. Their goal was 132 miles of road suitable for automobiles between Rio Grande, Alberta and Hansard, British Columbia, where it would connect with the Cariboo Highway. By the summer of 1937 the road was mapped out and the first volunteer work crews, mostly farmers who had just finished planting their crops, were chopping down trees, building bridges and culverts and working on the grade. "That year," wrote Stacey, "20 miles of road and bridges were built. The largest bridge was over the Kinuseo River, a span of 112 feet built at a cost of $80 plus labor. At times there were 90 men working on the road."

Those men— and women— came from all over the Peace River Country. Farmers who could not spare the time to work on the road, lent horses or sent a side of beef or pork, sack of potatoes, garden vegetables or some hay or grain for the horses. Businessmen donated what they could. Women did the cooking and baking. It was the kind of community effort that only a pioneer settlement could ever hope to muster. Alex Monkman, though getting on in years and suffering from a severe rupture, was probably as happy as at any time in his life, and rode the trail, giving advice and occasionally spinning a yarn of what he had seen and anticipated two decades before. He must have been gladdened when a lake and a creek, as well as the Pass, were also named in his honor.

The Monkman Pass Highway Association looked far and wide for financial support and received promises of funding from the Edmonton Chamber of Commerce— if and when the MPHA pushed a car through the route. Fair enough, said Francis Murphy, who had contacted the Edmonton people. Louis Stojan then donated the car, a 1927 Model-T Ford with two-speed rear axle. His two sons, Jerry and Charlie, proceeded to put it in shape. The Imperial Oil Company promised to donate the gas once the car made it through the Pass.

On September 3, 1938, the car headed west with 18-year-old Charlie Stojan at the wheel and 17-year-old Jerry acting as co-driver and mechanic. They cannot be faulted for the car's not getting through, for it ran smoothly and negotiated hills and mud-holes with relative ease. But, deep in the mountains, trouble began to pile on trouble. Radio contact failed, supplies did not arrive and a snowstorm made the trail sloppy and treacherous. The boys plugged on, however, and, finally, on November 6, reached the Herrick River. They were a day too late— the river was icing over and unsafe for them to ferry the car across. The goal— Hansard— was still 60 miles away. Next spring, 1939, finances were slow in coming. Then, in September, the war erupted in Europe and all thoughts of finishing the highway or pushing the pathfinder car through were put aside for the duration.

That car did get through, eventually, although not immediately after the war as everyone hoped. In fact, it did not make it until June of 1967. And it was not the Monkman Pass Highway Association that got it through, but 17 men from the Grande Prairie River Rats Association. The River Rats started out from Prince George in five jet-propelled boats. They

Here, Peace River volunteers carve a roadway through the wilderness for a dollar a day and board. Their goal was 132 miles of road suitable for automobiles to link Rio Grande, Alberta, and Hansard, British Columbia, where it would connect with the Cariboo Highway. But construction ground to a halt with the outbreak of the Second World War.

spurted up the Fraser River to the mouth of the McGregor, up the McGregor to the Herrick and to the spot where the old Model-T had been abandoned for the 28 years. It was still there, almost buried in leaves, its body rusted, its tires shot and its upholstery rotted away. The River Rats gingerly loaded it on to the boats, ferried it back to Prince George, then hauled it back to Grande Prairie via the Hart Highway and Dawson Creek. Today, after partial restoration, it sits in the Stojan Garage in Sexsmith, where Jerry, the only surviving brother, acts as its guardian.

As for Alex Monkman's Highway, it still has not been completed. Presently there is controversy over whether the highway should be built and paved, or the area turned into a wilderness park. Until the argument is settled the road will remain incomplete. Whatever the decision, Alex Monkman has long since ceased to care. He passed away in 1941 and is buried in the Lake Saskatoon Cemetery. An article titled "Funeral of Alex Monkman Held Wednesday, October 1," which appeared in the Grand Prairie *Herald Tribune* paid the following tribute to its earliest trailblazer:

"Notwithstanding the condition of the roads, there was a large turnout at the funeral services of

Trailblazer Alex Monkman on his saddle horse, Tramp.

Alex Monkman, held in Lake Saskatoon Hall on Wednesday, October 1. Oldtimers came in wagons, Bennett buggies, and on saddle horses, many over long distances, to pay their last respects to a great pioneer.

"The service was conducted by Reverend Eric Wright of Wembley and Captain C.R. Gillingham of the Grande Prairie Salvation Army.

"Mr. Wright in referring to the life of Alex Monkman, said: "I think Alex Monkman would face the transition (from this world to the next) in the spirit of a great warrior. I salute his memory, as I salute all who have pioneered and pushed ever onward the frontiers of civilization. He was our oldest resident and as long as we continue to work for a westward route to the Pacific, his name and work will be remembered."

Even without that westward route he visualized, with a mountain pass, lake and creek named for him, Alex Monkman has achieved the kind of immortality many strive for, but few achieve. If and when the Monkman Pass area is turned into a national wilderness park, what better name for it than the Alex Monkman Park. ●

Ma's epicurean cooking was truly something to behold, both in quality and quantity, and was known from the Peace River country to the four corners of the globe. When a new highway bypassed her little road house, customers continued to come and were well compensated for the effort.

MA BRAINARD'S

NOT too many travellers travelling to or from the outside over that old buffalo trail that passed for a road between British Columbia's Peace River Block and the little town of Hythe prior to 1950 could ever resist the temptation to stop off at Ma Brainard's for a snack. Ma's epicurean cooking was truly something to behold, both in quality and quantity, and was known from the Peace River Country to the four corners of the Globe. Many a northwestern Alberta resident still vividly recalls how, during the Second World War when the building of the Alaska Highway was in full swing, it was not uncommon to see a dozen or so Canadian or American military vehicles from the base camp at Dawson Creek parked among the farm trucks and tractor-drawn wagons in front of Ma's. They also recall that in the rambling log house facing a little lake, captains, majors, colonels and even generals sometimes rubbed elbows with the locals, while waiting their turn for a seat at Ma's sumptuous table.

And no wonder when you consider that the table would be loaded with, besides Ma's specialty of Southern fried chicken complimented with hot biscuits, a half-dozen kinds of vegetables and maybe 10 varieties of pickles, jams and jellies, all from her own garden. Finish this off with at least two cups of excellent coffee and apple pie so good it was seldom equalled let alone excelled, and you had partaken of a meal fit for the gods.

Even when you had gorged yourself to stupefaction, chances are pretty good that Ma still was not completely satisfied she had done her best for you and would say something like: "What's wrong with me? Here I plum forgot the salad. Danged if I ain't becoming forgetful in my old age."

If not too many people were around to occupy her time, Ma could be nearly as good a storyteller as she was a cook. She liked to tell of her home in North Carolina, of how she married Minnesota-born

W.L. "Leo" Brainard who, by the turn of the century, had established himself in Montana as a pretty successful horse and cattle rancher.

Then in 1905, when Alberta became a province, Ma remembered, Leo took a trip north to have a look around. What he saw convinced him that southern Alberta had far better grazing land and more accessible water than they had in Montana. From Alberta ranchers he learned that the Chinook winds generally kept the snow down so well that cattle could graze all winter. After a consultation with Ma, he decided to move north.

Trouble was, claimed Ma, by even that early date the only land still open for homesteading and ranching on the scale needed for their 600 cattle and 200 horses was north of the Red Deer River, actually outside the area usually swept clear by Chinooks. This did not seem to worry Brainard, though, for luck had been with him until then. The spot he chose was some 15 miles northeast of the present town of Hanna, close to the little village of Scapa.

"When Leo began driving the herd north (in) the summer of 1906," Ma said, "I stayed home in Montana to look after things 'til he got settled up there." With Brainard went a half-dozen ranch hands, his son from a previous marriage, and an old ranch hand who had been with him for years. As it was getting on towards fall when he moved the herd across the South Saskatchewan River at Medicine Hat, oldtimers in the area warned him not to go any farther north that year. For, they said, he would not have time to put up hay and if there happened to be a hard winter ahead he was liable to lose his whole herd. But Leo still believed luck was with him and pressed on, sure that the Chinooks would come as he had heard they always did.

Actually, claimed Ma, Brainard got his herd to his chosen ranch with no problem, where he paid off

FAMOUS CUISINE

the extra hands and let them go home. Though his neighbors offered to supply him with hay for the winter, because he was by then short of cash, he refused, still trusting to luck. And everything went fine through September and October, just as he had hoped. But, in November, the first bad blizzard struck and scattered the herd for miles. Then, when the looked-for Chinook failed to come, he decided he had better take advantage of his neighbors' offer of feed and set off with his son and the old ranch hand to round up the cattle. The horses, he figured, could rustle for themselves.

But there was more bad luck ahead—another blizzard, even worse than the first one, came howling from the west. While trying to keep the herd headed toward the ranch, the old cowhand over-extended himself, suffered a heart attack and died. Brainard's son too became exhausted and while Leo struggled to a neighbor's house for help, froze to death before Brainard could return. "My husband, himself, almost froze to death," Ma claimed, "and spent most of that winter in a Montana hospital, where all but one of his toes had to be amputated because infection had set in."

After that experience, most men would never have returned to Alberta. But Leo was a determined man and in the spring he and Ma set out for the homestead. Surprisingly, though most of the horses were never found, some 70 cattle survived the winter, one of the worst blizzard-plagued in Alberta history. Before he, Ma and their daughter Inez moved to the Peace River Country after the First World War, Leo had rebuilt that herd to its original size, had bought himself a steam tractor and had become well-known in the district for his custom plowing and threshing.

Ma's voice would invariably soften as she recalled how Leo had suddenly taken sick and died of a heart attack in the summer of 1938. By then other settlers were filing in, the land was being divided into quarter sections and fenced and ranching was no longer possible. It was then that Ma turned the ranch house into a stopping place and her cooking began to win international acclaim.

Ma liked to tell how she once served British diplomat, Sir Henry Thornton, and his entourage, when he passed through during the late thirties. Sir Henry was a connoisseur of good food and had eaten in many of the world's most famous restaurants. Small wonder, then, that Ma was proud that, when he signed the guest book, he wrote: "To the author of the best meal I ever ate." He was so impressed with her cooking that he found time to write to her every now and then. He expressed special concern, when, during the early years of the Second World War, he learned that Ma had fallen from her barn roof while making repairs to the shingles and broken her hip. He sincerely hoped, he wrote, that this misfortune would not in any way harm her cooking.

When, in the late 1940s, the Department of Highways straightened out the old buffalo trail between Hythe and the Alberta-British Columbia border, it bypassed Ma Brainard's stopping place and Ma never bothered to move to the new road. Too old, she said. Nevertheless, she continued to operate at the old location overlooking the placid little lake. Anyone taking the trouble to travel the old dirt trail was well compensated for the effort.

But time respects no one—not even one of the finest cooks that God ever placed on the face of His good earth. Old age forced her to retire in the early 1960s and she passed away a few years later. With her leaving, the Peace River country—and indeed the world—is the loser.

For Ma Brainard's was a stopping place par excellence—one of which any country could be truly proud. ●

A black and white reproduction of a full-color painting depicting the murder scene as Lemon is about to slay his sleeping companion with an axe. The painting is by artist Joe Adams.

THE LOST LEMON MINE

***Does the Lost Lemon Mine exist? Is it jinxed? No one knows for sure
but men still look for a murderer's gold near the headwaters of the Highwood
and Livingstone Rivers. At least four men have died in the attempt.***

THE Lemon Mine — did it ever exist? If it does
not, many men have wasted countless hours in
trying to find it, only to meet, at best, with disappointment and, at worst—death.

According to legend, the story begins in the
spring of 1870, when some miners from the
Tobacco Plains, which extend from southeastern
British Columbia into northwestern Montana, headed north to try their luck at panning gold in the
North Saskatchewan River, near Fort Edmonton.
Two of these men, "Blackjack" and Frank Lemon,
were experienced prospectors who were staked on
this expedition by a well-known frontiersman named
Lafayette French. French, who was born in Pennsylvania around 1840, had knocked around the
western United States and what is now southern
Alberta from a very early age. Some claim he himself was a prospector, but most knew him primarily
as a trader whose main customers were Indians.
Lemon was said to be the best prospector in the
West, purportedly having located some very rich
claims. Some maintain that he was the real dis-
coverer of the 1858 Cariboo strike in British
Columbia. Near Edmonton, so the legend goes, the
partners found some gold, but not in large enough
amounts to be worthwhile, so that fall they decided
to return to the Tobacco Plains.

On the return journey they were heading for a
mountain pass used by British Columbia Indians—
possibly the Kootenais — to slip into the Alberta
plains, knock off a supply of buffalo, then high-tail it
back with their meat before the Blackfoot tribes
learned of their coming. Somewhere near the headwaters of the Highwood and Livingstone Rivers the
two partners found a rich gold deposit. Lafayette
French, who later saw a sample of the rock in Fort
Benton, described it as a body of gold laced with
traces of rock.

What happened that night after the discovery is
not completely known, but it seems the partners
were not cooperating very well and an argument
arose over whether they should stay awhile and try
to develop their claim, or stake the claim and head
over the mountains, to return the following spring.

That night Lemon, apparently deeply angered
over something Blackjack had said, or perhaps
succumbing to greed, waited until Blackjack was
asleep and dispatched him with several hefty blows
of an axe. A short time later he was struck with the
enormity of his deed and headed across the
mountains to the Tobacco Plains where he confessed his hideous crime to a priest. What Lemon
did not know was that two Stoney Indians had
witnessed Blackjack's murder and had immediately

reported it to their chieftain. Chief Bearspaw knew
that if word of the rich gold strike spread, the
southern part of his hunting territory would soon be
swarming with white men. Not wanting that to
happen, he swore his two men to secrecy, telling
them never to divulge the whereabouts of the strike
even on pain of death. The two made a promise and
as a consequence their secret did follow them to
their graves.

Although a remorseful Lemon almost lost his
sanity immediately after the killing of his partner, he
recovered sufficiently to give directions to his claim
and the priest who had heard his confession
dispatched a man named John McDougald to locate
the spot. Apparently McDougald found the claim,
buried Blackjack's body, marked the grave with a
mound of stones, then returned to Tobacco Plains.
Chief Bearspaw, however, had had his men
watching the area and, as soon as McDougald left,
they tore down the mound and did an excellent job
of obliterating all signs of the claim. They did their
job so thoroughly, in fact, that the mine has never
been found since. Lemon himself apparently led at
least two parties in search of the mine. On the
second, when apparently close to the spot, he
became violently insane and had to be taken back to
the Tobacco Plains. He never recovered sufficiently
to lead another search.

Since then dozens of parties have searched for
the Lost Lemon Mine. If the legend is true, it is still
out there, incredibly rich, just waiting for the right
person to come along. Hopefully, the person who
does find it will have better luck than some of the
others who have searched. John McDougald, who
was to lead a party to the mine the year after he had
been there to bury Blackjack, went on a drinking
spree at Fort Kipp a short time before he was to meet
the rest of the searchers. He apparently drank too
much bad booze and it killed him. William Bendow,
one of the Stoney Indians who saw Lemon kill
Blackjack, after being promised a fine herd of cattle
was finally persuaded to lead Lafayette French to
the mine. For some unexplained reason Bendow
died on the way. And French himself was badly
burned when the house in which he was sleeping
burned to the ground. Although in terrible pain, he
wrote a letter to an old friend, Senator Dan Riley,
saying he had found the mine and would tell him
about it when he got to the Senator's home in High
River. But by the time French reached High River he
was no longer able to talk. He died soon after,
taking his secret with him.

The Lost Lemon Mine — is it out there? Is it
jinxed? Maybe some day we will know. ●

THE AMAZING MR. O'B.

Eugene Francis O'Beirne was the greatest hazard that travellers ever had to face in the Canadian West. From Edmonton to Fort Kamloops, he had to be extricated from one disaster after another, and his companions were delighted to see the last of him.

WE all tend to think of our early explorers and adventurers as fearless, resourceful fellows— always prepared to meet any emergency. Well it seems that not all of them were that way. Least-wise, not Mr. "O'B.," who travelled through western Alberta and the Yellowhead Pass with Viscount Milton and Dr. W.B. Cheadle from Edmonton to Fort Kamloops in the summer of 1863. A real stumblefoot, Mr. O'B. had to be the antithesis of our general concept of hardy pioneer.

For many years not even his real name was known. Not because no one wrote about him— Milton and Cheadle mentioned him constantly in their book *North West Passage By Land*— but because writers of the Victorian era had an irritating habit of abbreviating a name—particularly a name of someone they did not like. And no one who

wrote about him had a very high opinion of the amazing Mr. O'B.

Thanks to research carried on for six years by the late Tommy Tweed, a CBC actor and writer whose specialty was adapting Canadian history for radio and television, most of the mystery of O'B.'s life was cleared up in an article he wrote for *Alberta History*, the journal of the Alberta Historical Society. Mr. Tweed found that the Canadian West had been host to three Mr. O'B.s, none of them an asset to the country. But the one we are concerned with was born in Ireland, the grandson of a famous Irish bishop, sometime between 1809 and 1811. His real name was Eugene Francis O'Beirne, a long, gang-ling man who attended Cambridge University, al-though he apparently never earned his degree. Though raised a Catholic, O'B. later turned against

(Opposite page) The Milton-Cheadle party crossing the Fraser River. Time and again the useless Mr. O'B. fell behind the others — a habit temporarily cured when one of the others pretended to be a grizzly bear and frightened him out of his wits. (Above) The raging forest fire on McLeod River, which O'B. tried in vain to quell with his drinking cup. (Right) A fine sketch showing Lord Milton, in headband, second from left, and Dr. Cheadle. Unfortunately for posterity the infamous Mr. "O'B." is not shown.

the church after being expelled from one of their schools in Ireland and, for the next decade or so, he toured England expounding the evils of his former religion.

During the next quarter of a century, quite possibly because he never seemed to make friends, he never spent much time in one place. By the late 1850s we find him in the United States where he had strayed after serving some time as a journalist in India. He was working as secretary to a wealthy Louisiana planter when the American Civil War broke out. Appointed to the Home Guard with the rank of captain, Mr. O'B. envisioned flashing swords and bayonets, all directed at various parts of his anatomy, and promptly fled northward to Canada where, in 1861, he showed up at the Red River Colony in Manitoba.

"Alas for the colony, O'Beirne had no money and a well developed taste for alcohol," wrote Mr. Tweed. ". . . By the spring of 1862 he had predictably worn out his welcome and it was suggested he move on. This was a sad prospect for a man of 52."

Luckily for O'B., he was able to attach himself to a group known as the Overlanders — some 150 men, women and children from Ontario who were heading for the gold fields of the Cariboo in British Columbia. Altogether this group travelled 3,500 miles, including a 900-mile jaunt across the prairies by ox-cart, at an average rate of 2½ miles an hour. Some of them drowned while rafting down the Fraser and Thompson Rivers, but most eventually did get to the Cariboo.

Mr. O'B., however, did not arrive there with

them. It did not take the Overlanders long to find out that O'Beirne was inordinately lazy and a trouble-maker to boot. Consequently, they dumped him at the first opportunity, which was at Fort Carlton on the Saskatchewan River in what is now Saskatchewan. The residents of Fort Carlton likewise found O'B. an insufferable nuisance and sent him upriver to Rev. Woolsey's mission at Smokey Lake on the first Hudson's Bay Company York boat heading that way. "O'Beirne," wrote Mr. Tweed, "found a sort of temporary refuge with the Reverend Thomas Woolsey, a Wesleyan minister." The Rev. John McDougal met O'Beirne at Woolsey's Smokey Lake mission, but obviously was no more impressed with him than others had been. In his book *Forest, Lake and Prairie*, he remarked:

"He was an old Wandering Jew kind of man, one of those human beings who seem to be trying to hide from themselves... He had come to Fort Edmonton and was thrown out by the rule made by Governor Dallas that no Hudson's Bay officer should allow stragglers to stay around the posts. The fine for doing so was 10 shillings a day per stranger. When Mr. O'B. came to our home we found him to be an educated man...but a victim of the liquor curse. His was another life blasted by the demon from the bottomless pit. In rummaging around our quarters, Mr. O'B. had found a keg which had, sometime or another, held liquor. I saw him smell this, then fill it with water. Then every little while he would go down and shake the keg. One day I heard him say, 'It is getting good.' So I thought I would make it better. I secretly took the keg, emptied it and

filled it with fresh water. Mr. O'B. took great pleasure in drinking this, though the taste must have become very faint indeed."

Mr. O'B. had been stuck in Edmonton for a time when Viscount Milton and Dr. Cheadle came along in June, 1863. These two English gentlemen, both of whom were geographers among other things, were attempting to establish a land route across Canada to British Columbia by one of the northern passes through the Rocky Mountains. Immediately upon their arrival in Edmonton, O'Beirne began filling their ears with tales of ghastly experiences he had been having with huge grizzlies and packs of wolves, which he claimed roamed within feet of where he was quartered in a cabin in some willows a quarter mile from the HBC post, and said he was in imminent danger of being eaten alive. Learning that Milton and Cheadle were heading for the Cariboo by way of the Yellowhead Pass, O'B. begged to be taken along. Much against their better judgment, Milton and Cheadle finally consented.

Not too surprisingly Mr. O'B. had no trouble equipping himself for the trip. He had long since worn out his welcome and the HBC people were so anxious to see the last of him that each chipped in a pound to speed him on his way. A Mr. Sinclair donated two pounds just to be sure. With the money O'B. purchased himself a horse, blankets and 40 pounds of pemmican to eat on the way.

It was a motley crew that left Edmonton about the second week in June. There were seven in all, travelling with 12 pack and saddle horses. Included were a Metis guide who accompanied them part

(Opposite page) The expedition's pack horses caught in the rapids of the Fraser River near Yellowhead Pass. Not the least of the dangers of the journey was the company of the amazing Mr. O'B., who made his presence felt every painful step of the way.
(Right) One of the many exciting moments on the trail. Here, their raft goes adrift on the Canoe River, as illustrated in Milton and Cheadle's North West Passage by Land, *published in 1865.*
(Below) The Milton and Cheadle party cross the Athabasca River just downstream from Jasper. Here, they almost lost their unruly guest but, alas! Mr. O'B. was rescued from drowning.

way, an Indian guide, Louis Batenotte, known simply as The Assiniboine, his wife and their 12-year-old son. Mr. O'B. immediately got things off to a fine start by accusing The Assiniboine of every crime in the book, including murder. The Assiniboine was not too enthralled with O'B. either, having heard from some of O'B.'s fellow travellers how useless and quarrelsome he had been on the trail from the Red River Settlement. Rumor became reality when O'B. refused to pack his own horse and even required help to roll his blankets. It was shaping into an interesting journey.

On the trail O'Beirne insisted on being last and every mile or so he would lose his way. Rather than attempting to find the trail on his own, he would sit back and bellow at the top of his lungs until someone came to his rescue. By the third day The Assiniboine had developed a full-blown loathing for O'B. and decided to cure him of his new habit. Knowing O'B.'s morbid fear of grizzlies, The Assiniboine hid by the trail and, as O'B. passed, trailing far behind as usual, he let go with some fearsome roaring and growling. Scared witless, O'B., for a few days at least, kept well up with the group.

Unlike the well-defined trail the travellers followed to Lac Ste. Anne, the trail from that point

on was almost undistinguishable, being but a vague path used occasionally by employees of the Hudson's Bay Company. There were deadfalls to scramble over, muskeg to sink into, and creeks and rivers to cross. And at every step they were plagued by swarms of mosquitoes and horseflies. Then, while struggling through the area between the Macleod and Athabasca Rivers, they encountered an even worse hazard.

While camped for lunch in some heavy timber, they lit a smudge fire to drive off the horseflies which were particularily vicious that day. In attempting to get as close to the smudge as possible, one of the horses kicked some hot coals into the tinder dry undercover and in a few moments the forest was ablaze. Most everyone immediately picked up an axe or blanket to beat out the flames. Everyone, that is, but Mr. O'B. While others fought the fire he struggled with his boots, removed to ease aching feet. It was only when Cheadle suggested, "You can burn as easy with boots on as off," that O'B. sprang into action. Seizing his drinking cup, he filled it with water and marched boldly out to quell the inferno.

True to form, O'B. showed the same aptitude for raft-building as he had in all his other endeavors when, on June 30, the voyagers crossed the Athabasca River to reach Jasper House in what is now Jasper National Park. While the others cut logs for a raft to float their supplies across, O'B. conveniently disappeared to smoke his pipe and read his book, Paley's *Evidences of Christianity*, which he studied throughout the trip. When the logs were cut Milton went looking for O'B. and found him seated comfortably nearby. "Terribly sorry to disturb your studies," Milton said sarcastically, "but would you mind terribly helping carry the logs down to the river?"

"Oh, are they ready?" asked O'B. "I can assure you I've been waiting with eager anticipation for a chance to help." With that he seized the small end of

From river rapid to mountainside, the Milton and Cheadle party pushed onward. Here, a protesting pack horse is encouraged up a steep mountain trail near Jasper House.

the nearest log, leaving the heavy end for Milton. Several times on the way down to the river he complained bitterly about the damage being done to his delicate shoulder and without warning, dropped his end of the log, jarring Milton unmercifully.

Later that day O'B. nearly drowned himself while crossing the river. Because his horse had earlier refused to climb a steep mountain trail, O'B. now refused to ride him across the river. Instead, he strolled into the river leading his horse, stepped into a deep hole near mid-stream and lost his balance and his grip on the horse. Then, rather than heading for shore he headed for even deeper water. He was floundering around and would have drowned had not Milton ridden out and dragged him to safety. From then on O'Beirne crossed deep streams by holding on to his horse's tail.

And so it went all the way to Fort Kamloops, Mr. O'B. being extricated from one disaster, only to stumble into another. The travellers arrived in Kamloops on August 28, emaciated, their clothing in tatters, their identification papers lost in the Fraser River when one of the pack horses was swept away by the river in flood. Had they not eaten two of their horses in the heavy timber between Tete Jaune Cache and Kamloops it is doubtful they would have survived.

Despite their lack of identification, their haggard appearance, their unshaven faces and tattered clothing, they were welcomed at Fort Kamloops, wined and dined copiously and fitted with new outfits of clothing. To the relief of both Milton and Cheadle. Mr. O'B. quickly headed for Victoria.

Did O'Beirne find his niche in this civilized sector of British Columbia? Not so you would notice. For a while he was employed as a church secretary in Victoria. But when Milton and Cheadle were returning to England after an interesting sojourn to the Cariboo goldfield, they learned that O'B. had moved on to San Francisco and from there to Melbourne, Australia. At Melbourne, they learned, he had moved on to New Zealand. It seems O'B. was a natural wanderer. To him any place was fine for a while.

Any place, that is, but the wilds of frontier Alberta. ●

SAM LIVINGSTON
Calgary's First And Most Colorful Pioneer

Sam Livingston lived for the future. He proved this by becoming Calgary's first citizen — as well as one of its most colorful.

WHEN it comes to a man like Sam Livingston, as with many of our first and most colorful pioneers, it is difficult to differentiate fact from fiction. One reason is that he did so many things in his lifetime that it seems difficult to credit them all to one man. Another reason is, as one of his daughters stated, "He lived for the future and not the past. He was always looking ahead." As a result, except for letters preserved by relatives in Wisconsin, he never wrote any of his adventures down and when he told his stories in later years, the listener was so enthralled that he or she also forgot to write them down. Too bad, for his adventures were undoubtedly as exciting and colorful as any ever written about any of the characters of the Old West. Still, there is plenty to tell.

What is known is that he was a fairly tall man with a whisker-covered face and long blond hair to his shoulders, who as far as anyone remembered always dressed in a slouch hat and the fringed buckskin garb of a frontiersman. He was born about 1830 in Ireland in the village of Blessington—a place called the Vale of Avoca. Ireland's almost continuous state of unrest plus the terrible potato famine of the 1840s caused Sam to head for America where some of his cousins had taken up farming and owned a mineral claim in the state of Wisconsin.

Perhaps he found the place too tame or, perhaps, it was his adventuresome nature. Whatever, in 1850 Sam and some friends headed for California. The famous gold rush begun in 1849 was on. Various writers have given Sam various methods of travel, some having sent him around the southern tip of South America by boat, some by way of the Panama Canal. But a letter he wrote to his brother states he headed out by wagon train across the prairies. His biggest worry was hostile Indians whose territory he had to cross. Anyway, his California adventure did not prove very profitable and during the next eight to 10 years he drifted as far south as Mexico and as far north as Montana, prospecting, hunting buffalo and getting into a few skirmishes with Indians along the way. Eventually he joined a couple of partners and headed into Canada on a new venture.

Sam Livingston, Calgary's first settler in the 1890s.

Again we have conflicting versions of his destination and direction of travel. One version has him making his way with the two other men westward through Idaho and Washington, then north into British Columbia. They then either followed or preceded the gold rushers up the Fraser River to the Cariboo, where they spent the winter. Again Sam somehow missed finding the rich gold lode that others struck on Williams Creek and around Barkerville, so he and his partners followed the Fraser to its source, crossed over to the Parsnip River and followed it to its confluence with the Peace. They drifted down the Peace by canoe all the way to its mouth in the Slave River, followed the Slave to

Great Slave Lake, turned around and paddled back up the Slave to Lake Athabasca, then up the Athabasca River all the way to Athabasca Landing, now the town of Athabasca, which is about 80 miles north of Edmonton. On their way the men saw and probably shot wood buffalo, a larger version of the plains bison once so plentiful on the prairies.

Another version has Sam making and blowing several fortunes in Montana before joining with two partners and going north into British Columbia's East Kootenays to Wild Horse Creek, where Fort Steele was later built. When he did not hit the bonanza there, he teamed with James Gibbons, the man who gave his name to the village of Gibbons, 15 miles northeast of Edmonton, and together they crossed the Rockies by way of the Kicking Horse Pass, heading for Fort Edmonton to wash gold on the North Saskatchewan River. On their way they had their horses stolen by Indians near the Red Deer River, after which they struck out on foot for Rocky Mountain House, where Factor Richard Hardisty of the Hudson's Bay Company, let them stay over winter. The following spring Hardisty lent them horses to travel to Fort Victoria, which was originally named Victoria Mission by its founder the Reverend George McDougall. To add to the confusion, the place was later named Pakan after Chief Pakan of the Crees, a good friend of Reverend McDougall's. One thing that has not changed over the years is its location, which is on the north bank of the North Saskatchewan River south of the modern town of Smoky Lake and some 60 miles downstream from Edmonton.

Both versions of Livingston's travels could be at least partially correct, for the Cariboo Gold Rush began in 1858 and the Wild Horse Creek rush not till six years later, in 1864. Considering the way Sam moved around in those days, there is a possibility he was in both places. (According to Jim Gibbon's Diary, he met Sam Livingston at Wild Horse Creek and travelled with him to Fort Edmonton.) Anyway, in 1865 or 1866, he arrived at Fort Victoria where he courted and married Jane Mary Howse, daughter of Henry Howse and granddaughter of Joseph Howse, Hudson's Bay Company employee who lent his name to the Howse Pass in the Rockies. By the time he married Jane Howse, Sam was already an experienced trader. One version has him getting started in that field after obtaining horses from some Metis upon splitting with his two partners after his sojourn in the north. These horses he traded with the Indians around the Fort Edmonton area, stayed over winter there, then headed south the following spring with loaded pack ponies on a prospecting trip to the Livingstone River, a branch of the Oldman River which was later named for him. After that prospecting trip, he again drifted back to Fort Victoria.

After his marriage Sam got into the bartering business in earnest. He obtained more ponies and

Group of Blood Indians at Fort Calgary, 1878. L-R: R.W. Fletcher; Cst. T. Christie on horse; Sam Livingston leaning on wall; Insp. Cecil Denny, seated on chair; Joe Butlin, standing in wagon in background; Const. Van Courtland; Cst. Schofield, with rope; Sgt. James Barwis, seated on ground, front right.

probably some oxen, a string of Red River carts and began freighting between Fort Garry (now Winnipeg) and Edmonton. On the way he would stop at the various trading posts as well as drifting into the occasional Indian encampment for a busy session of trading. Occasionally, perhaps for a change of scenery, he journeyed down to Fort Benton, Montana to exchange his load of furs, buffalo hides or whatever for trading goods—everything from guns to beads to dried fruit. Obviously he finally decided he liked the southern part of Alberta better than the Edmonton area for, about 1873, he established a trading post in the Jumping Pound area west of Calgary. (To say it was west of Calgary is perhaps misleading for at that time Calgary simply did not exist).

It did not get its start until 1875 when a detach-

ment of North West Mounted Police rode in from Fort Macleod and founded the post that was originally named Fort Brisbois, but later changed to Fort Calgary by Commissioner James F. Macleod. There is a story that Sam, who had by then moved his trading post eastward to the bank of the Elbow River, spotted the Mounted Police, led by Captain Cecil Denny, approaching, laid down his field glass and told his wife there were men approaching who were not Indians, for they sat differently in the saddle. It seems, though, that Sam would immediately recognize the police even from a great distance, for when the force arrived in southern Alberta and built Fort Macleod, in 1874, he obtained a contract to freight for them and supply them with buffalo meat.

There is also a story still told that when the Mounted Police arrived to build Fort Calgary, Sam Livingston decided that the country was becoming downright crowded and that he had better grab some land before it became overrun with white settlers. Some state that Sam's first holding in the Calgary area was the spot chosen by the NWMP for their post and that he let them have the land while

he moved to the district adjacent the present Glenmore Reservoir. There he built a bigger home for his family which had expanded to five children. Although a frontiersman of Sam's caliber could never be completely content, tied to one spot, he became a farmer and a darn good one, too. According to an article written in the Calgary *Herald Magazine* in March of 1966 by Denny Layzell, "He brought the first mower and rake from Fort Benton and introduced the threshing machine to this part of the country. He raised pigs, cattle, oats and vegetables and it wasn't long before he had 300 head of cattle bearing his Quarter Circle L brand."

The big ranchers who then held sway in what is now southern Alberta did their best to convince government officials that this part of the country was fit only for ranching. Apparently they thought if they harped on the subject long enough and loud enough, they would convince the government that the land was unable to grow anything but grass and the government would attempt to keep homesteaders out. Sam Livingston, however, did not take long to repudiate the ranchers' claim. He grew beautiful oats and vegetable crops and, later on, even imported some fruit trees from the East. Some of the trees did not survive the first winter but some of his apple trees did and bore fruit. When, in 1884, Calgary formed an agricultural society, it not surprisingly chose Sam Livingston as the director. In that capacity, he travelled to Toronto with the area's first agricultural exhibit, where he enthralled hundreds of admirers with his frontier garb and tall yarns of his adventures in the early West.

None of his stories would require much embellishment, for Sam had a surfeit of hair-raising tales. He told of the time when he was freighting from Fort Benton and was halted on his way back to Fort Macleod by a posse of six Montana vigilantes, who had captured a suspected cattle rustler. The kangaroo court consisting of the six men was deadlocked as to whether to hang the man on the spot or to let him go. Sam was enlisted to resolve the debate and elected for acquittal of the accused, though he suspected the man was an outlaw. That decision later paid dividends when on another trip an outlaw gang overtook his bull train. They were about to dispatch Sam and his drivers forthwith when the leader of the gang rode up, recognized Sam and ordered the men to let the freighter and his people go. The leader was the same man Sam had freed from a neck-tie party a year or so before.

Undoubtedly in his 67 years Sam Livingston did more living than most men who live 30 years longer. By then he was the father of 14 children, the last one born in November of 1896. But on October 4, 1897, the heart of the man who was Calgary's most colorful citizen just gave out. On that day the *Calgary Herald* carried the report that Sam Livingston had passed away suddenly after a remarkable career. It described his passing in the following article:

"Sam Livingston drove into town this morning not feeling very well. He visited Wendell Maclean's and Marsh's stores where he made some purchases and afterwards went to the Windsor Hotel.

"While in the stores he complained of a pain in his chest. At the hotel Mr. Donohue asked him if he would drink something but he declined it, and going into the inside room sat down on a mattress that Mr. Donohue gave him. He said he was sick and wanted a doctor. Dr. Rouleau was phoned for. When he went into the room, Sam was kneeling on the mattress. He had complained frequently about his health in the last six months and his friends were in the habit of joking with him about it. So the doctor remarked, 'Hello, Sam. You are on your knees at last.' 'Yes,' said Sam, 'and only just in time.'

"Shortly after he dropped suddenly and died within a few minutes. His death occurred within two feet of the spot where, 10 years ago, he said he would like to die, surrounded by his friends, whom he named.

"He was about 67 years old and leaves a wife and an unusually large family... People through the Great West will regret to learn that Sam Livingston, a link with the old time frontier life and the present, has joined the great majority. He was a picturesque character and a typical example of the old time Westerner. He was familiar with the West from Mexico to the south to the Mackenzie River in the north, and has conducted many parties through the country in the capacity of prospector, hunter and guide.

"He was about the first white man to settle in this part of Alberta, and that at a time when the Indians were still hostile to the whites. While plowing he was obliged to carry a rifle with him at all times. He was never quite forgiven by the Sarcee who gave him a name which means 'Big White Devil.' They threatened to shoot him if he came outside the fence.

"His first shack was located on the Elbow River, not far from his late residence... At that time the buffalo were as yet, in all appearances, far from extinction, and it was not an uncommon experience to find them rubbing themselves against the walls of his shack.

"When the surveyors started to lay out the country, some effort was made to dispossess him of the land on which he squatted. Sam, however, stood off the surveyors with his rifle. Old timers discussing this may be heard to say, 'He did quite right!' Matters, however, were settled by giving him two sections of land.

"Alberta can ill afford to lose one of her old pioneers, one of the few remaining picturesque characters linking her with the past—and his sudden demise will be regretted not only by personal friends and acquaintances, but by those who knew him by reputation.

"It may be remembered that last year Sam was nominated as a delegate of the Conservative convention. He was always a staunch supporter and admirer of Sir John A. Macdonald."

Four days later the *Herald* carried the story of his funeral, which was attended by hundreds from miles around. His wife lived until 1919 and two of his children, Mary Ann and Margaret, lived until 1970. There is a mountain range named for him, supposedly, though history states that the Livingstone Range was named by Lieutenant Thomas Blakiston of the 1858-60 Palliser Expedition for famed Africa explorer Dr. David Livingstone, and not Sam Livingston. Thanks to people like Grant MacEwan, author, historian and one-time Calgary alderman, mayor and Lieutenant-Governor of Alberta, some of Sam's early buildings are preserved. There is a Livingston display in the Horseman's Hall of Fame in Calgary's Aquarium and a large federal building bearing his name.

Hopefully these monuments will ensure that Sam Livingston, Calgary's first and most colorful citizen, will never be forgotten. ●

*In a kite-like contraption he had designed
himself, and powered by an engine of his own making,
this Edmonton carpenter made Canadian aviation history
on September 7, 1909, when he soared aloft for
an amazing 33 minutes.*

REG HUNT
First Western Flyer

MOST Canadians are aware that in February of 1909 James McCurdy made the first recorded airplane flight in Canadian history by staying aloft for two minutes over Baddeck Bay in Nova Scotia. But how many know that, that same year, an Albertan made an equally great claim to fame? Yet it is true. For on September 7, 1909, Reginald Hunt, an Edmonton carpenter, flew an airplane he designed himself and stayed in the air for an incredible 33 minutes!

It certainly has to be a historical oversight that Reg Hunt is not recognized as one of the country's pioneer airmen. For while McCurdy had a group of engineers placed at his disposal by the Bell Telephone Company, Hunt designed and built his airplane almost entirely by himself. Moreover, he even designed and built his own engine. Then, on Labor Day, 1909, he nosed his masterpiece skyward over what is now West Edmonton and stayed aloft more than long enough to have established his niche in aviation history. His single failing was the fact that he did not stay in the aviation field long enough to secure his claim to fame.

But if his flight did not gain him aviation immortality, it did provide a thrill for those who witnessed it. Strangely enough, it did not seem newsworthy enough to attract reporters from Edmonton's two newspapers—the *Journal* and the *Bulletin*. Only the *Journal* bothered to send out a cameraman. His photographs reveal a strange kite-like contraption with dual wings and a tail assembly that looks more like a packing crate than anything associated with an airplane. Hunt built the landing gear from bicycle wheels with a couple of smaller wheels at the rear. He sat in the open between the wings and in front of the motor. The propeller was mounted to the rear. The fuselage was an open skeleton of welded pipe. Compared to modern aircraft it was definitely lacking in aesthetics. However, it had something in common—it flew.

It took Hunt three years to design and build his plane. He and another carpenter named Carruthers began tinkering around with it in 1906 and in two years had a glider they thought was airworthy. At least it stayed in one piece and sailed a short distance when pushed down a ramp. The motor was Hunt's masterpiece and took him a whole winter to assemble, his propeller being four-bladed and based on air-circulating fans he had seen in restaurants.

Just how well his plane was designed can be judged by comparing it to a factory-built plane of the same era. On September 8, 1909, Samuel Cody of the British Army made headlines by staying aloft for 63 minutes in the factory-built aircraft. The day before, Hunt had stayed aloft for 33 minutes in a plane he built himself!

Reg Hunt, however, was not designated for immortality for, at the Edmonton Exhibition in 1910, he wrecked his plane by crashing it into a fence. Though he was not hurt, for some reason he chose not to rebuild his flying machine. Instead, he decided to go north to build boats for the Hudson's Bay Company.

One wonders how famous he might have become had he remained with aviation. ●

PROHIBITION
AND THE RUNNERS OF RUM

Bootlegging was not new to Alberta, but, during construction of the Canadian Northern and Grand Trunk Pacific Railways, rum-running became an epidemic as Provincial and Mounted Police attempted to stem the flow of illegal liquor to the thirsty construction workers.

(Left) Alberta Provincial Police barrier, Blairmore, Alberta, 1922.
(Below) Seizure of liquor at Crowsnest Pass by Alberta Provincial Police in 1925.

FOR Albertans who liked their beer and hard liquor, July 1, 1916 — Prohibition — was welcomed with all the enthusiasm of an earthquake or a prairie tornado. For the members of the Temperance and Moral Reform League like T.H. Miller, W.F. Gold, A.T. Cushing, authoress Nellie McClung and many others, it was a day for celebration —without liquor, of course. For some—bold men who were eager to make a fast buck—it was a day of challenge. With liquor and beer over 2½ per cent alcohol declared illegal, well, they would just have to see that, somehow or other, burning thirsts were quenched. A bit risky, perhaps, but with huge profits involved…well, they would just have to take a few risks.

Bootlegging, of course, was not new to Alberta. It predated the arrival of the North West Mounted Police in 1874. It waned for a time but bloomed again with the arrival of the construction gangs building the Canadian Pacific Railroad. Since liquor was banned along the right-of-way when both the CPR and CNR were being constructed, the Mounted Police had their hands full trying to outsmart the bootleggers. Some of the problems encountered in trying to keep rum-running to a minimum along the right-of-way during the construction of the CPR are covered in the chapter entitled, *The Legendary*

Sam Steele. A quarter century later, men of the Royal North West Mounted Police experienced the same problems during the construction of the line that became the Canadian National Railway.

Of all the members of the oldtime Mounted Police who struck terror in the hearts of the makers and distributors of illicit hootch, probably none surpassed Sergeant 'Nitchie' Thorne. Between 1910 and 1915, when the Canadian Northern and Grand Trunk Pacific lines were being pushed through Alberta and the Yellowhead Pass towards the Pacific Ocean, a five-mile stretch on either side of the road-bed was declared a prohibition area and Sergeant Thorne and a detachment of Mounted Police were assigned the task of keeping the western end of the Alberta section whisky free. It was no easy task, for hundreds of thirsty construction workers with money burning holes in their pockets were clamoring for booze and dozens of eager bootleggers were doing their best to see that they got it.

For quite a time one lovely blonde woman led Nitchie and his men a merry chase. Time after time she would show up at one camp or another, ostensibly looking for her brother. As sure as the sun rises in the east, after each visit, singing, shouting and sometimes fighting would break out in camp and

many of the men would portray all the well-known symptoms of acute intoxication. None of the Mounties could ever recall her bringing anything more sinister looking than a batch of cookies into camp. Yet the evidence was almost overwhelming that somehow the lady was sneaking in booze.

Finally it dawned on Sergeant Thorne that the lovely lady invariably appeared considerably thicker around the middle on her arrival than on her departure. He quickly summoned a police matron and waited for the next time the blond bombshell appeared in one of the camps. The resultant arrest and search revealed a rather startling development. For around her waist the young lady wore a rubber tube that held a full gallon of hootch. A nozzle protruding from an ingenious belt buckle made dispensing quick and simple. A flip of the buckle, a slight contraction of abdominal muscles and presto!—whisky squirted forth in a stream sufficient to fill a two-ounce shot glass in a couple of seconds.

Another time Sergeant Thorne stopped a man who was delivering a wagon-load of freshly butchered hogs to one of the camps. Nitchie had long suspected this fellow of delivering more than fresh meat, but previous searches had revealed nothing illegal. When another thorough search again turned up nothing untoward, Nitchie, acting on a hunch, inserted a long, slender, sharply-pointed steel rod between the ribs of one of the hogs and gave a firm push. To his delight a thin stream of fluid that looked and smelled surprisingly like Scotch whisky spouted up. Further examination revealed that every carcass contained a rubber bag holding a couple of gallons of liquor—enough booze to keep the whole camp in a euphoric state for a week.

Not suprisingly Nitchie Thorne and his men never did completely stop the flow of booze into the railroad construction camps. He simply had too much territory to cover and too few men. But after some of his more noteworthy successes the mere mention of his name was enough to make the most intrepid bootlegger extra wary and the less brave tremble in their boots.

But shortly after prohibition was declared in Alberta, bootleggers no longer had to contend with Nitchie Thorne and other stalwarts of the Royal North West Mounted Police. The First World War was in full swing and with its ranks badly depleted by enlistments into the armed services, Ottawa decided to withdraw the NWMP from policing rural Alberta. In their place, A.L. Sifton, Premier of Alberta, announced a new force for the province, the Alberta Provincial Police. The new force had a formidable challenge to meet, for the no-booze act had more holes in it than 10 pounds of imported Swiss cheese. Moreover, with prohibition in effect, whereas bootlegging until then had largely been the work of amateurs, professional rum-runners soon took over. Most of the new breed had fast cars—sometimes substantial fleets of McLaughlin Buicks, Hudson

THE LIQUOR TRAFFIC MUST GO

THE REVENUE IS SMALL COMPARED WITH THE COST

IT CAUSES Poverty, Misery and Crime

THE REMEDY

NATIONAL CONSTITUTIONAL PROHIBITION

Poster, "The Liquor Traffic Must Go", used by Women's Christian Temperance Union for campaigns.

Super Sixes, Nashes and occasionally Cadillacs. The Alberta Provincial Police under their newly appoint Superintendent, Major A.E.C. McDonnell, were not as yet fully organized. Their transport consisted only of horses and a few Model T Fords, which gave their adversaries a decided advantage.

At first liquor was not difficult to obtain in Alberta for prohibition did not close down the distilleries and breweries. It also did not make it illegal for Albertans to import liquor into the province for personal use. The big liquor factories simply shipped their produce out to warehouses in Saskatchewan and British Columbia and thirsty Albertans just as simply sent out to those warehouses for their quota of booze. Moreover, doctors were permitted to prescribe liquor for medicinal purposes. Prescriptions were filled at drugstores—always a 40-ounce bottle no matter the ailment.

Things went along fairly smoothly until July of 1917, when flavoring extracts, some of which had contained over 80 per cent grain alcohol, could no longer be sold at grocery stores, only at drugstores with a doctor's prescription. Moreover it became illegal for either private citizens or businesses to store more than two gallons of beer or one gallon of hard liquor; thus effectively closing Alberta warehouses. Provincial legislation was making it increasingly difficult for Joe Citizen to obtain liquor legally, but at the same time it was throwing an impossible load on

Seven carcasses of dressed hogs containing contraband liquor seized at Jasper. Many and devious were the methods used to smuggle booze.

the APP, for it paved the way for professional rum-runners to take over from the small-time bootleggers and moonshiners who had always been around.

The federal government installed the final rung in the ladder to complete dominance for the rum-runners when, in December of 1917, it passed an act making it illegal for anyone to import any liquor containing more than 2½ per cent alcohol into Canada or to ship non-temperance booze from one province to another. Government legislation, however, cannot change human nature. Albertans—some of them anyway—wanted stronger beer and booze to drink and big-time rum-runners set out to see that they got it.

Montana in 1918 was still 'wet' so it is not surprising that the biggest rum-running operations took place along the Montana-Alberta border. One of the biggest operators reportedly was an ex-Edmonton tavern owner who sold his hotel soon after prohibition started. There were strong rumors, never substantiated, that he had great influence with government officials on both sides of the border. Anyway, he apparently was able to import liquor in carload lots, which he then stored in various caches in southern Alberta. From these he ran his booze in high-powered cars to secret buyers. Whatever his connections, they must have been good ones, for he became very rich in the trade and never was caught.

Probably the best known of the big-time runners of rum was Emilio Picariello, also known as Mr. Pick, The Bottle King, and Emperor Pick. A friendly heavy-set fellow with a flashing smile, he emigrated to Canada from Sicily around the turn of the century, married a Toronto girl of Italian descent, then moved out to Fernie, British Columbia, in 1911, where he worked at and eventually took over C. Maraniro's macaroni factory. A man with a keen business sense, Mr. Pick got into the liquor business in the pre-prohibition days as a representative for the Pollock Wine Company. He later branched out into the food industry and began making and selling ice-cream. Then, unobtrusively, he began buying beer bottles and eventually corralled the empty beer bottle market in the Crowsnest Pass area. By 1916 the following ad appeared regularly in the Crowsnest Pass area newspapers: "E. Pick, the Bottle King, requests that all persons selling bottles hold them until they see E. Pick, who pays top prices." In 1918 Mr. Pick purchased the Alberta Hotel in Blairmore and also became the sole representative for the area for Sick's Lethbridge Brewery. Of course the only beer the Bottle King could sell was the 2½ per cent temperance stuff. But Miners from the surrounding coal mines wanted something with a little more kick to it and Mr. Pick decided to find a way to give it to them.

At first Mr. Pick ran liquor into Alberta through the Crowsnest Pass from exporters in British Columbia, using Model T Fords equipped with concrete-reinforced bumpers—ideal for running the occasional roadblock. He later switched to fast, more powerful McLaughlins, which by then were aptly named the Whisky Special. He stored his illicit booze in a special room dug off to the side of the basement of his hotel. Vehicles could drive right into

(Left) Emilio Picariello, right, and partner, Charles Lassandro, with pet bear. Picariello was known as Emperor Pick, whisky runner of Crowsnest Pass.
(Opposite page) Emilio Picariello and family, 1915. Convicted of shooting a policeman he went to the gallows.

the basement and any noise of loading or unloading was effectively muffled by a player piano played at full volume in the beverage room above. Not that Mr. Pick had to try to conceal his activities from the local citizens. Most were aware of his sideline and condoned it. For he was not only filling a wanted service, he was also respected for being the most benevolent man in the district.

Just when some of the needy in the area were in direst of straits, they could expect a delivery vehicle at their door loaded with groceries, courtesy of the kindly Mr. Pick. In 1918 he reportedly bought $50,000 worth of Victory Bonds in aid of Canada's war effort. With his good standing in the neighborhood it is not surprising that his rum-running became a lucrative business. After switching to the speedy McLaughlins, he expanded his trade and not only ran booze through the Crowsnest Pass, but also through the aptly-named Whisky Gap from Montana as well. He had some strong competition from men in Calgary, Drumheller and Lethbridge but there was plenty of business for all.

When the United States declared prohibition in July of 1919, rather than hurting Alberta's rumrunning industry, it doubled the demand for operators. He and his colleagues had established good contacts in Montana, Idaho and Utah, along with numerous Canadian customers. Somehow Mr. Pick managed to import 100-proof rum from overseas which, when cut with water, made an acceptable drink. He also obtained an adequate supply of some very good 'mountain dew' from moonshiners who had set up their stills far back in the hills. This he was able to distribute to his local customers and also to his former American suppliers, now turned customers, by running it over the poorly-guarded border into Montana.

There are dozens of stories of border guards looking the other way to let the rum-runners pass. In his book The Rum Runners Frank Anderson tells an anecdote of those days that bears repeating: "On one of those trips through Whisky Gap, Mr. Pick ran into a severe rainstorm which mired down his whisky-laden car. Going to a nearby farmhouse, he

discovered two APP constables on patrol duty who had sought shelter from the storm. Enlisting their help to free his car from the mud, he waved a cheery goodbye, flashed his famous smile and drove on his way. The constables, never dreaming that the affable, farmerish-looking man in the sloppy-blue overalls was the noted 'Emperor Pick', returned to the house to await the cessation of the storm so that they could resume their vigil for rum-runners."

Mr. Pick's reign as Bottle King and rum-runner supreme came to an end in 1922 through the work of a stool pigeon employed by the APP. Naturally as time went on the APP grew more proficient in tracking down the peddlers of illicit hootch. On September 21, 1921, Constable R.M. Day of the Blairmore detachment got word from a stoolie that Mr. Pick would be coming through the Crowsnest Pass from Fernie leading a convoy of vehicles loaded with booze. Sure enough. that afternoon Mr. Picariello, his son Steve and J.J. McAlpine, a mechanic who worked for them, passed through Blairmore, each driving a McLaughlin car. When the little convoy reached the Alberta Hotel, Sergeant James Scott and Constable Day were waiting. When Mr. Pick saw Sergeant Scott approaching with a search warrant, he quickly ran back to his car and leaned on the horn, a signal to young Steve, who was carrying the booze, to head back for British Columbia. Steve got the message and roared off in a cloud of dust and gravel with Mr. Pick close behind, trying to prevent the police, who were by then in hot pursuit, from overtaking Steve. When a couple of attempts to get past the Bottle King failed, Scott realized other tactics were necessary, so he stopped and phoned ahead to Coleman to have Constable Steve Lawson intercept young Pick there. Lawson stepped out onto the highway which is also Coleman's main street just as Steve Pick's car came barrelling toward him. When the fleeing rum-runner ignored Lawson's command to halt and almost ran the policeman down, Lawson fired a couple of fast shots at the rapidly disappearing car, one of which wounded young Pick in the hand. That, however, failed to stop the fleeing Steve and Lawson had to

give up the chase when the car he commandeered blew a tire. Steve Pick, in the meantime, disappeared in a cloud of dust towards Fernie, British Columbia, and out of APP jurisdiction.

Perhaps the affair would have ended there as charges of rum-running and escaping arrest would have been hard to prove. But when Emperor Pick learned that his son had been shot, he naturally assumed the worst, such as his son stopped somewhere down the road with his life-blood oozing away. He cornered Constable Lawson and, at gunpoint, ordered him to go with him to find young Picariello. A struggle ensued and Mr. Pick's gun went off serveral times, although no one was hurt. But Mrs. Florence Lassandro, a close friend of the Picariellos, witnessed the struggle and fearing for the Emperor's life, opened fire with a gun she was carrying, hit Constable Lawson in the back and killed him almost instantly. Why she was armed, or indeed why she had followed the chase from Blairmore, has not been fully determined. What is known is that she was there, she shot Constable Lawson and both she and Mr. Pick were charged and convicted with the murder of Constable Lawson. When Mrs. Lassandro and Emilio Picariello dropped to their death from a gallows at the Fort Saskatchewan jail on the morning of May 3, 1923, it spelled *finis* to one of the most colorful chapters of the Prohibition and rum-running era.

Constable Lawson, Florence Lassandro and Emperor Pick were not the only ones whose deaths were directly attributable to Prohibition. In 1918 railway worker B.K. Bradley was shot and almost killed when he was mistaken for one of the hijackers who were looting a CPR boxcar loaded with booze

in the Calgary freight yards. In Drumheller, on May 2, 1923, Constable C.M. Paris was killed while trying to apprehend rum-runner Elmo E. Trider. Chief of Police Fletcher and Constable Paris waved down a McLaughlin roadster on the outskirts of Drumheller, which they suspected—rightly as it turned out—of carrying contraband hootch. Instead of stopping, however, Elmo Trider floor-boarded the McLaughlin's throttle. Fletcher and Paris opened fire in an attempt to shoot out Trider's tires, missed, when, somehow, Paris managed to jump on the running-board as the McLaughlin zoomed by. It was a daring but fatal mistake for, at the next bend, Trider lost control of the car. It smashed through a wooden fence, rolled over, and killed Constable Paris instantly.

Trider was charged with murder but, luckily for him, he faced a much more lenient jury than had Emperor Pick. They found him not guilty of murder. Instead he was found guilty of an infraction of the Alberta Liquor Act and fined $200.

Although most people had long realized that Prohibition created more problems than it solved, it was not until the Alberta Hotelman's Association compiled a 51,000-name pro-liquor petition in January of 1923 and presented it to the government that something was finally done. By then the government knew that something like 10 per cent of the drugstores, 40 per cent of the cafes and more than 160 poolrooms were violating the liquor act to greater or lesser degrees, and that many supposedly legitimate businessmen were actually becoming rich from rum-running. It was long past time to act. Despite heated argument from the Temperance League people, on May 10, 1923, Prohibition in Alberta officially ended.

Since Montana remained 'dry,' rum-running across the line continued. But the illicit booze trade no longer had the unofficial sanction of the average citizen as it had when Alberta was dry. Consequently, the APP got more cooperation than they had previously and many of the formerly successful booze-runners were caught. But neither the APP nor the RCMP who again took over policing the province in 1931 ever completely stopped the trade. There always has been and probably always will be the little guy—the local bootlegger who sells the odd bottle to thirsty customers when beer parlors and liquor stores are closed. Then there is the moonshiner with his one-man still. He brews a few gallons of potent hootch, generally just enough to keep himself and a few friends happy and probably put a few groceries on the table for his growing family.

Those we will always have with us, but they can be more or less controlled and do not create much of a problem. At least nothing like the problem created by Prohibition when hundreds of ordinarily honest businessmen turned to making a fast buck and quenching the parched throats of thousands of thirsty customers. ●

Colonel James Walker — left, in NWMP uniform, and right, in Canadian army uniform.

Calgary's Citizen of the Century:

Colonel James Walker

*Soldier, policeman, rancher, lumberman, homesteader
and businessman, Colonel Walker contributed to Calgary's growth
from a trading post to a bustling, modern city.*

HIS name is practically synonymous with Calgary. When Colonel James Walker first saw the place that was destined to become a great city, Calgary consisted of a Hudson's Bay Company post, an I.G. Baker store, a few houses and shacks, a dozen or so tents and a couple of churches. Surrounding it was a wild, rolling prairie divided by the Bow and Elbow Rivers. The year was 1880 and Colonel Walker, then a North West Mounted Police superintendent, was travelling with Edgar Dewdney, Lieutenant-Governor of the North West Territories, distributing treaty money to thousands of Indians scattered across the Alberta and Saskatchewan Plains.

That trip took Colonel Walker west of Calgary to the Stoney Indian Reserve at Morley. The country so impressed him that, the following year, he was back as a civilian in the employ of Senator Cochrane

of Montreal in charge of the first large cattle ranch to be formed in what became the Province of Alberta. Except for a hitch in the Canadian Army during the First World War, when he took a forestry regiment overseas, Colonel Walker lived continuously in Calgary until his death in 1936 at the age of 89.

During those years, besides managing Cochrane's ranch for a time, Walker operated a sawmill, homesteaded, built a barracks for the NWMP, built many of Calgary's frame and sandstone buildings, helped start the first school and the first regular mail service, and was involved in many of the first business enterprises.

He was a soldier, policeman, rancher, lumberman, homesteader and businessman—but probably known best as the "grand old man of Canada's defense forces," for he was a member of one military movement or another almost continuously for 70

Big Bear (fourth from left) led those Indians who refused to sign Treaties with the White Man, preferring his nomadic life to a reservation, and to what he thought was a poor deal. He is shown here at Frog Lake in 1884 with Four Sky Thunder, Sky Bird, Matoose and Napasis, as well as local people. Against violence, like Poundmaker, Big Bear was dragged into war the following year, when his son Imasees perpetrated the Frog Lake Massacre.

years. At his death in 1936 he was honorary colonel of the 15th Canadian Light Horse, a militia unit he formed in 1905.

James Walker was born in April, 1874, in County Wentworth, Ontario, about 12 miles south of Hamilton. By the time he was 18, besides being a member of the local militia, he was operating his father's farm as his older brother John was unable to do so because of crippling injuries and his father had apparently passed away.

When James Walker joined the first contingent of North West Mounted Police in Toronto in 1874 he was 27 years of age and already a seasoned veteran of military service, having attended several military schools and served with the militia during the Fenian raids. He had also helped organize the 77th Wentworth Battalion, where he served as adjutant with the rank of major. Consequently, upon joining the NWMP he was made an inspector and placed in charge of one of the original six troops.

One of his first major achievements was at Dufferin, Manitoba, where the six troops had joined (three that had trained at Fort Garry and the other three from Toronto) prior to the force's historic sojourn into the west. Just before the force began its momentous journey, a terrible wind and electrical storm stampeded the 240 horses which had been held in an enclosure formed by a ring of wagons and tents. Inspector Walker was almost run down in the pandemonium as the frenzied horses, terrified by the lightning and driving rain, took off for quieter

country across the American border. Somehow he managed to catch one of the runaway animals, throw saddle and bridle on it and race after the hightailing herd. He followed the horses almost to Grand Forks, North Dakota, when he managed to catch them, turn them around and bring them back to Dufferin (now Emerson). In all he travelled nearly 120 miles, most of it in a driving rain. Had it not been for James Walker, the NWMP might have been forced to delay their westward trek or complete the 1000-mile journey on foot. As it was, Walker helped guide the westward odyssey with compass and sextant.

In a letter to Colonel Walker that is now preserved in the Glenbow-Alberta Institute files, Dr. A.E. Porter, who served for a time as temporary surgeon with the NWMP, told of some of James Walker's exciting experiences during the six years that Walker served with the force. The letter was written to Walker in 1930.

"Few people are now living who know the dangers and hardships we, the early pioneers, passed through in the molding of a Great Empire," wrote Dr. Porter. Walker, then a superintendent, who was in charge of the detachment stationed at Battleford and Fort Carlton in Saskatchewan. He was also acting as an officer for what is now the Department of Indian Affairs. "Then came the treaty with Big Bear at Sounding Lake (Alberta) and all kinds of trouble was expected from him and his renegade Sioux," wrote Porter of Treaty Six, signed there in

1878. "These warriors, after the massacre of Custer and his command on the Little Big Horn in the United States, came via Fort Walsh and joined Big Bear. You, anticipating trouble from these cut-throats (racism obviously is not a new characteristic) engaged me as Temporary Surgeon of the Police... I can remember passing through the Ghost Woods just before coming to Sounding Lake, where hundreds of Indians died of smallpox some years before (1870)... I remember seeing thousands of Indians and traders assembled for the grand pow-wow on the banks of Sounding Lake. It was an awe-inspiring sight to see the numberless teepees and the Indian smokes curling up to the sky. There were at least 2,000 braves and many more women and children. You made a stockade of wagons and traders' carts behind which the police and traders had their tents... The Governor, when conferring with the Indians, met them outside the stockade and surrounding us was a semi-circle of two or three thousand hostile Indians. Here we expected to meet a detachment of 100 Mounted Police from Fort Walsh, but owing to a delay in crossing the Belly (Oldman) River where they lost a constable in the quicksands, they did not arrive until the following afternoon and then only about 10 or 15 had been sent.

"The first night we were there was principally spent by Big Bear and his rowdies in shooting through our tents, much to our annoyance, discomfort and danger. I know I did not sleep much that night but kept close to Mother Earth, fearing a bullet through the head. The next day the fire-works started when thousands of war-painted Indians squatted on the ground in a great semi-circle with their loaded rifles gleaming in the sun, just outside the council circle where Lieutenant-Governor Laird attempted to address them through interpreter John Saskatchewan. The Indians called the governor the 'Talking Crane,' for he was an exceptionally tall slim man and they even spat at him.

"The psychological moment came when an old squaw was sent into the ring to talk to the representative of the King (actually Queen Victoria). This was the biggest insult the Indians could offer. You were a young man then, Colonel, but it was magnificent to see how you handled the situation. I could see Big Bear get very white under his war paint when you told him, through the interpreter, that if his braves fired your men would kill 10 Indians for every white man killed. This I thought strange at the time as they had 50 armed men for every one we had. A long time afterwards I learned that this was no empty bluff but that you, fully expecting trouble, had ordered your men to load with buckshot or slugs. You were not going to be caught napping, and at close range every policeman had (the equivalent of) a gatling gun. Big Bear, hero of many bluffs, thought discretion the better part of valor and without taking treaty, like the Arabs, folded his tent

and stole silently away—a beaten man—outgeneralled at every turn. You saved the country millions of dollars and many lives by avoiding an Indian uprising and massacre of the few settlers in the Territories. By this you stopped the renegade's activities for seven years until he became active again in the rebellion of 1885 and made more trouble..."

On another occasion, in 1876, Superintendent Walker was accredited with having prevented an uprising at Duck Lake, Saskatchewan. The first signings of Treaty Six were about to take place that summer but some of the Indians under Chief Beardy, fearing that the treaty would not be fair to the Indians, lay in wait at Duck Lake to force the treaty commissioners to sign a treaty meeting their terms.

According to an article that appeared in the Calgary *Albertan*, April 7, 1936, "Colonel Walker led a troop of 50 men in a forced march from Fort Carlton and surprised the Indians halfway between Fort Carlton and Batoche. The Mounted Police appeared so suddenly that the Indians were taken by surprise and readily agreed to peaceful proposals. Colonel Walker continued on, met the commissioners headed by Lieutenant-Governor Morris, and escorted them back to the meeting place (Fort Carlton) where the treaty was finally signed."

The following year the Duck Lake Indians headed by Chief Beardy decided that they had not received a fair deal under Treaty Six. They began demanding a better set of terms and threatened to seize the stores at the Duck Lake post. According to the *Albertan* article, "The agent persuaded them to wait another day and managed to notify Colonel Walker, who was stationed at Fort Carlton.

"With only a sergeant and two troopers, Colonel Walker proceeded to Duck Lake, reaching there at daybreak just as 100 warriors, half-naked and covered with war paint, rode up to the store, singing war songs and shooting under their horses' necks. Without stopping, Colonel Walker and his three men rode through the gates, singled out Beardy, chief of the tribe, and told him they were there to prevent any looting of the stores. Cowed, the chief and the warriors retreated and accepted the terms of the treaty..."

Despite his anything but kid-glove treatment, the Indians came to realize that Walker, though stern, was always fair and honest. In later years they made him an honorary chieftain with the title, "The Eagle That Protects."

In 1880, after six hectic and colorful years of policing the area around Battleford and Fort Carlton, Superintendent Walker was placed in command of Fort Walsh. Just before he started out for his new posting, he received a telegram from Ottawa instructing him to proceed to Winnipeg first and meet Lieutenant-Governor Edgar Dewdney, who had succeeded Laird and Morris as governor of the North West Territories. He was to travel with the Lieutenant Governor and distribute $100,000 in

Half-breed Scrip Commissioner at Grand Rapids, 1899. L-R: Seated—Major James Walker and J.A. Cote, commissioners; Standing—J.F. Prudhomme and Charles Mair, secretaries.

one dollar bills to the various tribes of prairie Indians due them under Treaties 4, 6 and 7. After leaving Winnipeg in July the party passed through Calgary in September, on its way from Edmonton to Pincher Creek. Most of the Mounted Police detachment had moved away from Calgary the previous year and when Walker and Dewdney passed through, the "force" consisted of two men, Sergeant "Doc" Lauder and Constable MacDonald. Angus Fraser was the factor of the Hudson's Bay Company post, while C.C. King was in charge of the I.G. Baker store. The rest of Calgary then consisted of a few houses and a couple of churches.

One of Superintendent Walker's first duties after taking charge at Fort Walsh was far from pleasant. Captain Dalrymple Clarke, a close friend of Walker's, was sick when Walker arrived and died a week later. In a 1934 interview with Walker, the Calgary *Albertan* noted: "Colonel Walker did not realize it at the time, but his last official duties with the force were to take charge of his friend's funeral. He obtained a leave of absence to escort Mrs. Clarke to Ottawa, where her husband's aunt, Lady Macdonald, wife of Sir John A. Macdonald, lived..."

If the trip to Ottawa was a sad one for Walker, it nevertheless turned out to be a beneficial one. During his safari through the West with Lieutenant-

Governor Dewdney, the two had formed a deep friendship. Governor Dewdney was a good friend of Senator Cochrane of Montreal, who was interested in starting a large ranch in southern Alberta. When Walker arrived in Ottawa Governor Dewdney told Senator Cochrane he thought Walker would be an ideal man to manage such an enterprise. Approached by Senator Cochrane to take the job, Walker told the Senator he knew just the place to start such a ranch—the area west of Calgary along the Bow River, an area of rolling hills and good grass land that stayed free of snow most winters. Walker decided to take his discharge and accept the offer.

The resulting Cochrane Ranch took in 100,000 acres on both sides of the Bow extending 50 miles to the west to Morley. It was Walker's intention to have 10,000 head of cattle grazing those acres within two years. According to the Calgary *Herald*, "He made his first purchase in Walla Walla, Washington, giving (Mose) McDougall enough money to buy 500 head. While waiting for a stagecoach in Dillon, Montana, he (Walker) met some cattle ranchers and bought 3,000 head from them. They reached the ranch in August, 1881."

One of the interesting sidelights of forming the Cochrane Ranch was that NWMP officials in Ottawa had set aside a parcel of land in Calgary west of the

Col. James Walker's sawmill, Calgary, early 1880s. Col. Walker crouched at far right.

junction of the Bow and Elbow Rivers. They tried to persuade Walker and Senator Cochrane to use this land as a headquarters for the ranch. Had Walker and Cochrane accepted the offer, and built there instead of at the more central location chosen, there is a possibility that the city of Calgary might have been named Cochrane and the town of Cochrane might never have come into being.

Though the 3,000 cattle that Walker bought in Montana arrived in August without serious difficulty the drive from Walla Walla met with tragedy when Mose McDougall was drowned while crossing the Hell Gate River near Missoula with his herd. The Cochrane Ranch seems to have been ill-fated from that point on, as two cold winters with deep snow decimated the herd and forced Senator Cochrane to lease land farther south, between the Belly and Waterton Rivers. By then Walker had resigned from the company and had gone into the sawmill business.

In 1882 Walker had persuaded Senator Cochrane to send out a sawmill, which Walker set up between the Kananaskis River and modern day Canmore. The mill was needed, Walker realized, to supply the needs of a growing Calgary, which was soon to grow even faster when the westward stretching Canadian Pacific Railway arrived. Walker had invested several thousands of dollars in the Cochrane Ranch Company and when the cattle were moved south, he resigned as manager and took over the sawmill as his equity in the company. About the same time he took up a homestead in East Calgary where the Inglewood Bird Sanctuary and Inglewood Golf Course are now located. It was the start towards a considerable fortune, for that

year he obtained a contract to build a new barracks for the NWMP. He bought the Methodist Church which had not been used for a few years and around it built the barracks at a cost of $35,000. By then he was married and the father of a baby boy.

The following summer, 1883, he built a boat and took his wife, son and sister-in-law down the Bow River to Medicine Hat. His family continued on east for a vacation in Ontario via the CPR which, by then, had reached Medicine Hat, while he returned to Calgary by horse and wagon—a long journey over the prairie compared to the less-than-a-day trip it soon would be with the coming of the railroad.

By 1883 Colonel Walker was probably as well known as anyone in the West, although as far as Calgary was concerned, his fame was only beginning. Just a few of the things he is remembered for are: his posting as the first immigration officer in the area; his establishment of a twice-monthly Pony Express when he became dissatisfied with the length of time it took to get mail, which came by bull-train from Fort Benton; his starting of Calgary's first telephone service in 1884; his appointment as the first president of the exhibition association when he was responsible for having the land set aside for Exhibition Park; his construction of many of Calgary's first frame buildings with lumber from his sawmill, as well as many of the city's first sandstone buildings; his helping to organize the first school and his service as a school trustee for 15 years, during which time he was chairman of the building committee and responsible for the erection of all but three of Calgary's early stone school buildings; his starting of the cadet movement in the area and organization of the Alberta Boy Scout movement, which he served as first president; his service as a member of the first hospital board until the city assumed control of the hospitals many years later.

With all his civic and business activities, Walker still managed to find time for his first love, the militia. During the 1885 North West Rebellion, when Calgarians feared an attack from surrounding Blackfoot and Sarcee tribes, he organized a contingent of 109 special constables to patrol the area between the Highwood and Red Deer Rivers. He personally put in so many long hours in the saddle during those dark days that his friend, George Murdoch, fearing for his health, asked Walker when he was going to stop for a rest and a decent meal. "When the Blackfoot and Sarcee have washed the war paint off their faces," was Walker's reply.

In 1900, on the occasion of a visit by the Duke and Duchess of York to Calgary, Colonel Walker organized a cadet corps of school-aged boys and equipped them with rifles, Sam Brown belts and caps borrowed from the North West Mounted Police. The smart appearance of the lads so impressed the Duke that when he met Walker in England during the First World War, the Duke, who had become King George V, remembered the boys and commended Walker for turning out such an impressive group. In 1905 Walker formed the militia regiment known as the 15th Canadian Light Horse and commanded the unit for five years. It was at that time that he was promoted to the rank of lieutenant-colonel.

When the First World War started Colonel Walker, then 68, saw no reason why he should not be eminently well qualified to lead an infantry battalion to France. He was still erect and looked and felt much younger than his actual years. Military authorities however, proved stuffy towards Walker's suggestion but, two years later, in 1916, changed their minds and appointed him a captain with the authority to recruit a company of men from southern Alberta and southeastern British Columbia for the 238th Forestry Battalion. Captain Walker, soon promoted to Major, took his company overseas, inspected timber reserves in England and Scotland, then set up several sawmills that for the remainder of the war turned out much needed timber and lumber. His sawmill experience in earlier years had served him well. His enlistment into the Forestry Corps caused General Sir Arthur Curry to make the wry comment: "Walker is a man who breaks out every 50 years and goes to war."

After the war Walker returned to Canada and took up his civilian life where he had left off. He remained busy, hale and hearty until just a few months before his death in 1936 at the age of 89. His wife had passed away a few years before and he was survived by his son, W.J. Selby Walker, and a granddaughter, Mary.

Calgary has seldom if ever seen a funeral procession to surpass that of Colonel Walker. He was buried with full military honors with high ranking army officers from all over Canada attending as well as officers and men from the Mounted Police. Reverend Doctor W.F. Kelloway of Knox United Church gave a fitting tribute during the eulogy when he said:

"In the promotion of Colonel James Walker to higher services, Knox Church has lost her member of longest standing and the man who was most instrumental in building the old church. He was one of the 'old guard' of whom so few are left, and because of his sterling qualities all Calgary, and indeed, all the West, is glad to honor him.

"...One word that stands out above all others in my mind as I think of his eventful and colorful career...is the great word 'Service.'

"Truly Colonel Walker was among us as one who served. The oldest soldier in the Canadian Militia; member of the first contingent of the North West Mounted Police, who blazed the trails to this great west land. Older than the Province of Alberta, older than the City of Calgary, he played an active part in laying the foundations and building thereon of both these institutions.

"The heroic service rendered Canada by the early police who guarded her frontiers...in the wild days now gone, and preserved the safety of human life and property, has not been sufficiently recognized. When that time comes, Colonel Walker cannot be kept out of the picture. Of this we may be sure: no history of the West will ever be complete without a prominent place being given to the records of those men who in pioneer days suffered isolation far out on the lonely plains and upheld law and order against freebooters, whisky smugglers and outlaws. It seems incredible that such a handful of men could have accomplished so much in such a short time and in a territory almost as large as Europe.

"My acquaintance with Colonel Walker covers a period of 33 years and I recognize his great and invaluable service to this community. As one who held very responsible positions from time to time, I can say that he fulfilled all with conscientious endeavor and fidelity. As a friend tried and true, he was always ready with a helping hand and an encouraging word. He served well his country, his city, his community, his fellow man and his Maker, and in doing so fulfilled the injunction of the Scripture to 'honor all men, love the brotherhood, fear God and honor the King.' James Walker has answered the Last Post and entered the great adventure."

Following Dr. Kelloway's tribute, Reverend Dr. G.W. Kerby read a message from one of the Colonel's long-time friends, the Right Honorable R.B. Bennett, former Prime Minister of Canada, who wrote:

"I sincerely regret my inability to join with my fellow citizens in paying a final tribute to the memory of the late Colonel James Walker... The last officer of the members of the original Police Force, whose achievements command universal admiration, he assisted in maintaining law and order in the territories but recently opened for settlement. A pioneer settler, he saw the frontiers of civilization pushed farther and farther into the wilderness, the railway supplant the prairie schooner, the motor car the pack pony. Territories became provinces and mere settlements thriving cities and towns.

"Active in every movement for the development of the West and the welfare of its people, he finally succeeded, despite his age, in serving overseas in the Great War. In the closing years of a long life of service and sacrifice in many fields of human endeavor, he became not only our beloved 'Old Timer,' but an institution of our city and district. We shall not see his like again."

The final and perhaps the greatest honor came nearly 40 years later. In 1975, although Calgary has been the home of many great men—Senator James Lougheed, Prime Minister R.B. Bennett and Premier William Aberhart to name three—in its Centennial Year it chose Colonel James Walker as its "CITIZEN OF THE CENTURY."

Surely no one can claim a higher earthly tribute than that! ●

*"Throw the skunk out!" Bredin once roared
at a political opponent during a campaign meeting.
These were harsh words indeed for a man who was
supposed to be the strong, silent type!*

FLETCHER BREDIN
Liberal Member For Athabasca

VARIOUS sources portray W.F. Bredin—Fletcher to his friends—as either the strong, silent
type, or as a vociferous campaigner ready to swap
insults and possibly fists with the best of them. He
probably was both, depending upon the
situation—silent and resourceful on a back-country
trail or paddling down some lonesome river as he
did for many years of his life, or noisy as the most
ardent of politicians when campaigning for a seat in
the Alberta Legislature, or arguing the merits of his
beloved northern Alberta as the foremost farming
area of Canada, if not of the whole world.

The Grande Prairie *Herald* recorded some of his
noisier campaigns while fighting to retain his seat in
the Alberta Legislature, particularly in 1913 when
he was running as a Liberal candidate for Peace
River. W.A. Rae, a well-known Grande Prairie
lawyer, was contesting Bredin for the Liberal
nomination, while Alpheus Patterson, Grande
Prairie businessman, carried the banner for the Con-
servatives. At the height of the campaign all three
men attended a meeting at a Grande Prairie school
to try to convince a skeptical audience of their
relative merits. It soon became obvious that there
was little love lost between Bredin and Rae, for
Bredin, while making his speech, flatly told the
crowd that if—Heaven forbid—they chose not to
vote for him, to change parties and vote for Patterson the Conservative. Then, as Rae stood up to
protest, Bredin shouted, "Throw the skunk out!"

When the crowd stoically failed to comply with
the order, Bredin proceeded to do the job himself.
As a parting gesture, after he had propelled Rae to
the door, Bredin proclaimed, "You're worse than a
skunk. It has a white streak down its back—yours is
yellow!"

*(Top) "The Northern Lights," High Prairie and district
personalities. Fletcher Bredin, second from left in
center row.*
*(Center) Main Street, Grouard, 1914. Many of these
buildings were moved to High Prairie.*
(Bottom) Main Street of Lake Saskatoon in 1916.

Harsh words, indeed, for a man who was supposed to be the strong, silent type!

It was finally resolved that Fletcher would run as
an independent Liberal while the skunk—er, Mr.
Rae—would stand as the Liberal candidate.

At the time of the campaign Fletcher Bredin had a
column in the Grande Prairie *Herald*. In one of
them, as a little propaganda promoting his can-
didacy, he wrote the following:

"Who at his own expense built the first sleigh road
into Grande Prairie?—Fletcher Bredin.

"Who at his own expense built the first wagon
road into Grande Prairie?—Fletcher Bredin.

"Who was the first to secure government assistance for the building of a railroad into Athabasca
and Peace River?—Fletcher Bredin."

Obviously there was one man who did not agree
with Bredin's claim—Dave Sexsmith, early
trailblazer who had had a town named for him and
who replied as follows:

Editor Grande Prairie *Herald*
Dear Sir:
In your issue of the 16th I see in Mr. Bredin's
column the statement that he built the first wagon
road into Grande Prairie.
Now I don't mind a person claiming credit for
what he did or didn't do as long as their state-
ments don't conflict with those of my own.
But as I cut a wagon road to Grande Prairie a year
and a half before the one mentioned in your
paper, and have claimed it as being the first, I feel
it my duty to contradict the statement appearing
in your paper.

Yours truly,
(Signed) D. Sexsmith

Such was the stuff of politics in the early days.
Though Fletcher Bredin lost out to his Conservative
opponent in that 1913 campaign, he was by then an
old hand at the game, having been elected to the first
sitting of the Alberta Legislature, soon after Alberta became a province in 1905. He was the Liberal
Member for the District of Athabasca and served two

terms, one under the first Premier, A.C. Rutherford, until he resigned in 1910, then under Premier A.L. Sifton for another three years. During his first term Bredin was called to Ottawa as one of the principal witnesses during a special Senate Committee in 1906 and 1907 inquiring into the natural resources of the Canadian Northwest. Fletcher Bredin was eminently qualified to testify, for he had been in the Canadian West since 1882 and had spent the past 10 years tramping the vast area north of Edmonton as a trader, explorer and homesteader.

He told the Senate Committee of those travels, of how he had seen the country from the Alberta-Montana border north as far as Fort Wrigley in the Northwest Territories, the Peace River Country from Fort St. John in the B.C. Peace River Block to Fort Vermilion, and the Athabasca River system from Athabasca Landing to the Arctic Circle on the mighty Mackenzie. He praised the Peace River area as being the best anywhere in Canada for agriculture. That was hardly news, for many others had spread the word before him. But his statement that the country north of Fort McMurray on the west side of the Athabasca River all the way to Lake Athabasca was also excellent for farming must have raised a few eyebrows, for this claim has not been proved almost three-quarters of a century after. Of that area he said:

"The elevation of the plateau above the river is very much less than it is on the upper river. It looks like a great alluvial plain from the (Clearwater) River all along from McMurray to Lake Athabasca, 200 miles. The country is more or less timbered and the soil is excellent...

"The muskeg between the Athabasca and the peace can all be drained and cultivated. These muskegs are from a foot to three feet deep until you strike hardpan. The moss keeps the heat of the sun out. In fact there is ice in some of those muskegs all year round (permafrost), covered with moss."

He spoke of the dimensions of the Peace River Country suitable for growing crops and claimed it was at least "equal to the Saskatchewan River valley for agricultural purposes." He told the committee of his farm near Grouard where he raised fine crops of oats and vegetables, but either boasted or was misquoted when he told of keeping cattle over winter and only having to feed them for five to six weeks during each of the five previous winters. Possibly that should have been, "five to six months each winter."

He estimated there was twice as much land north of Edmonton suitable for farming as there was south of that city. He likewise gave a glowing report of the natural gas in the North, especially along the Athabasca River where he told of cooking a meal over a gas jet issuing from a fissure in the rocks, as well as seeing gas bubbles rising in the river in many places. He told of the vastness of the oil sands, although if he realized their eventual worth to the

United Farmers of Alberta, board of directors, 1919. Front–L-R: Perrin Baker; Mrs. J.F. Ross; Mrs. Paul Carr; Henry Wise Wood; Mrs. Irene Parlby; W.D. Trego; Rice Sheppard; Middle–G.A. Forster; Charles H. Harris, George G. Huser; Lawrence Peterson; F.W. Smith; Herbert Greenfield; W.F. Bredin; Back–A. Rafn; Henry E. Spencer; H. Higginbotham; G.D. Sloane; George F. Root and Joseph Stauffer.

country, he seems not to have given them the same emphasis as the land's potential for agriculture and timber.

Fletcher Bredin was born in 1857 on a farm 15 miles west of Cornwall, Ontario. He headed west 20 years later, in 1877, when he followed his father to Winnipeg, where the elder Bredin had purchased some land. Young Fletcher got his first taste of real adventure in 1878 when he joined the militia unit commanded by Colonel Osborne Smith who later led the Winnipeg Rifles during the North-West Rebellion, and was sent to help quell a strike of construction workers building the CPR east of Winnipeg. To W.D. Albright, longtime superintendent of the Beaverlodge Alberta Experimental Farm, Bredin recounted:

"We got out there in the evening and arrested some prisoners. The next morning 800 men came walking down the track, four abreast, every man with a club in his hand and made a demand for the release of the prisoners. The Colonel went forward and harangued them declaring that no prisoners would be released, but gave them to understand that the troops were there to see fair play all around... We remained for a week until the matter was straightened up and then went back to Winnipeg...."

The following year Fletcher decided he did not like Manitoba very much and headed for North Dakota, where he got a job driving stage carrying the U.S. mail. Like Kootenai Brown before him, he soon learned there were safer jobs elsewhere and pulled out to work on construction gangs building the Northern Pacific Railway through Montana. He worked at anything and everything from cook to dishwasher until he began hearing glowing reports of southern Alberta from men like Liver-Eating Johnson, one of the builders of Fort Standoff, who was town mar-

Members of the first Alberta Legislature, 1905. Fletcher Bredin is right centre of "Alberta."

shall for the town of Coulson, Montana, when Fletcher met him; from J.J. Healy, Fort Benton sheriff and one of the founders of Fort Whoop-Up; and from Joe Kipp, another Montanan who founded Fort Kipp. He decided to have a look for himself and headed north from Fort Benton, accompanying an I.G. Baker Company bulltrain consisting of three yokes of 10 to 12 oxen, each pulling three wagons hitched one behind the other. They followed the Benton-Whoop-Up Trail to Fort Whoop-Up where Bredin left the train and rode on to Fort Macleod. There he met such early North West Mounted Policemen as Superintendent John Cotton and Inspector Francis J. Dickens, son of the famous author, Charles Dickens.

"I pulled out from Macleod up along the Willow Creek and crossed High River, Sheep River and Fish Creek to Calgary," Bredin told Albright. "I camped overnight at Fish Creek, eight miles below Calgary and there was an old Irishman named John Glenn who was farming on Fish Creek and had taken out an irrigation ditch, probably the first in the province. He rode into Calgary with me the next day...."

While reminiscing before a meeting of the Young Liberal Club in Lethbridge in 1907, Bredin told of looking down at Calgary from a hill. Said he: "It was a beautiful sight, but a great contrast to the handsome stone city of today. The whole valley was green and a single shack stood way up the valley. I.G. Baker had a store just over the Elbow River... There was a small Mounted Police barracks... Captain French, afterwards killed at Batoche, was in command. The Hudson's Bay Company had a post near the mouth of the Elbow and on the east side. The Cochrane people had their ranch about 20 miles west of Calgary at this time... It was one of the Cochrane cowboys, 'Tex,' (in the Albright papers he gives the cowboy the name of 'Buckskin Shorty') who directed me north and stayed with me all night at McPherson's Coulee about 20 miles north of Calgary. Add. McPherson and the buffalo traders had been in the habit of wintering at this point..."

Bredin remembered that Sam Scarlett had settled at Service Berry Creek and that he crossed the Red Deer River three miles above the present city. "After leaving Lacombe," he said, "the next point I struck was the Battle River. Here I met Father Leduc, who was traveling up the river and I enjoyed the hospitality of his camp. He had some fine bread baked by the sisters of the St. Albert convent. He was on the road to Benton and had a young half-breed, now Father Cunningham, and was taking him east to be educated. I likewise enjoyed a night with Reverend E.B. Glass who had come out the year before as a missionary for the Methodist Church…"

At Edmonton he learned that his brother had died shortly before his arrival. "He had been buried three days," he told Albright. "I crossed John Walter's ferry on the Saskatchewan and went to Donald Ross' hotel below where the *Journal* office now stands. He had a log building with a pool room and about 16 beds in an upper room. I stayed there all night…" Bredin mentioned that there were only a handful of people living in Edmonton at the time. Some of the names he remembered were Mat McCauley, Alex Taylor, A.D. Osborne, Kenny McLeod, Jim Gibbons, John Cameron, George Sandison, Frank McDougall, and Frank Oliver who had recently opened a printing office and started his Edmonton *Bulletin*. Bredin's brother had willed him a piece of land on the south side of the river. Fletcher settled on it, broke a few acres, but succumbed to wanderlust again that fall and headed for Winnipeg via Fort Walsh, accompanied part way by Ad McPherson, who later operated a stopping house on the Calgary-Edmonton Trail.

For the next couple of years Bredin led a nomadic existence, farming at Edmonton in the summer, helping his father, who had started a store in Calgary, part time in the winter, as well as hauling coal from a mine at Fish Creek. Most of the coal went to the NWMP barracks and was probably the first coal sold in Calgary. When his crop froze in Edmonton in the cold summer of 1883, he became disgusted with the place, sold his farm for $150 and headed for the Kicking Horse Pass, where he spent the next couple of years freighting for the various construction companies building the Canadian Pacific Railway. During the summer of 1885, he headed north to Lac La Biche with a government party who were issuing scrip to the Metis. (Ironically, each adult male Metis who had settled around Lac La Biche was entitled to a land grant of 240 acres. Many sold their scrip for a mere pittance and were no better off than before).

This task completed, Bredin followed the crew back to Calgary, outfitted himself with a trading packet and the following winter, 1885-86, headed to Buffalo Lake near the present village of Mirror and south of the town of Bashaw, where he started a trading post on Spotted Creek.

"This was a favorite place in spring for the Indians to meet after their winter's fur hunt," he explained. "They killed and dried great numbers of Jackfish and suckers (caught) in this creek and consumed great numbers of gull eggs which they got in the Spotted Lake. This lake is all dotted with rushes and when viewed from an elevation has a spotted appearance. I have eaten many gull eggs myself and used to make custards from them. The eggs are a little strong but not bad…."

He remembered thousands of gulls nesting there when he first arrived but when the settlers came, after 1900, they robbed the nests so shamelessly that the gulls left and did not come back. "I remained at Spotted Creek trading with the Indians until 1896," he continued, "when I sold out and went to Lac La Biche to prepare the voter's list for the coming Dominion election…" Only two candidates ran in that election—Frank Oliver, Liberal, and Lieutenant Cochrane, R.N., Conservative. Oliver won and served for many years, becoming Minister of the Interior under Prime Minister Wilfred Laurier.

Although Bredin did not mention it in his diary, he apparently named the post office that operated from his post, Lamerton. At least the village of Lamerton blossomed on the spot and flourished until 1912 when the Grand Trunk Pacific Railway ran a line through the area. The railway company wanted to build a station, roundhouse and maintenance shop in Lamerton, but apparently the man who owned the land held out for a higher price than the railway wanted to pay. They haggled for a time, then simply bought land two miles south and built their own town, naming it Mirror. Within two years all Lamerton businessmen had moved to Mirror, taking their buildings with them. The only thing left of the village of Lamerton was a cemetery and a building, now a farm house, that was built originally to house the one-man detachment of the North West Mounted Police.

Fletcher Bredin's next big venture was a trip down the Athabasca and Mackenzie Rivers with a couple of partners and a 10-ton boatload of trade goods. They started at Athabasca Landing and kept going far into the North West Territories, looking for a likely place to set up shop. At a stop-over at Hay River, NWT, Bredin met his future wife, Anna Marsh, who was assisting her brother, the Reverend Thomas Marsh, with missionary work among the Indians, and also helping with an Anglican school for Indian children. Fletcher and his partners spent the winter of 1896-97 in a log cabin they built north of Fort Wrigley on the bank of the Mackenzie River.

The partners did a brisk business with a band of Indians who, after arguing for a better deal with the Hudson's Bay Company factor at Fort Wrigley, had become angered and begun their winter hunt without any food or ammunition. Having none of the white men's goods, however, did not seem to bother them much. For when Bill McLeod, one of the partners, caught up to them somewhere in the Nahanni River area, he found them well supplied with meat — moose, bear and Big Horn sheep — besides which they had trapped or snared some 600 pounds of beaver, marten, mink and various other furs. The Indians accompanied McLeod back to the post and Bredin said of them:

"They stayed with us a couple of nights and they had no article of European dress on them. They had moccasins and sox of rabbit skin and rabbit skin shirts

—that is the rabbit skins had been cut in strips and woven together to make these garments. They wore goat skin leggings with the fur on the outside, goat skin jackets with a capote on them, a rabbit skin muffler and of course, moose skin mitts...."

Trade with the Indians was sufficiently profitable that Bredin was able to sell out to McLeod and leave the North in the summer of 1897. McLeod and his brother Frank were later involved in one of the most mysterious stories of the North when their headless bodies were found in the Nahanni River valley, giving rise to the naming of the Headless Valley. But that is another story and, long before, Fletcher Bredin and his remaining partner, John Burker, were paddling and tracking their way up the Mackenzie, across Great Slave Lake and up the Athabasca all the way to Athabasca Landing. About the last lap of that trip Bredin remembered:

"In the morning we were preparing our boat to start for Athabasca Landing on the last lap of our trip from Wrigley. We were about 12 miles below Athabasca Landing when there was an explosion over at the well where a party of men hired by the Dominion Government were drilling and there was a great eruption of gas. This explosion was heard three miles away. We went over to see what was up and there was light oil spattered on the derrick. The man in charge put his finger on that and said 'That's what we're after.' We reached Athabasca Landing on the 9th of September, having left Wrigley on the 7th of June." Strangely, though the well Fletcher Bredin witnessed blowing in must have been one of the first oil wells in the province, this area has not produced any great underground oil field as might be suspected. However, not far downriver from the Grand Rapids on the Athabasca begins the great oil sands deposit, probably the largest in the world.

By some strange quirk of fate there does not appear to be very much written about Bredin from the time of his leaving the Far North, although he was really only hitting his stride. However, from short news items in various newspapers such as the Grand Prairie *Herald* and Edmonton *Journal* we know that in 1898 he joined in a partnership with "Peace River Jim" Cornwall and established trading posts at Grouard, Lake Saskatoon and Fort Vermilion. From these news items we know, too, that he homesteaded near Grouard where he ran for and won a seat in the Alberta Legislature in November of 1905. He retained his seat in 1909 but, in 1913, when he ran in the Peace River constituency, he received only 47 votes.

From the files of the Edmonton *Journal* we learn that in September of 1907 he married Anna Marsh, the lady whom he met at Hay River. The wedding took place at Clarksburg, Ontario, Anna's old home town. They spent their first years of married life at the Bredin homestead near Grouard. From there they travelled each year, usually by caboose—a sort of sleigh-mounted, horse-drawn version of the

I.G. Baker Store in Old Fort Macleod.

modern motor-home—to attend the annual sitting of the Alberta Legislature. About 1911 they moved to their Twinshacks farm on the northern shore of Bear Lake, near Clairmont, north of Grande Prairie. Although his time was now taken up by farming, Fletcher retained his trading interest for, as late as 1934, he still had a trading post at Rio Grande, southwest of the town of Beaverlodge.

Ask anyone who remembers the Bredins and their Twinshacks farm and the word that will be used to describe them is 'hospitality.' Their home was open to all and both Mr. and Mrs. Bredin seemed happiest when helping others. Perhaps Reverend R. Little, Archdeacon of the Anglican Church, who served Grande Prairie for many years, said it best upon Fletcher Bredin's passing away in an Edmonton hospital in December of 1942.

"When we arrived at Grande Prairie in Holy Week of 1921, it was the Bredins who came to Grande Prairie from Clairmont to give us a royal welcome. Fletcher Bredin erected the porch on the rectory kitchen to keep out the northern winds. When we needed potatoes, it was Fletcher Bredin who always brought them. On one occasion he brought a whole washtub full of corned moose meat as his offering. At one of our camps he gave us the meadow by the shore; he built a cupboard in the lake bank; he gave us the use of a granary and brought all the ice we needed. His stories about Winnipeg in the 70s or about Edmonton or the Arctic in the early days were always so thrilling. Mrs. Bredin took charge of the Junior Girls' Auxiliary every week, holding the meetings as the girls came from school. It was no uncommon incident to serve 20 people without notice being given. Fletcher also had a farm near Grouard which he called 'Meyanook' (Cree for good camping place) but soon after moved to Clairmont to a place called 'Bredin' and Mr. Bredin himself was postmaster... He contributed much to the development of this part of Canada's Northland and he will be greatly missed."

This, then, was Fletcher Bredin, intrepid pathfinder and one of the best promoters the Peace River Country ever had. He was obviously a man of great contrasts, for in politics he was a tiger, in domestic life a man whose greatest thrill was helping his fellow man.

W.F. Bredin—1857 to 1942. May his spirit always endure. ●

DISASTER AT THE HILLCREST MINE

The Crowsnest Pass area was no stranger to tragedy. But even the most pessimistic could not have anticipated the disaster of June 19, 1914, when an explosion in the Hillcrest Mine snuffed out the lives of 189 men.

THE Crowsnest Pass area in southwestern Alberta is certainly no stranger to disaster. Coal mining districts seldom are. Few indeed are those living in the area who are not acutely aware that, on April 29, 1903, the whole face of Turtle Mountain— some 90,000,000 tons of it— came tumbling down, burying part of the village of Frank and killing 76 people. Over seven years later, on December 9, 1910, another 30 men lost their lives at Bellevue when an underground explosion devastated the mine.

Miners and their families everywhere are painfully aware that mining is dangerous— that at any time a miner's life can be snuffed out by a rock-fall, an explosion, a runaway mine car. Those things happen and miners live, or die, with it. But even the most pessimistic could hardly have anticipated the disaster at the Hillcrest Mine that fateful morning of June 19, 1914, when an explosion and its aftermath snuffed out the lives of 189 men.

Actually, there seemed to be no reason for the disaster. Hillcrest, named for Charles Plumber Hill who established the mine in 1905 and sold to Hillcrest Collieries Limited in 1909, was purported to be the best operated and safest mine in the Crowsnest Pass. Because of over-production the mine had been idle for a couple of days, but, early in the morning of that terrible Friday before the miners

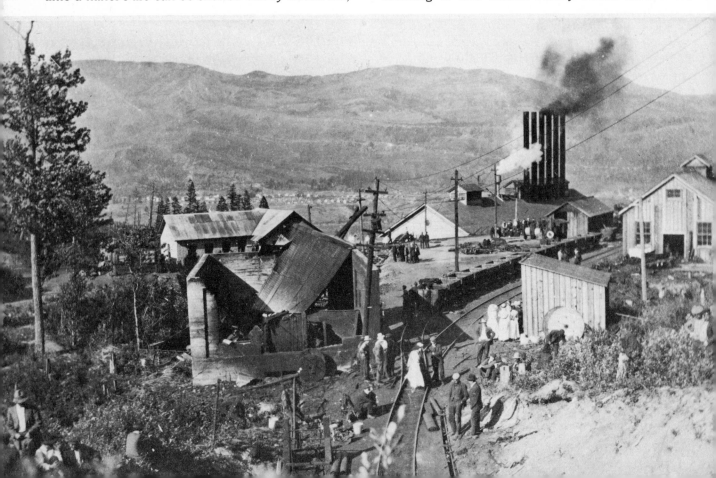

returned to work, William Adkin, one of the mine fire bosses, had made a thorough investigation of the diggings. He reported a few small pockets of methane gas, some small rock-falls, but nothing out of the ordinary. Ventilation was good and there seemed to be no reason why the men should not resume work. Moreover, a committee of three men from the mine-worker's union — Frank Pearson, James Gurtson and George Pounder—had likewise toured the mine and pronounced it to be safe for the men to return. With no reason to think it was anything but another working day, most of the 377 Hillcrest Mine employees filed to their jobs, 235 picking up their lamps and identifying tags before heading underground to resume work at the various coal faces. It was a bright sunny morning. For 189 of those men it was the last time they would ever see daylight.

The first indication that anything was wrong came about 9:30 a.m. when, just as electrical engineer Alex May turned from inspecting one of the huge outside fans that ventilated the mine, he was knocked flat by a tremendous rush of air from behind. Partially stunned, he turned to see a cloud of heavy brown smoke emanating from the airshaft. At that same instant General Manager John Brown, who was walking towards his office near the entrance to Mine No. 1, saw the roof of the building that housed the mine hoist collapse as though some great weight had dropped on it. He realized immediately that somewhere deep in the bowels of the mine something, or someone, had set off a tremendous explosion.

Just how devastating the explosion had been was soon brought home to the men working outside the mine. Sixty feet from the entrance to Mine No. 1, Charles Ironmonger, a 19-year-old rope-rider whose job it was to unhook coal cars from the cable that drew them from the mine and shunt them onto tracks leading to the tipple, lay dying. He had been caught in a blast so forceful that it crumpled an eight-inch-thick concrete wall in the hoist house and plugged the mine entrance with a jumble of twisted mine track, broken mine cars and fallen rock and timbers. Nor had No. 2 Mine entrance been spared. Here the blast had killed the other young rope-rider, 22-year-old Fred Kurigatz, and blown down the hoist house. But, miraculously, it left the mine hoist engine and cable intact.

Since the entrance of No. 2 Mine was relatively clear of debris, some of the outside workers, knowing that every second counted, rushed in to help the men underground, only to be driven back when they ran into choking carbon dioxide, the poisonous black damp that miners fear so much. Despite the gas concentration, three men staggered from the mine entrance. George Wild, Antonio Stella and Arthur Crowther, who had been working close to the mine mouth, had survived the blast and the gas by nothing short of a miracle.

(Opposite page) Hillcrest, Alberta. This view shows the remains of the pump house and No. 2 mine entrance after the June 18, 1914, blast which took the lives of 189 men. The mine closed forever in 1938.
(Top) The No. 1 hoist house at Hillcrest.
(Center) Some of the horses used in the mines at Hillcrest, showing the heavy leather pads that protected their heads when underground.
(Bottom) The crowds gather at the scene of the disaster.

It was a quarter of an hour before any more survivors emerged from the mine on their own. The total count came to 19—the rest were down in the mine. Some were undoubtedly still alive, but if they were not rescued quickly, they would succumb to gas and smoke.

It did not take long for the rescuers to organize and acts of heroism that day were more the rule than the exception. Hillcrest Collieries was actually two mines interconnected below by a labyrinth of tunnels. It had two entrances, but since No. 1 Mine entrance was hopelessly jammed with debris, all efforts were concentrated on clearing the entrance to No. 2 Mine.

Mounted Police Corporals F.J. Mead and Arthur Grant, and Constable William Hancock, raced to the scene from Burmis Mines to assist the Hillcrest men. Unfortunately, the Mounties' initial task was to control the women and children who had rushed to the scene and were pushing and screaming in an attempt to learn if relatives were safe. They were impeding rescue efforts and had to be driven back by the police.

Meanwhile, mine workers, knowing that every second counted, quickly got the hoist engine in operation, cleared the track and piled aboard the first car heading into the mine. Although oxygen masks had not yet arrived, these rescuers, led by a man who only moments before had emerged from the mine half-suffocated from gas, smoke and dust, kept up their search, ignored the dead and hurried those still breathing to the surface and the emergency hospital set up at the entrance. At 10 a.m. came the good news that oxygen masks had arrived from Blairmore, along with a doctor and pulmotor equipment, and that 100 miners from Blairmore were on their way. The oxygen masks were immediately sent underground — and none too soon, for, although the ventilation fans had been restarted, some of the rescuers were all but done in by the bad air.

For all too many, however, oxygen masks, pulmotors and heroism were too late. Some of those caught near the center of the explosion were literally torn apart. Others who had tried to save themselves after surviving the initial explosion by dipping their shirts in shallow pools of water, then breathing through them to filter out gas and smoke, were still alive although unconscious. Others had succumbed to gas before they could do likewise. At least 30 men, clustered in a group, lay dead, face down in a pool of water. So it went all through the mine— some dead, killed outright, some suffocated from gas and smoke, some unconscious, but still breathing — hopefully to be revived when taken to the surface. Unfortunately, of the 235 who went into the mine that morning, only 46 survived. No words adequately describe a tragedy such as this. For those who waited in vain on the surface there was only numbing, sickening shock.

But the work had to go on. First came the job of bringing out the bodies and identifying them for burial. Later came the task of attempting to find out what went wrong. Initially there was a tendency to blame fireboss Sam Charlton for somehow setting off the explosion. He was the powder man that day, responsible for placing the charges at the coal face that would bring down, or at least loosen up, the first batch of coal the men would have mined that day. It turned out, however, that although Sam had set his charges that morning, he had not detonated them. When rescuers found his body, his firing cable was still wrapped around his waist, the battery lay disconnected several feet away, and the key that he used to turn the switch was still in his pocket. It seemed as though Sam Charlton, sensing something was amiss, had delayed setting off his charges. Either that, or the explosion had taken place before he had time to hook up the wiring and turn the switch.

What had touched off the explosion remains a mystery, although one man advanced the theory that a rock-fall in one of the tunnels had caused a spark, which had in turn ignited a pocket of methane gas. The gas flame had then jumped from one small gas pocket to another until, near the coal-face, it had hit a pocket of concentrated coal dust which, when dry enough and in the right concentration, is like gunpowder. It was thought that the resulting explosion caused the disaster. This was the theory advanced by Harry White, a former fireboss at the Hillcrest Mine and one of the first men to go through the mine from end to end after the blast. His idea was ignored by the board of inquiry, but later proved feasible when, on September 19, 1926, another terrific explosion tore through the Hillcrest mine. At the time there were only two men in the mine. Both were killed, but neither had been near the spot where the initial explosion took place.

When the last of the survivors were brought to the surface, rescuers began the grim task of bringing out the dead. Efforts were often held up while blocked mine shafts were cleared of jumbled mine timbers and cars and fallen rock. At least twice rescue operations had to be suspended when fires broke out in the shafts far underground and firefighters had to be rushed to the scene. Always there was the danger of another explosion, but the miners stuck tenaciously to the task until all the dead, some of whom had been dismembered, were brought to the surface.

The grim task of identifying the bodies fell to the men of the RCMP. Corporals F.J. Mead and Arthur Grant spent seemingly endless hours in the mine wash-house, cleaning bodies, piecing together sundered bodies, or touring the mine with Constable Hancock in search of missing arms and legs. Nobody envied their job and despite the fact that the miner's union, the United Mine Workers of America, had no use for policemen in general, and

(Top) The official team inquiring into the Hillcrest mine disaster pose at No. 2 entrance during rescue operations.
(Center) A mine rescue team at Coal Creek in 1912. Organized by John Shanks (extreme right, with hand in pocket), these miners assisted in the Hillcrest mine disaster in 1911.
(Bottom) Burial for the victims of the Hillcrest Mine disaster.

the Mounties in particular, they grudgingly had to admit that this group of Mounties, led by Inspector Christen Junget who had driven in from Pincher Creek, were doing a magnificent job. For almost a week Grant, Mead and Hancock stuck with the task, eating and sleeping in the wash-house until the job was completed. For their efforts each was later granted an extra $50 in pay and all were later promoted.

Surely one of the saddest funerals in the history of the country took place on Sunday, June 21, 1914, when 150 men were placed in a mass grave at the Hillcrest cemetery. Others were buried in private ceremonies at Hillcrest and Blairmore, while four men took the long cross-country ride to their hometowns in Nova Scotia and their final resting place. In all, some 130 women were widowed by that terrible blast and 400 children, most of whom were under the age of 10, left without fathers.

It is at times such as this, however, that people show their best. Although Hillcrest Collieries was to pay out $1,800 to each family in compensation, it takes time to process compensation claims and for most families the need for money was immediate and great. Fortunately for them, a relief committee from Hillcrest was immediately formed and donations of money and food readily made available. Donations from far and wide soon followed. The federal and provincial governments soon forwarded their contribution — $50,000 from Ottawa and $20,000 from Edmonton. People in cities and towns across the nation donated to relief funds set up for the sorrowing town, the response being spontaneous and generous. Unfortunately, no amount of money could return even one miner to his grieving family.

What of Hillcrest today? As already mentioned, another horrendous blast tore through the mine in 1926. Two men were killed in that blast, but had it happened a couple of hours later when the night shift was on duty, the toll could have been 150 more. Despite damage as severe or worse than that caused by the 1914 explosion, the mine was soon back in operation. It was supposed to be one of the safest mines in the country, yet, twice, devastating blasts ravaged its workings. Nevertheless, it remained a productive mine until 1949. By then natural gas and fuel oil had dethroned coal as king of fuels, and mines were closing all across the country.

To insure that no one could enter the mine and injure himself, the mine entrances were permanently closed with well-placed dynamite charges. Mine equipment has been moved away and, although the town remains, the population has been reduced by almost half.

Only an inordinately large number of markers in the cemetery remain as a grim reminder of that fateful day in 1914 when a terrible explosion snuffed out the lives of 189 men at the Hillcrest Mine. ●

BLUE-COATED MOUNTIES
THE ALBERTA PROVINCIAL POLICE

MOST Albertans tend to think of the Royal Canadian Mounted Police as Alberta's police force, for they were here long before Alberta became a province and are still here, doing a tremendous job. But for 15 years Alberta had its own "Mounties," and a topnotch force it was too. Moreover, when the Alberta Provincial Police began enforcing the laws of the province, they actually took on more duties than the RNWMP ever had. Besides general police work the APP were responsible for bringing in any isolated homesteader to the nearest hospital should he fall ill; they were responsible not only for escorting the insane to the various institutions, but also for administering their estate after hospitalization. The APP was also responsible for

the administering of the Mothers' Pension Act, seeing that women who were widowed or deserted by their husbands received a pension to feed their hungry children. The force was likewise given the job of distributing relief.

Those were only a few of their extra duties. The APP also inspected theaters in towns that had no police force of their own, likewise poolrooms and cafes, to see that all were operating according to Alberta law. They acted as brand inspectors and watched for diseases in cattle; they were required to collect unpaid bills from country patients who had used city hospitals. They investigated cases for the Workmens' Compensation Board, they acted as game wardens and fishery guardians, and assisted

x Illustrating how Bassof appeared when shooting Bailey dead. Bailey was unharmed in the buildi[?]

(Opposite page) *The Alberta Provincial Police at closing out ceremonies, March, 1932.*
(Above) *Re-enactment of the shooting of Const. Baily by Tom Bassoff at Bellevue, August, 1920.*
(Right) *Commissioner Willoughby Charles Bryan (1865-1947) of the Alberta Provincial Police.*

For 15 years Alberta had its own "Mounties" in blue. Under the able direction of Superintendent W.C. Bryan, the APP gave Alberta the reputation of being the province where gangsters, thieves and murderers came to be arrested.

the forestry department in enforcing forest fire regulations as well as rounding up firefighters when forest fires started. They were required to report attendance at country schools to enable school boards to collect grants from the provincial government. Then there was the job of attending cattle roundups to supervise the distribution of branded animals and see that monies accrued from the sale of unbranded animals went to the rightful owners. Still another extra-curricular duty was to help Indian agents with their work whenever the need arose.

Then, of course, there was the regular police work of maintaining law and order, highway patrol work, criminal investigation, as well as the biggest job of all, particularly during the years when

prohibition was in effect, keeping the bootleggers in check. An article that appeared in the Edmonton *Journal*, December 10, 1928, gives a good example of how efficient the APP became at apprehending rum-runners through constant practice. It states:

"This year Christmas will not be what it used to be in Montana and adjacent states. Inhabitants of these sections long accustomed to having Santa Claus and imported Yuletide spirits from Alberta at Christmas will have Santa Claus but they won't get their Yuletide spirits.

"Monday morning as part of the relentless war the Alberta Provincial Police have declared on rum-runners, three private cars loaded to their tops with Christmas cheer in bottles, were seized at Blairmore by the APP...The drivers of the cars were arrested for illegal possession of liquor under the Alberta Liquor Act... The cars captured were making their way to Montana at top speed through the Crowsnest Pass from British Columbia.

"For some time the APP has been steadily plugging the holes along the border through which liquor has been trickling into the land of the 'Parched Eagle' despite heart rendering wails from bone-dry throats.

"So acute had the situation become due to prohibition in the United States that rum-runners are offering princely bribes to any policeman who will take a beauty sleep while they roar through his territory. One APP constable from Edmonton who was sent into the southern part of the province recently claims he was offered $3,000 to change the name on the charge laid against one rum-runner who apparently had a previous conviction against him.

"With bars down against the contraband runners, Americans are becoming desperate. Prices of Canadian liquor are soaring to unheard of heights...."

Despite being offered great bribes simply to turn their backs, there were few if any incidents where members of the APP accepted. Though ill-equipped and badly organized when the force assumed its duties in 1917, the Alberta Provincial Police soon became as efficient as the force they succeeded, the Royal North West Mounted Police, who were reorganized and renamed the Royal Canadian Mounted Police in 1920. The new force should have been as efficient, for 85 per cent of its members were former members of the federal force. Though many Albertans were against the idea of a provincial police force and voted against it, they had little choice in the matter. With the First World War raging, its ranks badly depleted by enlistments into the armed forces, the RNWMP decided they had their hands full looking after the internal security of the country. Consequently, in 1916 the federal government told both Alberta and Saskatchewan that the Mounties could no longer handle the policing of the two provinces and that they would have to form their own police forces. The Alberta government asked Major A.E.C. McDonnell, a former Mounted Policeman, to form a new force and act as its first superintendent.

The new force officially went to work on March 1, 1917. They took over with little training, though this was no serious drawback since most of its members had served, some for many years, with the RNWMP. What was a serious drawback, however, was the lack of adequate equipment. The APP had only three cars, Model T. Fords, at the start and a serious shortage of horses, uniforms and other equipment. At first the uniforms were cast-offs from city police forces, which badly angered the members of the new force who had been former Mounties. That problem was solved by adopting a uniform quite similar to that worn by the RNWMP, the tunic being blue rather than the Mounties' familiar red. But the theory advanced by some members of the Alberta Legislature prior to the takeover, that a provincial force would be cheaper to maintain, was soon shot down in flames. For, while the province had paid $75,000 per year for the RNWMP, the annual cost of the APP soon rose to over a half a million dollars.

It would be false to claim that the APP was an immediate success. In its first year of service, of the 216 original members, there were 66 resignations. Fourteen were dismissed for various reasons such as being unsuitable (three); disgraceful and immoral conduct (five); making a false statement (one); for allowing a prisoner to escape (one); for mutinous conduct (one); for taking part in a civil action (one); and for being absent without leave (one). By the end of the first year the force was down to 139 men and Major McDonnell had resigned. Lieutenant-Colonel W.C. Bryan, also a former Mounted Policeman, took over as Superintendent, later changed to Commissioner. Under him, the force was soon organized to a high state of efficiency.

Headquarters of the new force was Edmonton, also the home of "A" Division. "B" Division had its headquarters at Red Deer, "C" at Calgary, and "D" at Lethbridge. There was also "E1" at Peace River and "E2" at Grande Prairie. Initially the force had 48 detachments stationed throughout the province. It gradually expanded to 100. It also had a Criminal Investigation Branch, composed of specially trained men under Inspector K. Duncan, ready to go anywhere in the province to assist in tracking down criminals. They did a masterful job for, throughout its lifetime, the force maintained an 80 per cent conviction ratio. Some of the Force's top-notch men were Inspector E.W. Bavin, Inspector J.D. "Blood Hound" Nicholson, Senior Inspector, later Assistant Commissioner, W.F.W. Hancock and many others.

According to the annual report submitted by Inspector Bavin in 1930, when he was in charge of the Calgary Division, of 2,954 arrests his men made that year, he had 2,492 convictions, with 19 still awaiting trial, for a conviction ratio of 89.9 per cent. That meant that of every 10 arrested, nine were convicted. "And in many cases," stated the report, "the one in 10 was allowed to escape APP jurisdiction only because some other force in another part of Canada or the U.S. had already arrested the man." It led to a saying among gangsters, thieves and murderers who had operated for years in other parts, that they had to come to Alberta to be arrested. The APP's record was an honorable one, admired around the world—that is, by everyone but the criminals.

Two of the APP's more notable cases were the Basoff, Arkoff, Auloff train robbery and the Union Bank robbery at Foremost.

The Basoff, Arkoff, Auloff case began on August

2, 1920, when CPR train No. 63 was on its way from Lethbridge to Cranbrook, British Columbia. As the train neared Sentinel way station in the Crowsnest Pass, Conductor Sam Jones was taking tickets when, suddenly, a man stood up and pointed a handgun at his head. Jones, perhaps foolishly, ignored the threatening gun and reached for the emergency cord, bringing the train to a screeching halt. Thrown off balance by the lurching stop, the bandit fired, but fortunately missed Conductor Jones. Just as the train ground to a stop, two more men jumped up and began waving guns and warning the passengers to stay in their seats. It took them only a few minutes to relieve the men of money and watches, though the women were simply ignored. There is a rumor that Emilio Picariello, the Crowsnest Pass' famous Mr. Pick, Bootlegger and Bottle King, was carrying $10,000 that day, but somehow managed to slip it under a seat and escape detection. As it was, the bandits got away with $400 in cash and several watches. It was one of those watches, the one belonging to Conductor Jones, that eventually led to the arrest of one of the men. As the train robbers stepped from the train, they fired another shot to keep everyone inside, then disappeared in the direction of Coleman.

From descriptions given by the passengers, the three holdup men were identified as Frank Allen, alias George Arkoff; Jimmy Attin, alias Tom Basoff; and Alex Godzees, alias Ausby Hollof (alias Aulcoff). The combined police forces of the APP, RCMP and CPR soon had a manhunt underway. But the robbers seemed in no rush to get away as, four days later, they were seen in the village of Coleman. There they apparently split up, Aulcoff heading west and eventually into the United States, while Basoff and Arkoff went east, finally showing up in Bellevue on the morning of August 7, where they read about themselves on a "Wanted" poster displayed in the window of Justice of Peace J.H. Robertson's office. Then they casually sauntered into the Bellevue Cafe for breakfast. Perhaps they would not have been so nonchalant had they known that Mr. Robertson had recognized them as they stood reading the poster and quickly phoned Constable James Frewin of the APP at Blairmore. Constable Frewin soon contacted Constable F.W.E. Bailey of the APP and Corporal Ernest Usher of the RCMP and all three climbed aboard a passing CPR train for the short run to Bellevue.

Accounts differ as to what actually happened when the police reached the Bellevue Cafe, but one story has Constable Bailey guarding the back door while Corporal Usher and Constable Frewin entered the front. Frewin, states the one version, stepped up to the men who were sitting in a booth behind drawn curtains, drew his gun and told him they were under arrest. Since Frewin was wearing civilian clothes, perhaps the two train robbers did not know he was a policeman. Anyway, they both went for their guns

and all hell broke loose in the Bellevue Cafe.

According to an article in the Glenbow-Alberta Institute files, publication unknown, but written by Dan E.C. Campbell in 1931: "Frewin, telling the men they were under arrest, ordered them to throw up their hands. They reached for their guns. Frewin fired at one of the men known as George Arkoff, wounding him. Usher held his fire until too late.

"Bailey, hearing the shooting, rushed in from the back. Frewin, having emptied his gun, backed out to make room for Bailey. Both Arkoff and his companion known as Basoff, had opened fire at Usher and Bailey, the former with a heavy Mauser and Basoff with two guns of the same make.

"Usher, shot in the back as he passed sideways through the front door to the street, fell and Bailey, stumbling over his body, struck his head on the pavement and lay stunned. Arkoff and Basoff, working their way along the wall, reached the door about this time. The former plunged through the door and fell to the street, dead.

"Basoff, standing in the doorway, a gun in each hand, saw Bailey move and shot him in the head, killing him instantly. He then fired a succession of shots into Usher's body and, though badly wounded in the leg, made his get-away. Frewin, badly shell-shocked during the (First World War), did not recover himself until Basoff was out of range. There, in less time than it takes to tell about it, two policemen, both of different forces, and one bandit had lost their lives."

The country in the Crowsnest Pass area is hardly conducive to an easy manhunt. Nevertheless, the APP, led by famed Detective Inspector J.D. Nicholson, and the RCMP under Inspector J. McDonald, were determined that Basoff would not get away. However, he eluded pursuit until August 11, four days after the shooting. That night he was seen by a CPR engineer just west of the Pincher Creek station. The engineer poured on full steam and roared into Lundbeck, where he notified company police. Four CPR policemen jumped aboard the locomotive and were hustled back to Pincher Creek, where they found Basoff hiding behind a shed near the station. It was all over. Basoff, weakened by loss of blood, hunger and little sleep, put up no resistance. The CPR police swarmed over him, handcuffed him and took him to Inspector Nicholson. On December 22, 1920, after a trial at Lethbridge, Tom Basoff died on the gallows for his crimes.

This left two down and one to go. In the meantime, descriptions of Ausby Auloff had been sent all over the United States and Canada. But it was not until four years later, on January 18, 1924, that Auloff made his first serious mistake by hocking Sam Jones's watch in a Portland, Oregon, pawnshop. According to Dan Campbell: "Auloff was subsequently tracked to earth in a mine in Butte, Montana. He was later sentenced to seven years in the Prince Albert Penitentiary, where he was lodged just

10 days after word of the pawned watch had been received from Portland."

Another crime that received front page coverage on almost every newspaper in the Northwestern States and Western Canada was the August 29, 1922, robbery of the Union Bank at Foremost, Alberta. Inspector E.W. Bavin who later became the commander of Calgary's "C" Division, was in charge of that case. Not only did he and his men solve it, but in so doing they helped recover $860,000 in bonds and securities and helped break up what was probably the best organized bank robbery network ever to operate on the North American continent.

Apparently there were five gangs all told, working out of Shelby and Havre in Montana and Minot, North Dakota, but organized from a headquarters in Chicago. They had pulled off so many bank holdups that clerks in both Canadian and American banks were holding lotteries on the chances of their banks being hit.

After the Foremost job, Inspector Bavin headed for Montana where, with the help of the Montana police, he apprehended two men named Reid and Wilson. Both were identified by the clerks at the Foremost bank. Under a barrage of questions, Reid finally confessed to his participation in the robbery and agreed to help locate the stolen money, securities and bonds taken not only from Foremost, but from Ladner, B.C., Dollard, Saskatchewan and Mathers, Manitoba as well. Some of the loot was recovered from various hiding spots, the biggest amount being hidden in Stanley Park in Vancouver. It totalled $860,000 and for his help Reid received a suspended sentence. Wilson was not as lucky—he spent the next nine years behind bars.

The rest of the bank robbers were soon rounded up by American authorities in various towns and cities. Since they were all sentenced to terms in the United States, Canadian police did not bother to press further charges. They considered that justice was served and being paid for by American rather than Canadian citizens.

Ben Shantz, long-time constable with the Alberta Provincial Police, when interviewed in 1939 by Clifford Awcock of the Calgary *Herald*, claimed that Rocky Mountain House was once one of Alberta's toughest towns. The reason for its toughness was the fact that, in the early 1920s, it was the supply center for dozens of logging camps. "From 1,500 to 2,000 men were employed within a radius of 25 miles and they depended on Rocky to show them a good time, especially on Saturday nights and payday," wrote Awcock.

Constable Shantz, who retired from the force in 1939 to farm near Rocky Mountain House, told of serving from 1922 until 1926 in that town. "Rocky was tough in those days," he said. "I prosecuted as many as 50 cases a month when I first took over—mostly liquor charges. All liquor going to

Nordegg had to go up on the train as there was no road then. Of course, there wasn't supposed to be any booze going in as Alberta was dry till 1923. The first day I was in town I nailed two fellows with suitcases loaded. They were easily spotted. A suitcase loaded with liquor is as heavy as lead, so spotting the fellows carrying them wasn't really that hard.

"We seized bottles in trunks and baggage, too. One man even used to send his daughter up to Nordegg on the train to carry the stuff in her baggage. Next day or so he would follow her in and peddle the booze."

Much of the liquor being sold was moonshine made in local stills. Shantz claimed that he managed to slow the trade down but never did stop it altogether. "There was just too much profit in it," he claimed.

Besides trying to curtail the illicit liquor trade, Constable Shantz's life was kept busy investigating the many hunting and logging accidents as well as the occasional suicide. He acted as coroner and assisted doctors with autopsies. For a time he even served as the truant officer for the Rocky schools.

Shantz told of a bizarre incident when he accompanied a doctor to a logging camp near Horburg to investigate the case of a logger having been killed by a falling tree. By the time he and the doctor arrived, the body was frozen stiff. However, he and the doctor assured themselves the man had been killed by the tree, then loaded the body in the rear seat of the police car and started for town.

"That was quite a trip," he remembered. "He was frozen with his arms outstretched, so we set him on the seat in a natural position and tied a rope around him. I was nervous as a cat with that fellow riding behind us. We had to drive across the railway bridge as the ferry was out due to drifting ice. About halfway across a hand fell on my shoulder. It was only the Doc, but it startled me so I nearly drove off the bridge."

Shantz told of apprehending a murderer who was accused of murdering a man named Faulkner at Sylvan Lake in 1924. "I was washing my car about 10 o'clock in the morning when a call came saying the suspect was believed headed west toward Rocky. I jumped in the car and drove to Eckville—made good time, too, though the roads were none too good in those days. In Eckville I went into the telephone office to see if I could find out how the hunt was organized, but got no information. When I came out I looked east along the tracks and saw a fellow acting very queerly. He walked the tracks aways, then got down and walked in the ditch. He climbed the fence and went away from the tracks, then came back to the fence and finally disappeared under the big railway trestle.

"I started down the railway and when he saw me he ran south into the willows along the river. He certainly led me a merry chase, but when I caught sight of him and fired a shot over his head, he stopped and waited for me with hands up. It didn't take any smart detective work to know he was the bird we were after. His hands and clothes were covered with dried blood. He still wore the knife in his belt and carried a .22 rifle taken down and wrapped in a bundle. When I started to take the knife, he landed a hearty kick on my shins. I returned the compliment and roughed him up a little, after which he came along peacefully."

After legal liquor stores were opened in 1923 and the lumber industry began to decline, Rocky lost its toughness, Shantz said. "Those were good days for business, but mighty busy ones for the police."

Most other detachments of the APP were busy right up to April 1, 1932, when the RCMP resumed the policing of the province. By then the APP was under its third leader, Acting Commissioner W.F.W. Hancock, who took over when Commissioner W.C. Bryan resigned in February, 1932.

Perhaps an article that appeared in the Calgary *Albertan* on April 1, 1932, told the story of the demise of the Alberta Provincial Police as well as any. It stated: "The Mounties have taken over. Thursday at midnight the Alberta Provincial Police as such ceased to exist. Henceforth the policing of Alberta will be done by the Royal Canadian Mounted Police, a force which will incorporate into its ranks the majority of the men who made the Alberta Provincial Police known throughout the continent as one of the most proficient police organizations ever formed.

"As is a way with policemen, there was little outward sign of excitement as the last hours of the provincial police came near. But many of the men throughout Alberta could not help but feel sadness, as they had served with the force since its formation and had given 15 years of faithful service. They had built up a reputation for law enforcement unsurpassed by any force in the world. They had gained the respect of the citizens of Alberta as fair men and they had followed the hard and dangerous path of duty without fail.

"At midnight in police barracks and quarters throughout the province, the members of the APP automatically became members of the RCMP. To many of them the scarlet tunic of the Dominion force is familiar, for they served with the Mounties before the formation of the provincial police.

"Manitoba, Alberta, Nova Scotia and New Brunswick—all came under the jurisdiction of the Mounties on April 1,"

It was simply a matter of economics. Of course the Mounted Police were now seeking a wider role for themselves, but the deciding factor in their taking over in Alberta was an estimated saving to the province of $250,000. However, the change did not take place before a great deal of debate. It was D.M. Duggan, Conservative party leader, who first proposed the changeover in the 1930 session of the Alberta Legislature and estimated the saving that

(Top) Seizure of liquor at Crowsnest Pass in 1925. (Center) Cpt. R. Vise at Empress Detachment, APP, 1919. (Bottom) Alberta Provincial Police detachment, Claresholm, Alberta. Sgt. T. Hudson on step.

would come from it. Attorney-General J.F. Lymburn claimed that no such saving would result. Still others wanted the change as they felt the RCMP was the superior force, although that claim does not seem to be substantiated in light of the APP's incredible record. Labor groups, on the other hand, did not like the Mounties and feared their take-over.

Finally, however, money decided the issue. It was decided there would be a saving by utilizing the federal force and on April 1, 1932, the RCMP took over. Since the men of the APP became Mounties and since the uniforms of the APP had not been too different from those of the RCMP, it is doubtful if the casual observer even noticed the change. One thing did not change—Alberta retained the same high standard of law enforcement it had known since the Mounties first arrived in 1874. ●

Wild Horse Creek.

THE JAMES GIBBONS STORY

Gibbons watched Edmonton blossom from a trading post to a bustling city and provincial capital. Although he contributed greatly to the city's development, no Edmonton district or landmark honors this pioneer.

HE rubbed shoulders with Louis Riel, Factor Richard Hardisty, the Reverends George and John McDougall, Father Albert Lacombe, Colonel James F. Macleod, Malcolm Groat, Sam Livingston, Frank Oliver and dozens of others whose names are synonymous with the history of Alberta. Like his good friend Sam Livingston, he was a prospector, trader, buffalo hunter and farmer. And just as Livingston saw Calgary grow up around him, Gibbons watched Edmonton develop from a trading post to a burgeoning city and become the capital of the province. Strangely, though he homesteaded the land where Storyland Valley Zoo is located today and contributed considerably to the development of the city, no district in Edmonton is named for him, although the town of Gibbons, 15 miles to the northeast, bears his name.

Jim Gibbons was born in 1837 at Holly Hill, Donegal, Ireland, into a family of 10. His father owned a farm which was much too small to support such a large family so, at the age of 17, Jim left Ireland for America to see if all the stories of easily gained fortune were really true. "I think I got there in 1854," Jim told General W.A. Griesbach in 1922 in an article entitled "The Narrative of James Gibbons." The voyage by sailing vessel took two months, Jim recalled, and brought him to Philadelphia. Later, while visiting an aunt in New York City he met a man who had been to California during the 1849 gold rush. This man piqued Jim's interest no little for, as Jim told General Griesbach, "I sailed from New York to Aspinwall in Panama, crossing the Isthmus on mule-back to the Chagrass River and traveling by boat to Panama, and sailed from that place to San Francisco on the steamer *John L. Stevens.*"

He found plenty of adventure in California. San Francisco was then a wild place where gunfights and murders occurred daily. The bodies, however, were easily disposed of as the city was then built on piles. When the tide came in it reached floor level and bodies were simply dumped in and allowed to wash out with the receding tide. Gibbons did well in California, by working in a relative's liquor store, and in the gold fields, where he made a small fortune which he blew in the fleshpots of a hell-hole with the morbid but apt title of Hangtown, later more respectably renamed Placerville.

He did not stay broke for long. Word arrived that someone had made a big strike on the Fraser River in British Columbia and in 1859 he boarded a steamship bound for Victoria. Had he headed immediately for the Cariboo where some of the miners struck it rich on Williams Creek, he too might have become rich. Instead, he and three others tried their luck along the lower Fraser River between New Westminster and Hope. But they had little success, so headed overland to California. Until 1864 when he heard of a big strike at Wild Horse Creek, British Columbia, he worked as a teamster, did some prospecting, got into a skirmish with some Indians in Utah and was with General Connor in a bloody massacre of a band of Ute and Piute women and children who were hidden in what the Indians supposed was a well-concealed camp. Undoubtedly Gibbons felt considerable remorse for his part in that atrocity for, once in Alberta, he befriended many Indians, but at the time he was under army orders. At any rate, he did not brood long for he mentions he later led a carefree life in Salt Lake City until he lost his money in a nearby mining venture.

At Wild Horse Creek, later renamed Fort Steele, where Jim arrived in either 1864 or '65 (he was not sure which) he had little success in the gold fields, so teamed with Sam Livingston for a trip to Edmonton. A man called "Flatboat" McLean had just come through the Kicking Horse Pass and told them there was gold along the Saskatchewan River, although it was so fine that it was hard to pan. But, said Jim, "Sam Livingston had been mining on the Ponderay and said he knew how to save fine gold, so we decided to give it a trial and started out. Our party consisted of Sam Livingston, Johnny Healy, Big Tex, Tom Riley, George Detweiler, Charlie Thomas and Joe Kipp... We traveled by way of the Kicking Horse Pass and Banff and washed our shirts in the Bow River just below where the CPR Hotel now stands...."

Altogether there were 15 men in the party. After leaving the Banff area and getting lost, they returned there, then followed the Bow River to where Calgary now stands. There they split up, some heading down the Bow which they thought was the North Saskatchewan, while Gibbons, Livingston and a couple of others headed north. "After we crossed the Red Deer River the Blackfoot ran our horses off," said Jim, "so we reached Rocky Mountain House on foot and without any provisions... Richard Hardisty was in charge... I stayed the winter in a shack near the fort and toward spring came to Edmonton. Hardisty lent me a horse."

The Edmonton of Jim Gibbons' first visit comprised 25 families, most of whom worked for the Hudson's Bay Company. Factor W. Christie was in charge. There were French Canadians, Metis and, as Gibbons stated, "two kinds of Scotch—those who could speak English and those who could not." Every language seemed to be spoken but one Gibbons could understand, so he asked Malcolm Groat who worked for the HBC if there were people who spoke only English. Groat directed him to Reverend George McDougall's Methodist Mission, Fort Victoria, which was some 70 miles down the Saskatchewan River to the east. So Jim, Sam Livingston, Mike Shannon and Sandy Anderson headed that way.

For the next couple of years Jim panned for gold along the North Saskatchewan, making as much as $18 a day. In 1867 he and Dave McDougall, Reverend George's second oldest son, planned a trip to Fort Benton, Montana for trade goods, but held off while awaiting the marriage of Victoria Eliza McDougall to Richard Hardisty. While plans for the wedding proceeded, Jim went on a buffalo hunting trip that took him 125 miles south, possibly to the area where Coronation and Consort now stand. There he joined about 100 families of Indians who were also hunting. In his "Narrative" he gave a vivid description of the method employed by the Indians to capture the buffalo. It is so different from the method used by the Metis as told by Kootenai Brown that is is worth repeating.

Said Gibbons: "They built a large corral of heavy timbers about two acres in extent with a narrow entrance and runway... Before attempting to drive the buffalo in the direction of the corral, a medicine man went out and planted a line of sticks about eight feet apart in prolongation of one side of the runway. Then the buffalo drive began. As soon as the buffalo came up to the line of sticks they appeared to fear it and galloped down along the line, thence into the runway and finally into the corral...some 300 were impounded and the slaughter began. All the buffalo were killed although some of them were in such poor condition as to be worthless. I called the attention of the chief to this and suggested that the poor animals should be turned loose. In reply he stated this was never done as the buffalo which might be turned loose would tell the others of the trap and thereafter no buffalo might be caught this way... I became on (sic) very good terms with those Indians and spent the winter of 1867-68 with them."

If Jim ever did make that trip to Montana with

David McDougall he failed to mention it. The Blackfoot had always been hostile to white intrusion and were particularly touchy at this time, just prior to the establishment of Fort Whoop-Up and the other so-called whisky forts by American entrepreneurs in southern Alberta. Instead, in the spring of 1868 Jim joined some men for a trip to Fort Garry, a months-long trip of 1,000 miles which he embarked upon as casually as his modern counterparts would embark upon a trip to their lakeside summer cottage. By August he was back in Edmonton, panning for gold with two partners, Charlie Stephenson and Charlie Clark, on the river at Clover and Rusty Bars. To wash the gold, "We invented the Grizzly," he claimed. "It worked all right and we made about $16 a day." The Grizzly was an adaptation of the sluice box used to wash gold from creek and river gravel. Whereas a sluice box was a long, sloping trough with cleats nailed crossways at various intervals, the Grizzly was shorter with a double trough. Gold was captured the same way, by shovelling gravel and sand into the upper end of the trough, then washing it down with water. Larger stones were screened out whereas finer sands and gold were caught on the upper edge of the cleats. Finally the sand was washed away and any gold trapped on the cleats was gathered by using mercury. Depending upon how well a sand or gravel bar yielded, it required shovelling from one to possibly five yards of gravel to retrieve an ounce of gold. It was back-breaking toil, but men like Jim Gibbons were no strangers to hard work and thrived on it.

Hard physical labor, however, induces hearty appetites and although there still was plenty of wild game available for the hunting and fish for the catching, Jim and his companions needed something more readily available. The HBC supplied its employees with pemmican and flour, and since some of the employees seemed not to place a very high value on flour, Gibbons would buy extra flour not normally obtainable at the post from the servants. It cost $30 a bag but, mixed with pemmican which was available from the HBC, they could make a pemmican stew that was much more palatable than a straight pemmican or wild game diet. Sugar, however, was almost as hard to come by and as expensive as the gold they sought. Tea was $3.00 a pound. Though the HBC had a garden, it was not well looked after and did not yield well. Their potatoes were scrawny things, not much bigger than a man's finger. It was not until Donald Ross, Edmonton's first hotelman, arrived in 1872 and started a market garden on the flats below McDougall Hill that vegetables were readily available. About this same time, said Gibbon, Malcolm Groat took up land west of 121st Street and began farming in a modest way. From that point on there was a much more dependable supply of nutritious food in the area.

Though gold dredging proved fairly profitable, it was strictly a summer job and Jim had to find other employment in the winter. In the fall of 1868 two men, Bob Hastie and George Chapman, pulled into Edmonton with a load of trade goods acquired in Winnipeg and immediately got into trouble with the Indians. They offered anyone who could handle the Indians a half share in the profits and Jim quickly accepted their offer. "I got a train of dogs and set out early in 1869 for the Mountain Fort (Rocky Mountain House). My goods were rum, powder, shot and some dry goods and trinkets."

He soon learned that the HBC people considered this area—in fact most areas—their sole domain and welcomed Gibbons and Thomas Bird, who went with him, with all the warmth and cordiality of an Arctic blizzard. No sooner were they camped near the post than a Blackfoot brave, probably at the instigation of the HBC, rode up and accused Gibbons and Bird of selling rum that induced smallpox. At the time a band of Blackfoot camped at the post were suffering from the disease and, as it turned out, smallpox was soon to decimate the whole Blackfoot Confederacy as well as play havoc with the Crees and Metis to the north. Though ordered to leave the country, Gibbons held his ground stubbornly and finally persuaded some of the Indians to take a drink.

Said Jim: "They waited to see if they would get the smallpox and when they found out they did not, they opened trade with us. I got 108 buffalo robes and nine horses for that keg of rum..." In light of modern trade practice his profit seems unwarranted but Jim had to earn every cent he could from that trade. To take his hides back to Edmonton he borrowed a wagon and six-horse team from an American who had planned to drive through the mountains to the coast before changing his mind upon seeing the obstacles he faced.

Shortly after starting out, Gibbons and Bird ran out of grub. Then the Blackfoot began harassing them and Jim began to suspect that Bird and an Indian named Mygosis, who accompanied them, were in cahoots with the Blackfoot. He was right. "When we reached where Wetaskiwin now stands," explained Gibbons, "Mygosis and Bird disappeared with all the horses, so I followed them on foot and finally got to Edmonton half dead...." He did recover his buffalo robes later, so his trip was not a total loss. He met Bird a few years later and, said Jim, "He was uncomfortable to see me and tried to make a joke of the whole thing." That joke could well have cost Gibbons his life.

In a way Gibbons had the last laugh on the HBC people at Rocky Mountain House as well. He and two partners were located on his holdings at present-day Laurier Park, then called Miner's Flat when, one morning, they heard someone hailing them from across the river, asking them to bring a boat over. "This we did and found that they were the Hudson's Bay garrison of the Mountain House

Fort, who had been driven out by the Blackfoot who were in close pursuit..." No sooner had Jim and his partners got the HBC people safely across the river than an estimated 400 Blackfoot warriors began filing down the south riverbank. They milled around for awhile before setting up camp on Walter's Flat across from the HBC post. Everyone at the post stood ready to repel an attack, but the river was too deep for fording, so the warriors contented themselves with a few war-whoops and firing their rifles in the direction of the fort. Fortunately, the range was too great and no one was hit. According to Gibbons, Dave McDougall who had a trading post at Pigeon Lake, and William Roland of the Hudson's Bay Company, just managed to cross the river before the Blackfoot arrived. Dave McDougall had been shot through the coat but was unharmed. Both had to leave their trading goods behind. These were promptly seized by the Blackfoot and either put to use or destroyed.

Fort Edmonton then had two brass cannon and a former American artillery man who was at the post wanted to open fire with them on the Blackfoot. Factor Christie, however, would have none of that. He realized the cannon would probably drive the Indians off but they would only go looking for another unprotected post and wreak their vengeance there. Left alone, the Blackfoot finally wandered away.

Next spring, accompanied by three men, Gibbons set out for Winnipeg to acquire a trading outfit, a journey that took three months. On the way he heard about the Riel-led rebellion in Manitoba, but did not learn how serious it was until he reached his destination. When he got there, said Gibbons, "Louis Riel was in power. I met Riel, also O'Donahue, who was Riel's right hand man. There were also a lot of Fenians there." One of the Fenians turned out to be a cousin to Gibbons.

Jim could do no business in Winnipeg because of the unrest, so bought a barrel of whisky and headed south to the American border. He did a brisk trade with American troops stationed there to deter any dreams Riel might have of crossing the border. Gibbons joined a man named Nelson, who farmed nearby and had a contract to sell milk to the Americans. Nelson had no trouble smuggling whisky over to the American troops along with his milk deliveries, but this transaction angered Colonel Wheaton who was in command of the troops. He would have liked to bring Gibbons in for trial but of course could not touch him as long as he stayed on Canadian soil. Gibbons wisely decided to get into a less volatile business by selling all his booze to Nelson, then taking a job rafting lumber down the Red River to Winnipeg at $5.00 a day. But he seemed unable to stay out of the liquor business for long and soon took a job as liquor salesman for a Winnipeg firm. Troops from eastern Canada had arrived to repel the rebellion, so the liquor trade proved a lucrative one and Jim stayed with it until

June of 1871.

"In June, 1871," said Gibbons, "I got from Bannatyne and Begg (the company he worked for) a democrat wagon and cart and all kinds of stuff suitable for trade and pulled out for Edmonton, where I arrived about August of that year." An interesting sidelight here is that while Gibbons and other traders thought little of making the trip from Winnipeg to Edmonton, and often made the trip a couple of times a year, when, in 1874, the first contingent of North West Mounted Police made their famous trek from Manitoba to Alberta, it took them five months. Many have portrayed it as being one of the greatest achievements in Canadian history. Their accomplishments after arriving in the West were indeed momentous, but their safari took so long and was so arduous primarily because of inex-

Edmonton's

Old Timers' Association

ORGANIZED 1894

(Opposite page) Pioneers in Yoho Valley, B.C. L-R: James Gibbons; Dr. Charles D. Walcott; Tom Wilson.
(Above) Old Timers' association group, Edmonton, May 6, 1920.

perience and because they used eastern horses which grew thin on a diet of prairie grass while the Indian ponies used by the traders gained weight on the long trek.

In 1871 Jim Gibbons not only made the trek from Winnipeg to Edmonton but, upon arrival, accompanied a band of Metis on a buffalo hunt along the Battle River, shot a large number of buffalo, prepared a great quantity of pemmican, and was back in Edmonton in October, when he made ready to trade with the Indians as soon as they came in from their fall hunt. By the spring of 1872, he was back in Winnipeg for another trading outfit which he took back to Edmonton that summer.

But, by 1873, Jim Gibbons decided it was time to take on added responsibilities, although settling down completely was still far from his mind. He married Mary Isabel, the 14-year-old step-daughter of HBC employee Gilbert Anderson, and set up housekeeping on his river flats holdings. "We were married by Father Leduc at St. Albert Mission," he related. "There was quite an establishment at St.

Albert then with lay brothers. They had a blacksmith shop, a carpentry shop and were doing some farming, also growing berries and vegetables." By that time the HBC was raising its own cattle and oxen. They had 65 milk cows and the oxen "were used to draw the old-fashioned Red River cart, which was made without nails and no axle grease was used on the axles. The result was that a train of Red River carts could be heard coming almost as far as you could see them…"

Being married did not curtail Gibbon's travels much. He simply took Mary Isabel with him. In 1873 they headed for Winnipeg for a load of supplies, took the supplies to Edmonton, then returned to Winnipeg for their second load. On the way back they were overtaken by a prairie blizzard near Portage La Prairie. When their horses disappeared, they were forced to remain in that area for the winter. During their stay Jim remembers meeting many of the Mounted Police who were training at Fort Garry, getting ready for their western trek. Jim met Major, later Colonel, James F. Macleod, who was courting a Winnipeg girl. Gibbons also met Donald A. Smith while on the trail from Edmonton to Winnipeg. Smith was on a tour of inspection of HBC posts. Said Jim: "He was Governor of the Company at that time and traveled in much state and at great speed. Fresh horses were ready for him at every post." Donald Smith, of course, went on to become Superintendent of the Canadian Pacific Railway and later was knighted with the title, Lord Strathcona.

In the spring of 1874 Gibbons recovered his horses, then went into Winnipeg and purchased 30 gallons of whisky, although his permit allowed him but two gallons. Luckily he sold his booze at Portage La Prairie, for the NWMP were already on the lookout for illicit booze. Consequently, when he was searched by Major L.N.F. Crozier at Shoal Lake while on the way back to Edmonton, the Mountie found nothing. Crozier, however, proved he could look the other way when it came to booze as long as it was not being sold to the Indians. For he took a drink with Gibbons and other travellers when all arrived at Fort Ellis and were invited in for a meal by the HBC Factor, Archie McDonald.

Gibbons continued trading until 1878 when he sold out to "two or three different parties." By then the buffalo, so plentiful when he first arrived, were fast disappearing. After selling out, he went on a buffalo hunt and followed the herds all summer, but shot very few. That hunt took him to Battleford in what is now Saskatchewan, where he met Frank Oliver who was heading from Winnipeg to Edmonton with a load of trade goods. Frank Oliver, of course, later started Edmonton's first newspaper, the Edmonton *Bulletin*, and still later became a Member of Parliament with the Liberal government and was appointed to the Cabinet as Minister of the Interior by Prime Minister Wilfred Laurier. When he returned to Edmonton Jim Gibbons filed on the land on which he had been squatting. But, before he could do much farming, he suffered a stroke that incapacitated him for four years.

"At first nobody knew what was the matter with me," claimed Jim. "There was no doctor in the country. I went out to St. Albert and was treated by Sister Superior St. Rock, who blistered the back of my head. Some time later Dr. Very arrived and treated me. Afterwards I went to Winnipeg and saw a number of doctors. They all told me that I might get better but that if I had another stroke I was done for. When I got back to Edmonton I told Dr. Very what those doctors had told me. Dr. Very said: 'Well, you might see those fellows dead yet.' And so I did, including Dr. Very himself." Later he threw away the medicine prescribed for him and except for bothersome arthritis, enjoyed good health throughout the rest of his long life.

The stroke would have put most men on the shelf for good, but for Jim Gibbons it was a temporary set-back and he was soon moving around the country again, often acting as "caller off" at dances.

When, in 1885, the North West Rebellion broke out, there was Jim in the midst of it. When Major-General Thomas Bland Strange and his Alberta Field Force started north from Calgary to take care of Chief Big Bear's Plains Crees, who were making threats at Frog Lake, Gibbons hired two teams to the government and went south to where Wetaskiwin is now located, where he met General Strange's force. "On the return journey my wagon carried the band of the 66th Battalion," he said. "Afterwards I went down to Frog Lake. At this place, Jimmy Roland, myself and some others dug up the bodies of the people who had been massacred there and reburied them properly, with religious rites."

The men Gibbons and his friends buried were the nine killed by Big Bear's rampaging warriors led by War Chief Wandering Spirit. The party then moved on to Fort Pitt, which had been put to the torch by Big Bear's people after the Mounted Police detachment stationed there had deserted it for Battleford. Jim Gibbons' account of the ensuing pursuit of Big Bear, the battle at Frenchmen's Butte, and his trip to Cold Lake with Captain Wright to round up the Chipewyan Indians who were with Big Bear at Frog Lake, is sketchy in light of the tough terrain traversed and the constant danger of being bushwacked by Indians. He spoke of it casually, it seemed like just another jaunt, if not a Sunday School picnic. Said he, "We had no difficulty rounding up the Chipewyan Indians and took their arms, horses and cattle from them for the meantime. General Strange and I became good friends. We were both very fond of horses. When the Rebellion was over we all came back to Edmonton and were discharged."

With the Rebellion behind him, Gibbons began living a much quieter life, though he was not yet ready to put up his feet and relax. The North West Territory, of which Alberta was part until becoming a province in 1905, was under prohibition until 1891. That year Gibbons returned to the liquor trade—this time legally. He obtained a licence and operated a wholesale liquor outlet until 1897. That year he was appointed Indian Agent for the Stony Plain Reserve. He stayed with that job until 1907 or 1908, he was not sure which. "Since that time I have not been doing anything in particular," he told General Griesbach in 1922.

The man who was "not doing anything in particular" had already done more than most do in several lifetimes. He had seen the West change from wild frontier to a settled, civilized place. He had seen the buffalo virtually disappear and Edmonton grow from a trading post to a burgeoning city. He liked to think he had played a strong part in the great transition, and he was not through yet. He lived on for another 11 years and passed away in 1933 at the age of 96. But his name will live on, commemorated by the town 15 miles northeast of Edmonton. They could not have named their town for a more colorful or enduring pioneer. ●

James K. Cornwall, Peace River pioneer, 1911-17.

PEACE RIVER JIM:
Empire Builder

From the time of his first visit to the Peace River country, Jim Cornwall became its greatest promoter. By the time of his death in 1950, he had seen this country become one of the best farming areas in the world and oil wells begin to pump their black wealth from its depths.

"HE was all man: big, broad-shouldered and strong as a buffalo. Down North they used to say: 'Jim Cornwall can outrun any man behind a team of dogs'."

Thus did Jim Coleman, probably Canada's most outstanding sportswriter, say about Peace River Jim Cornwall in a 1964 article in the *Edmonton Journal.* Dozens of others have written about him; most appear to have been somewhat in awe of a great man who spent much of his life promoting first the Peace River Country and later the Far North. For over 60 years he was the north country's greatest ambassador. He served four years in the Alberta Legislature—from 1908 to 1912—so that he could help promote his constituency, the Peace River district. During his long life he was a sailor, trapper, trader, builder of steamboats, promoter of railways and mining. Probably he was happiest when he was challenging the roughest weather a northern winter could throw at him, following a team of dogs while he looked for a new adventure beyond the next hill.

Even before he arrived in Alberta—and he was here long before it became a province—he had seen as much adventure as most see in a lifetime. He was born in Brantford, Ontario, in 1869 and left home at the age of 14. By the time he reached 21 he had been across the Atlantic several times. In his early years Jim read the stories of the great science fiction writers—books like Jule Verne's *Twenty Thousand Leagues Under The Sea.* He was intrigued by adventure and wanted to experience it for himself.

His first job after leaving home was the mundane one of selling newspapers on the streets of Buffalo, New York. But he soon tired of that and, the first chance he got, he shipped out on a sailing vessel plying the Great Lakes. By 1885 he had signed on with lumber boats sailing out of New York and Boston and eventually visited most of the ports of the world. He was no ordinary sailor. He was interested in anything and everything from art galleries to libraries, from farming to fishing. Ships could not take him to every place he wanted to visit, so, during his late teens and early twenties, he hiked throughout much of Europe and Asia. One of these hikes took him south from St. Petersburg across the Ukraine to Odessa on the Black Sea. Others took him through Mongolia, Manchuria and even into Tibet. In between his sailing and hiking he somehow found time to further his education through night school and reading. His favorite subjects were geography, geology and the adventures of the great explorers.

He found however, that his academic studies did not help him much as, in 1896, he tried speculating on the Chicago grain market and went broke. But it took more than one little set-back to deter a man of Jim Cornwall's stature. Later that year he wandered west through the United States, then crossed the border into Alberta. In the Crowsnest Pass area he found work helping to build the Canadian Pacific Railway through the Pass to Cranbrook in British Columbia. He was immediately intrigued by the fresh and ample opportunities he saw all about him. He looked to the North and was drawn to it like a magnet. This was the place for him—this was where he would make his home, where he could roam and stretch and work and build. This was his, this vast northern frontier.

"You see, I was ready for it," he told William O. Grenalds, writer for the now defunct American *Magazine* in 1932. "I'd had a lot of ordinary adventure. I'd even shipped out of New Orleans on a gun-running ship to a Venezuela revolution... But to go 'down North' was different..." It was a chance to lead the way. "Somebody has always got to go ahead," he told Grenalds. "Somebody's been doing it ever since the world began."

Jim's initial trip "down North" began in 1897. Some claim he went all the way to the Yukon. True, the gold rush began the following year and the gold fever certainly was as strong in Jim Cornwall as in any other man. But according to William Grenalds, who travelled quite extensively with Jim, Cornwall travelled north to Edmonton, passed on through and struck out for Athabasca Landing to trade and trap among the Indians. His adventure took him north of the Landing and it was not until he returned there the following spring that he met the first of the men heading for the Klondike. Before long there were a couple of thousand men hell-bent for the Yukon. Many took the overland route which led to Lesser Slave Lake, Peace River Landing, Fort St. John and beyond, while others started building boats for the trip down the Athabasca River to the Mackenzie, which they hoped to follow to the Peel River, cross over the Mackenzie Mountains to the Porcupine River and follow it to the Yukon River and the gold fields. Once they were past the dangerous rapids some 80 miles downstream from Athabasca Landing, they had smooth sailing for hundreds of miles. Cornwall saw that his Klondike was right there, helping the gold rushers to navigate those rapids.

"Those who followed him and other capable guides got through," wrote Grenalds. "Others mad with the thought of riches, struck out on their own. Some made it; others capsized, or crashed against submerged rocks. Indians found their bodies and buried them on the banks of the Athabasca..." Jim's bonanza and his start to a great fortune began right there at the Grand Rapids, piloting boats safely through at $25 apiece.

Although Jim launched many safely on their way and was well paid for doing so, he received no compensation for rescuing others who did not make it. He helped find many of those men who were reduced to living skeletons by a winter's stay in the bush and returned them to Athabasca Landing. But that was, and is, the way of the North.

While the great gold rush was underway, Jim Cornwall made his first trek into the Peace River country and was taken in with its vastness, its beauty and its deep, rich agricultural loam. For the rest of his life he would never tire of talking about this great empire to anyone who would listen. It was on one of his jaunts into this land that he met another great adventurer trader, "Twelve-Foot" Davis, whose name is known to almost everyone who ever set foot in the Peace River country. Cornwall and Davis became great friends and one evening, while talking and admiring the magnificent view from the top of the hill that overlooks the confluence of the Peace and Smoky Rivers where Peace River town now stands, Davis told Cornwall, "When I die, this is where I want to be buried."

Peace River Jim never forgot that wish and a few years later when he was told that on a trip out to Edmonton his old friend had died at Grouard and was buried there, he did not rest until many years later he gained permission to have Davis' remains exhumed and brought to the top of the Peace Hill. Thousands have since visited Twelve-Foot Davis' gravesite. It is easily found, for Jim Cornwall had a great stone of granite cut from Davis' home state— Vermont—and mounted over the grave. That stone is shaped to resemble a tree cut down by beavers. On it under Davis' name Jim had the inscription carved: *He Was Every Man's Friend, And He Never Locked His Cabin Door.*

It was the highest tribute Cornwall could pay to his friend, a man highly regarded by both Indian and white; a man who had traded up and down the Peace River for years and who was known for his square dealing. Davis had always left his cabins unlocked so that any hungry traveller could go in and cook himself a meal or have a rest.

From the time he first visited the Peace Jim became its greatest promoter. Over the years he made many trips into eastern Canada, extolling its virtues. It was also shortly after his first Peace River visit that he joined Fletcher Bredin, another frontiersman and trader who had called Alberta home for over a dozen years. Together they set up a trading post on the west end of Lesser Slave Lake where

Grouard stands today. Before long they were establishing trading posts at Lake Saskatoon west of present-day Grande Prairie and farther down the Peace at Fort Vermilion. In time their posts extended down the Mackenzie River to the Beaufort Sea.

Prior to Bredin and Cornwall joining forces, the Hudson's Bay Company carried on trade in the north without the use of money. The term "Skin," meaning beaverskin, had been used since 1607. In other words, each item of trade such as a gun or blanket required so many beaver skins to purchase. Bredin and Cornwall changed all that by paying cash for the furs they bought from Metis, Indian and Eskimo trappers. Naturally their policy did not sit too well with the HBC and it started a trade war that spread to the Arctic Ocean. But eventually Bredin and Cornwall won out. More correctly, it was the trappers who won out, for from then on they could pay cash for their purchases. At any rate, money became the medium of exchange in the North. From this time also, Jim Cornwall was a familiar figure, almost invariably dressed in Northerner's garb of parka and moccasins, whether in the North or "outside."

Bredin and Cornwall continued their partnership until 1903, when they sold out to the Paris-based company known as Freres Revillon. During those five years in business, Jim Cornwall had driven dogs in the winter and packed horses or travelled by boat in the summer until there was not a river or trail in the country that was not familiar to him. Freres Revillon bought out Bredin and Cornwall with the proviso that the two men would not do any trading for five years. It was no great hardship to Jim Cornwall, for there were plenty of other things to do in the North.

He became the first official mail carrier for the North by carrying the first mail packet in from Edmonton on his back. There are many stories about how he obtained the contract to carry the mail, for until that time the Hudson's Bay Company had considered mail for the North its private domain. The truth seems to be that Jim simply applied for the job and got it. But Robert Dunn in an article entitled, "The Settler's Fight For The Fur Land," which appeared in an 1914 issue of *Everybody's Magazine,* tells it more eloquently, if perhaps not too accurately. He wrote:

"We were walking over the great prairie north of the Peace, below Dunvegan, and I asked Cornwall to tell me the best thing he had ever done in the country. 'I won the confidence of the Hudson's Bay Company,' he said.

"'Every autumn I would go out to Edmonton,' he went on, 'to get the fur lists — the prices paid at the Company's fur auction in London in the spring. I was bucking them as a fair rival, but of course they could not see that. Each year I went hat in hand to their inspector in town, and asked if I could take any HBC mail back to the head post at Lesser Slave Lake. And every year I was coldly told "No". I knew

they had important letters, and that there was no other way to get them in. But they would not trust me. 'The Company carries its own letters, thank you', they said. It made me angry. I resolved to tell them I was fighting fair and that they were unreasonable. Year after year I went to them with the same offer until I finally broke them, and they gave me their sack. Yes, that's the greatest fight I ever won....' "

During the early years Jim was satisfied to move the mail and freight the hard way, on his back if need be, or with pack horses and boat in summer and dogteams in winter. But he saw the need for a railway and for more steamboats on the northern lakes and rivers. As soon as he and Fletcher Bredin sold their trading posts to Freres Revillon, Jim turned his energy to improving navigation. The HBC had a monopoly on freight on the upper Athabasca with its sternwheel steamboat *Athabasca River*, built and launched at Athabasca Landing by Captain Smith in 1888. Jim thought they should have a little competition and in 1904 built and launched his sternwheel steamboat, the *Midnight Sun*. Both his ship and the HBC *Athabasca* were confined to the upper river by the Grand Rapids, so ran their freight and passengers either upstream to Mirror Landing, or downstream to the Rapids. Jim hoped that his *Midnight Sun* would be able to ascend the Lesser Slave River from Mirror Landing. But when that hope was dashed by the treacherously shallow and twisting stream, he built and launched the sidewheeler *Northern Light* on Lesser Slave Lake in 1907. Freight then could be shipped from Athabasca Landing to Mirror Landing via the *Midnight Sun*, loaded onto wagons for the 16-mile portage to Salt Landing on the south-eastern tip of Lesser Slave Lake, then loaded aboard his *Northern Light* for the 100-mile trip down the lake to Grouard. Over the years his Northern Transportation Company also launched the *Northland Echo* and the *Northland Star* on the upper river.

From the time he first went into navigation, Peace River Jim began campaigning for telegraph lines and railways into the North. When he successfully ran for the Peace River seat in the Alberta Legislature as a Liberal candidate in 1908, he stepped up his persuasion ten-fold, for now he had a captive audience. What he was most interested in was a railway to Fort McMurray to bypass the barrier to navigation on the Athabasca — the Grand Rapids — but he also pressed strongly for a railway to Athabasca Landing and one into the Peace River Country. It was due in no small part to his persuasion that the Canadian Northern Railway pushed a line to the Landing in 1912 and the Edmonton, Dunvegan and British Columbia Railway built its line to the Peace River Country, arriving at Grande Prairie in 1916. But Jim's crowning achievement was in seeing the Alberta Great Waterways line pushed north from Edmonton over sandhill and muskeg and arrive at the Clear-

water River east of Fort McMurray in 1917. Even before the AGW arrived at its northern terminus, Jim saw the necessity of moving his home port from Athabasca Landing to Fort McMurray and set about doing that in a way described by historian James G. MacGregor in his book, *Paddle Wheels To Bucket Wheels On The Athabasca.*

"No one had ever taken a sternwheeler down the Grand Rapids but in 1914 the time had come to try that desperate venture. During high water that year the Hudson's Bay Company ran its *Athabasca River* and the Northern Transportation Company took two of its steamers through the dangerous passage. For the run through the Grand Rapids Jim Cornwall took command of his company's *Northland Echo* and with Joe Bird as pilot successfully made the leap through the foaming millrace. Eventually at Fort McMurray he replaced her with a new steamboat which was given the same name. Some of the steamers which had considered Athabasca Landing their home port were put on the run from Fort McMurray to Fitzgerald... With new railways reaching out to new railheads, Athabasca's days as the gateway to the North were over...."

While a Member of the Alberta Legislature, Peace River Jim, as well as pushing for rail lines, made his biggest bid to bring settlers into the Peace River country. When the Canadian Northern began building towards Athabasca Landing, he realized this was the first major link in a line to his beloved Peace and burned the ears of the Edmonton Board of Trade with a plea to them to help finance a tour of journalists through the country so that they could see for themselves what the country was like and help to promote settlement. Edmonton's businessmen were apparently suffering from a bad case of myopia and refused to give any help, so Jim decided to sponsor the safari himself. In the spring of 1910 he sent letters out to many well-known people whom he thought would be interested in the tour. Eighteen prominent people responded to his letters. Among them were noted writers for leading newspapers and magazines. Among them, also, were two noteworthy agricultural scientists, Professor Coats P. Bull, head of the Department of Agronomy at the University of Minnesota at St. Paul, and Professor J.H. Pettit of the University of Illinois. A reporter from the Calgary *Herald*, L.V. Kelly, who travelled with the group, later wrote a story entitled, *North With Peace River Jim*, which has been edited by historian Hugh A. Dempsey and is now available in booklet form from the Glenbow-Alberta Institute.

That journey, which started at Edmonton on the morning of July 27, 1910, was made by horse-drawn vehicles as far as Athabasca Landing. All returned to their starting point on August 29, after

Lt. Col. James K. Cornwall, Edmonton, 1917.

Main Street, Fort McMurray, Alberta, 1922.

having covered some 500 miles to Fort Vermilion. The excursion reportedly cost Jim $8,000 of his own funds. From Athabasca Landing the men travelled by his *Northland Sun* to Mirror Landing, then by wagon across the portage to Salteaux Landing, across Lesser Slave Lake on his *Northland Light* to Grouard, across the 90-mile portage by wagon to Peace River Landing, and from there down the Peace River to Fort Vermilion via the HBC sternwheeler *Peace River*.

Conservation at that time was unheard of and any swimming bear, deer, moose or other wild creature that was unfortunate enough to come within shooting range was hailed by a barrage of gunfire that would have put to shame a Second World War combat team storming a foreign beach in broad daylight. The scientists took daily samples of Peace River soils and wrote glowing reports of the depth and assumed fertility of the black loam. Journalists gathered such a wealth of material that they were still writing flowery reports two, three and more years later. Undoubtedly their prose helped to speed up the flow of settlers who were already beginning to head into the country.

Like so many trail-blazers of the Alberta frontier, Jim Cornwall could not be held to one province. After his five-year agreement not to trade expired he began building trading posts down the Mackenzie River to the Arctic Ocean. A memo that is now in the Glenbow-Alberta Institute files states: "You will find his trading and trapping friends wherever there is human habitation, from Athabasca to Victoria Land in the Arctic, and from the Yukon to Hudson's Bay.

"He finds time to collect copper specimens, iron ore, tar, oil, galena and asphalt, and they are given away where they will do the most good. He took a moving picture outfit (on an expedition) with one of the world's greatest outdoor operators of the Essany Chicago Company at his own expense. The party travelled all the waterways between Athabasca Landing in Alberta, via the Mackenzie, over the Mountains and down the Porcupine to the Yukon and up the river and out by Skagway (Alaska), over 5,000 miles, taking over 6,000 feet of film, which was shown all over the United States and parts of Canada, and pictured the most wonderful inland waterway system in North America."

In his years in the North Jim learned to speak Cree, Chipewyan, Dogrib and several Eskimo dialects, so perhaps it is not so strange that during the First World War he joined a unit that spoke almost every language known to the European continent. Actually Jim did not need to join at all for he was 45 years of age and technically exempt from service. But if there was action Jim wanted in and he formed a regiment known as the Irish Guards and accompanied it to France. His unit, according to chronicles, was so-named not because it was composed of Irishmen, but because it was made up of

(Right) James K. Cornwall, "Peace River Jim", in the late 1890s. (Below) Scrip Commission boat leaving Fort McMurray to ascend Athabasca, 1899. Pierre Cyr (or Sawyer), steersman.

took into partnership the man he placed in charge after a successful apprenticeship of three years. As he told William Grenalds, "I like to hire a married man to take charge of a post, or some proposition away from civilization. That is, if I can talk to the woman first.

"But I never hire him if the woman isn't right. I want intelligent wives... I want to know all about them. Two men, alone, may get bushed. Both of them may go crazy—they'll go for months without speaking to each other... But a man and a woman seem to be able to make the grade, and it's the woman who does the trick. She holds the man up some way or other." With a married couple taking over one of his posts Jim knew it would soon boast a garden, then children and finally it would become a village as others moved in—hopefully to stay. Thus Jim Cornwall's northern posts developed. Of course, by the time it had achieved village status it had become too crowded for him and he had moved on to remoter areas. He was still out there, exploring by airplane, when he died in 1950 at the age of 81.

By then he had seen the Peace River Country become one of the best farming areas in the world and oil wells begin to pump their black wealth from far below. He had seen Yellowknife grow from a tiny tent and shack town into a prosperous gold mining town. He had told of the oil he knew was in the Northwest Territories and persuaded Imperial Oil to come and drill. During the Second World War he saw a dozen more wells spud in at Norman Wells and American army engineers come flocking to build the pipeline across the Mackenzie Mountains to their refinery at Whitehorse in the Yukon, to supply fuel for the machines building the Alaska Highway. In fact, it was the barges and boats of his Northern Transportation Company, now taken over by the Canadian Government, that carried the steel pipe down the Athabasca and Mackenzie River System to build that needed pipeline. During the war also, he saw the uranium mines open up at Great Bear Lake, and later at Uranium City in northern Saskatchewan. Some of that uranium was used to build the bomb that ended the Second World War.

With peacetime he saw a new breed of prospectors flocking in—men who flew over the land and staked their claims with ticking geiger counters. His North was no longer a remote and deserted area, inhabited only by the caribou and Arctic fox and the dusky men who followed them for a living.

He was still out there blazing trails long after most men of his age were content to sit back in an easy chair and reminisce about it all. But age cannot be denied, not even by so sturdy a pathfinder as Peace River Jim. He became ill and passed away in Calgary's Colonel Belcher Hospital in November, 1955, at the age of 86.

He is gone, but the far North he promoted so fervently is finally coming into its own. ●

many Mikes—Irish Mikes, Polish Mikes, Lithuanian Mikes, Belgium Mikes, Italian Mikes, Swedish Mikes and many more. There were 16 interpreters in that outfit—17 when Jim was counted, for he was required to interpret for the 50 Indians who formed part of his 8th Battalion. Reportedly all of them could speak at least a little English when they reached the front, for Jim, since promoted to lieutenant-colonel, had started a school.

Many of those men never returned to Canada and are buried under the poppies of Flanders Field. But Colonel Jim came back—decorated with the Croix de Guerre for valor by the French and the Distinguished Service Order by King George V at Buckingham Palace. His only son, James Anthony, was not as lucky in the Second World War, going down with his ship, the *Valleyfield*, in 1944.

When Colonel Jim came back from overseas in 1918, he took his discharge in the East so that he would not have to attend all the banquets and speeches being prepared to welcome him home as a conquering hero. He wanted none of that and after a visit with his wife, Beatrice, whom he had married in 1908, he was off again for the North. As before the war, wherever he established a trading post, he

FRONTIER DOCTOR

Although not the first doctor in the Peace River country,
A.M. Carlisle knew what it was like to be the only doctor for
miles, when he had to answer every call in every kind
of weather. And this in the age before anti-freeze!

BY the 1920s much of the pioneering in Alberta, especially in the southern half, was over. But settlers were still flocking to the Peace River country. The road from Athabasca Landing was still only a poor wagon trail and in the great district named La Grande Prairie by early explorers, roads were not much better. Rains of summer and snows of winter made travel arduous, especially for men like Dr. A.M. Carlisle, who had to go when called to treat his patients, regardless of distance, weather or road conditions. Dr. Carlisle was not the first doctor in the area by any means, but when he arrived there was only one other medical man — Dr. L.J. O'Brien— serving the vast territory, and roads and means of travel were such that his story gives a pretty good picture of what it was like for all doctors who practised their profession on the Alberta frontier.

Dr. Carlisle first told his story, which he entitled "A Pioneer Doctor," after his retirement in Victoria, British Columbia, to a gathering of the Kiwanis Club. It later appeared in the book, *Beaverlodge To The Rockies*, edited by E.C. Stacey for the Beaverlodge Historical Association, which was published in 1976. "The people attending the Kiwanis meeting wanted to know what it was like to live where it got so cold," Dr. Carlisle stated. "That was why I went into such detail about starting my car."

Dr. Carlisle gave permission to use the story. It follows, the only changes being the addition of a couple of anecdotes and an ending:

"I practised medicine in the Alberta part of the Peace River country from June 1921 until June 1957. First, I would like to give you a brief resume of my background.

"I was born in Peterborough, Ontario, on March 6, 1896, into a family of seven. I got my senior matriculation there, started medicine in Toronto in September, 1913, joined the Second Division Canadian Army in March 1915 as a stretcher bearer and spent almost three years at the front in France. In September, 1918 I was sent home along with some other medical and dental students to finish our courses.

"I had just finished my exams in 1921 when I got an urgent telegram from my brother-in-law, Jack Archer, to come at once to Lake Saskatoon, Alberta. The only doctor in that district had left because his young wife had died. So not knowing whether or not I had passed my Dominion Council Exams, I left for Edmonton and I am glad I did. I found out in Edmonton that I had passed; I registered with the College of Physicians and Surgeons and in a few days left by the weekly train for Grande Prairie, then end of steel, a 500 mile trip that took 30 hours if it was on time, or if it got there.

"Mr. Archer was at the station to meet me and drove me out to Lake Saskatoon, where some calls were already waiting. I had only $10.00 to my name when I arrived there and there were so many things that I needed. One great need was a car, so my brother Dave (who lived) on the east shore of Lake Saskatoon, mortgaged his farm and lent me enough money to buy a brand new 1921 Model T Ford. That was the first year that Henry Ford had put a self-starter on them.

"It is a beautiful rolling country, so different from the Prairies, dotted with lakes and bluffs of trees, high and sunny skies with wild ducks and geese flying high in the fall, and always the snow-capped Rocky Mountains on the far horizon. It looked like the Promised Land to me. There were many men there who had just returned from the First World War on the farms and in the towns, some with English brides.

"Lake Saskatoon had been the distributing centre for the whole area until the railroad came in 1916, making Grande Prairie the end of steel. The big trading companies then moved away, The Hudson's

The village of Lake Saskatoon taken in the early 1920s.

Bay, Revillon Freres, The Diamond P. etc., so I rented the Diamond P. store mostly because it had a nice lean-to. It made a good warm office and I slept in the big, unheated store. During the first two winters there were usually a few blocks of ice piled five feet high about my bed as that was my water supply. A Scotch lady made me two big comforters, each lined with a good inch of carded wool, so I slept comfortably. For this luxurious accommodation I paid $5.00 a month, but after paying my large livery bill and my drug bill, it wasn't always easy to find that $5.00. I had to carry my own medicines. I couldn't just give a prescription to patients living 30 or more miles from a drug store.

"There was no anti-freeze for cars in those days and winters set in early. At first I used coal oil in my radiator, but the motor would get so cold the car wouldn't start, so I used just water, a tricky business in 20 to 40 degrees below zero; even with a good radiator cover, a large piece of cardboard behind the radiator and a thermometer visibly sticking out of the radiator cap. I used to keep two large pails of water boiling on my office stove. When I had to start the car in cold weather, I would pour one pailful into the radiator, leaving the drainage tap open, then shut the tap and pour in the second pailful. In four or five minutes when the engine warmed up a bit I would turn it over a few times with the crank, pour a kettle of boiling water on the carburator, get in, pull out the choke, step on the starter and it usually started. If not, I cranked it, then if the tires were not frozen to

the ground, or flat, I would get away. For some reason the very cold weather would make those early tires go flat. But in the winter I usually drove a cutter and team, and in the spring and fall, a buggy and team on the clay roads and prairie trails. These roads were like pavement when dry in the summer, but that was the shortest season of the year. When asked what he did up there in the summer time one fellow said, 'Oh, we played baseball that day.' The season for hockey and curling was much longer. I met an old army friend a few years ago who said I was looking young. When I told him I had lived up in the Peace River Country for 36 years he said, 'Oh that explains it. Anything will keep in a deep-freeze. Even you.'

"In 1928 I was lucky enough to get a great fur coat. It had been ordered by the Russian ambassador in England, but by the time they had it made for him, diplomatic relations had been cut off with Russia. A man who worked at the furriers in London sent it to his brother, a farmer south of Lake Saskatoon and I got it from him by a trade and some cash. It was a Reindeer Calf on the outside and wombat skin on the inside. With a thick woollen lining between and a high Beaver collar, it was huge and had been made for a much bigger man than I am. I had to get six or seven inches cut off the bottom before I could walk in it. I already had a coonskin coat and this new one slipped over top of the coon one nicely. I had large beaver gauntlets and a fur hat. When I would start out on a cold trip dressed conservatively in heavy Stanfield underwear, with all this fur on, which was like a mattress, with a charcoal footwarmer burning at my feet under a big buffalo robe, the weather didn't seem too bad.

"The worst time for getting around in a car was in the spring. The snow on the roads would melt all day in the warm spring sun, forming pools that would freeze over each night, just mining the roads like tank traps. I was coming home from Grande Prairie one April morning about 4:30, when I broke through the ice in one of these traps. There was just one thing to do — get a team to pull the car out. I walked to the farm of an Irishman I knew, Mike Cochlin. I threw some snowballs and pebbles at his window to wake him, helped him hitch his team and we walked down to the car in the spring dawn dragging a chain. On the way he said, 'Have you got your tooth forceps with you, Doc?' and I said, 'Oh yes, Mike, I always carry them.'

"So he hitched the chain to the Ford and we splashed through the water, ice and mud to firm ground. Then he pointed to a lower molar so I said, 'Sit down.' He sat down on the wide running board of the Ford and I lifted out his aching tooth. As he sat there afterwards spitting blood on the snow he said, 'Well, what do I owe you, Doc?" and I said, 'What do I owe you, Mike?' 'Well,' he says, 'I guess one good pull deserves another!'

"Then I went to help him up. His trousers were frozen solid to the running board and he said, 'You are a heck of a dentist; you don't freeze me up here but down there.'

"Dentists were scarce in Canada in 1921, so the University during our fifth year gave medical students some instruction on tooth extractions and local anaesthesia. When we got married I promised my wife I would give her all the money I made out of teeth, but I soon had to break that promise as that was the only service for which I usually got cash. I had many calls to the country and the farther out the patients were the less money they had, so I wrote to the Public Health Department in Edmonton and eventually they paid me $100 a month for the next three years for my work in the three unorganized districts west of Lake Saskatoon. I was the only doctor from there to the B.C. border, 45 to 65 miles, and the only ambulance. On one far out trip the only food in the bachelor's shack was eggs, so Miss Watherston, the district nurse, and I just boiled six eggs apiece for lunch with a mug of tea and were very, very grateful.

"On another occasion I was called out to visit a sick child south of Wembley. The caller told me he would put out a lantern at his gate so I would know where to turn in. It was a black night and I went on and on south of the community and nearly went over the bank into the Wapiti River. I was fuming; there was no lantern anywhere. Well I got back home only to have the same man call again. By then I was really angry and shouted, 'Why didn't you have the lantern out as you said you would?' 'Well, Doc,' said the caller, 'the child got better after I called so I took in the lantern.'

"In the summer of 1921 I first met a student from Toronto University home on her summer holidays. The next year we became engaged and in 1923, Jean McFarlane of Cutbank Lake Farm became my wife. She had graduated and I bought and fixed up a house. Housekeeping was no problem for her as her mother had died very young and Jean had capably managed the farm household when home on holidays, including the summer hired help and threshing crew. The office in those days was part of the house. The doctor's wife had to double as practical nursing assistant and at a moment's notice be prepared to serve sandwiches, cookies and tea to patients from a distance who could not afford even the moderate charge in the restaurant.

"The country was in recession when I got there in 1921 due to a Cow Bill passed to encourage farmers to buy cattle. The banks were allowed to lend farmers up to $500 for cattle. In 1920 the price of cattle went away down, the banks needed their money back and money was tight.

"The early days in this new country were the hardest for me, but the most interesting to look back on. Then there were the hungry twenties and thirties, so called, but few if any ever went hungry or cold. The settlers had not been there long enough to become established. They had no backlog especially when the great Depression came in the thirties. We knew thrifty farmers who said that all they bought in the stores during that time was sugar and salt. It was a very fertile, productive land. I have a newspaper article here that claims that the soil around the Lake Saskatoon area, later called Wembley, had grown more world championship grains for farmers than the soils of all the rest of Canada.

"Herman Trelle, whose farm was two miles south of Lake Saskatoon, won the World Wheat Championship four times and was crowned Wheat King of the World. In 1926 he won both world championships in wheat and oats, the first time in the history of the Chicago World's Fair that both championships had been awarded to the same exhibitor. His first and second prizes in grains at the various shows in Canada and the United States numbered more than 600.

"I had the honor of taking out the 'King's' appendix and bringing their first Princess into the world in their farm house. Other exhibitors from this area also won world championships in wheat, oats, timothy, peas, etc. It became a habit. Garden crops were very good. Wild game and wild fowl were plentiful. Wild fruits, raspberries, strawberries, saskatoons, blueberries, chokecherries were abundant. There was lots of poplar wood and open faced seams of coal in the banks of the Wapiti and Red

The legendary Dr. Carlisle, who gave 35 years of service to the pioneers of the Peace River region.

Willow Rivers close at hand to be had for the digging and hauling. So although few could pay cash for a doctor, we were kept well supplied with wood and coal, meat and fowl, milk and cream, butter and eggs, vegetables and sometimes homemade coffee, a ground-up, roasted mixture of grains tasting a little like Postum. I remember one young man who brought us a load of wood saying, 'Well, one more load and the baby is ours.'

"I stayed just 3½ years at Lake Saskatoon. Our railroad in 1924 was extended 15 miles west and eventually the whole town moved to the railroad, which became a new town named Wembley. The buildings were skidded down on logs in the winter, but I had been accepted as an intern for a year in surgery at the Sick Childrens' Hospital in Toronto. Then we looked over Ontario for an opening but, encouraged by a warm invitation from the new town of Wembley, we returned west again in April 1926. I knew that was the place where I was needed the most and where we both had relatives and good friends. Wembley was our home for the next 10 years. Our three children were born there. The only hospital was in Grande Prairie and I made that 15-mile trip each way nearly every day, often two or three times a day. Eventually we moved to Grande Prairie where we lived for 21 years.

"Most of the young mothers did not know how to feed their babies properly and there was no literature available to instruct them. I found many babies with rickets and had one baby die of it. I got literature from the Children's Hospital and gave it out freely and for years I gave to every mother on the birth of her first child a new copy of Dr. Alan Brown's book, *The Normal Child*, and most of them followed it explicitly. When doctors examined the youth from that part of the Peace River Country for the army in 1939, they reported they found the least disqualifying disabilities in them compared to any other of the Province. I gave Alan Brown's book a lot of credit.

"Our famous railroad was (originally) called the Edmonton, Dunvegan and British Columbia, ED&BC, generally known as the Extremely Dangerous and Badly Constructed Railroad. There were many funny stories about it. My wife was on it once when it ran off the tracks five times in 45 miles. It was the only connection we had with the outside world for eight years after I got there. There was no road out in any direction, no telephone, only telegraph. No radio, no aeroplanes, just a weekly passenger train, later increased to bi-weekly. We doctors had to cope with everything that came along and almost everything did.

"The Government started building a road to Edmonton in 1928 and finished it in 1929 by way of Sturgeon Lake, Slave Lake and Athabasca to Edmonton. For years it was called the Sunshine Trail for a very good reason— if no sunshine, no trail. Once in the 30s my wife and I left Edmonton on a sunny morning with our city clothes on and ran into rain. When it had stopped we had made only six miles in four hours. We had to get out every three or four hundred yards and with our bare hands claw the gumbo out from under our mud guards to free the wheels.

"In 1928 the Canadian Medical Association for all of Canada was meeting in Edmonton and I wanted to be there. The road was under construction, but my wife and her brother Wallace and I went on it anyway. We made it in 22 driving hours, beating a previous record of 27 hours. The men working on the road would say, 'Take a run at it. We will pull you through,' which they did many times, often for a mile or so. The next issue of the Toronto *Star Weekly* had an article and a cartoon about us, headed 'Doctor drives 555 miles to attend medical convention.' We had started out with a fairly new Durant but it wasn't quite so new when we got back. They let us run on the railroad tracks once for a way.

"Soon bush pilots started coming north, performing at fairs, etc. Some took supplies farther north to McMurray, Whitehorse and the Arctic. Soon we got a field for them to land on. Grant McConachie came up from Edmonton twice in a Ford Trimotor box car, a cargo plane, and flew me about 60 miles north to treat his mother-in-law. We landed on a back field of their farm, but couldn't get off it on the second visit. On one mercy flight I was on, 50 miles to the east, we crashed. A woman had been kicked by a horse, which split one of her kidneys and she was bleeding a lot. The roads were absolutely impassable and the Smoky River ferry was out. I flew out with a young pilot to Debolt, landed on a plowed field, got the patient bound up and loaded on our little plane. She was a big woman. A patch of straight road had been cleared by the local folk who pushed the plane out of the muddy field onto this 20-foot strip and we took off. We got just a few feet in the air when the right wing dipped and hit one fence post after another tearing a big rip in the wing canvas, but we landed back on the road with no one hurt. The patient was taken back into the house and the pilot and I spent the evening and night standing on boxes, sewing the rips in the canvas wing with our hands way above our heads, working by lantern light, very painful work with our arms aching badly and a chilly breeze blowing. Besides, we were in a hurry. I had two rolls of six-inch wide adhesive tape which we wound around the wing over the stitching to reinforce it. By the time we finished it was daylight. We got the plane pushed back on the road again and the patient back in it. This time we made it, got to the hospital in time to give the lady blood and operate. She made a good recovery.

"For several years I was the only doctor there who could blood group people and give transfusions. The first year we had to make our own serum to blood group with. Dr. L.J. O'Brien, a man in his late 50s and a skilled surgeon, was in group 2 and I was in group 3. When a transfusion was needed I would draw a syringeful of blood from him and he would draw one from me and when the blood settled, I had enough No. 2 and No. 3 serum to group the patient. A hundred or more people from the area would be the donors. We never had any serious reactions although we gave many transfusions.

"One afternoon a big income tax inspector from Edmonton, a Mr. Thompson, was waiting in my office to see me. I was blood grouping people to find the right donor for a patient, and driving four or five people to the hospital every hour. He got restless waiting, so on one trip I asked him to come along. He came; he had the right blood group and I had him donate a good quart of blood. For the next few years he used to tell his Edmonton friends, 'That's an awful country. I went up there once as an income tax inspector and they bled me.'

"In 1927 we had a wide-spread epidemic of very virulent smallpox. There were 35 deaths from it in the area from Grande Prairie to the B.C. border. My wife and I went to all the schools from Wembley to the border and vaccinated the children. The Government paid nothing for this, just supplied the vaccine. My Government allowance of $100 a month had stopped. The teachers had asked the children to bring 50 cents apiece for the vaccination —some did, some didn't. Some just brought the rest of the family, but all were vaccinated.

"The Indians had the least resistance to smallpox —almost none at all. There were a lot of Cree Indians west of Rio Grande, about 30 miles west of Wembley, that I looked after. A big Indian agent, Leo Ferguson, half French and half Indian, always went with me. He was a very dignified and comical fellow in his late 50s. To protect the Indians, we went to their camp first. Leo sent nine or 10 horseback riders out in all directions and gathered the tribe together and all that tribe was vaccinated except two families and two teen-age boys. They hid under a little bridge and were not vaccinated. They all died, all 16 of them. I have often thought that the whole tribe might have been wiped out if we had not gone out that early.

"House calls after midnight in the cold weather were never popular. I would try to get all the facts to be sure a cold trip was necessary, but they usually managed to get you out one way or another. One cold night in the 50s a man phoned about 2 a.m. and said, 'Come on down to the house, Doc, I think my wife has appendicitis.' I said, 'Appendicitis, why Wilf, I remember taking out your wife's appendix 15 or 16 years ago. I never heard of anyone having two appendixes.' 'Well, Doc,' he said, 'Did you ever hear of a guy having two wives?' 'Oh,' I said, 'I'll be right down.'

"The settlers as a rule were young, hard working people and mostly friendly. No settler was young enough to have been born there; they had all come from other places —almost everywhere. Some older men who had come down from the Yukon and Alaska were prospectors who had gone north in the gold rush of '98 and had great tales to tell. I treated one of them who claimed to have been so long in the North that he had Arctic Circles under his eyes!

"I was coroner there for 36 years until a younger man took over the job. I had many interesting cases and could tell some grim, but true, murder stories."

I will leave the murder stories for Dr. Carlisle to tell when he sees fit.

But as an example of some of the things he accomplished during his 36 years in the Peace, Al Hosker of Fort St. John would not be alive today if it had not been for the dedication and tenacious nature of Dr. Carlisle. As a two-and-a-half-year-old infant living on a homestead south of Wembley in 1936, Al suffered a ruptured appendix and it was many hours before his parents could get him to the Grande Prairie hospital. Ruptured appendixes in that era before the advent of antibiotics almost invariably meant death. Somehow, through his unwillingness to surrender anyone to the Grim Reaper without a tremendous struggle. Dr. Carlisle pulled young Hosker through to lead a happy and productive life.

Shirley Sorobey who now lives in Edmonton is also alive today because Dr. Carlisle refused to give up. She was clinically dead at birth, but Dr. Carlisle continued to dip her alternatively in warm and cold water long after others had given up hope. Finally he was awarded with a gasp and a scream of protest and the doctor had won yet another fight. The list goes on and on. In contrast to today when few doctors make house calls, when he was practising medicine few people came to his office. But when people needed help, he went. He continued to go regardless of weather or time of day or night until he finally retired to Victoria in 1957, where he still lives.

"I am a gardener now," he told Bill Scott of the Grande Prairie *Herald Tribune* in August of 1971, when, at the age of 75, he visited Grande Prairie to sell his Carlisle Building and thus sever ties with a town and district with which he had been associated for so long. If he gives his plants half the care and attention he dedicated to his human patients for so long, one can only assume that Dr. Carlisle must have one of the finest gardens in Victoria. ●

(Above) One of the many hazards of the Edson Trail. Here, a "bull outfit," or team of oxen, have upset the wagon owned by R.C. Lossing, and four fellow travellers are helping to right his wagon and outfit.

(Left) Bound for Grande Prairie on the Edson Trail — the hard way.

(Opposite page, top) Besides the hazards of the road, travellers on the Edson Trail had to brave flooded rivers. Here, D.C. Cranston and his outfit cross the Peace River at Peace River Crossing while heading to Grande Prairie in 1909.

(Opposite page, bottom) Another bull train on the trail to Grande Prairie in 1911.

THE EDSON TRAIL

*If ever a route deserved the title "trail" in the most derogatory sense, the
Edson-Grande Prairie Trail was it. In winter, storms, deep snow and ice impeded travel;
in summer, steep hills, endless mud, river rapids and swarms of blood-sucking
insects made travellers wish they had never heard of the trail.*

LIKE most of the bush trails of the frontier, the Edson-Grande Prairie Trail was called many things — few of them complimentary — by those who travelled it. For if ever a route deserved the title "trail" in the most derogatory sense, the Edson-Grande Prairie Trail was it. When the Grand Trunk Pacific Railway, now the Canadian National, reached Edson in 1910, land promoters, not surprisingly, saw it as the jumping-off place to the last frontier— the land along and beyond the mighty Peace River. What the promoters did not bother to explain was that the trail was then little more than a figment of fertile imaginations.

It was not until 1911 that the Alberta government sent in work crews to cut a trail through and to make improvements to the route. Prior to that there

were no stopping places and nowhere a traveller could obtain hay or grain for his horses or oxen. Nevertheless, those travelling the route in winter, providing they equipped themselves with enough provisions for themselves and their animals, could travel the 150 or so miles between Edson and Sturgeon Lake in reasonable comfort. That is, they could if they did not run into a bad storm, deep snow, ice, or a hundred other obstacles that impeded travel. But summer travel — that was another matter. Incredibly steep hills, endless mud, swift-flowing streams and billions of blood-sucking insects made the wayfarer constantly wish he had never heard of the trail. Yet people trekked over the route, and after ferries were installed on large rivers and smaller streams were bridged in 1911, hundreds of homesteaders used it to get to the Peace River Country.

One of the first pioneers to head over the Edson Trail was Harvey Switzer during the winter of 1910-11. He still had vivid memories of that trip many years later when he wrote a prize-winning article about it that appeared in the Summer, 1960, issue of the *Alberta Historical Review*. Switzer was a pharmacy graduate from an Ontario University who was looking for a spot in the West to build a practice. Although he went to the Peace River district for a look around, he decided not to stay, but instead returned to Edson where he settled for life.

Switzer, in partnership with Dr. R.N. Shaw and Elmer Davidson, started over the Edson Trail in March of 1911 in a sleigh drawn by a team of oxen. Since there were no stopping houses, they loaded the sleigh with everything they thought they and their animals would need during the long jaunt. One of Switzer's most vivid recollections was that of melting snow for drinking and washing water each evening. Snowshoe rabbits at the time were so plentiful that they left their tracks seemingly everywhere. Actually they left more than their tracks, for no matter how carefully the men selected the snow, almost invariably when it melted a few rabbit pellets would be found floating on the water. At first the tendency was to discard the water and try to garner snow where no rabbits apparently had been, but since pailful after pailful produced the same results, the men finally concluded that the best way was to simply skim off the rabbit raisins and grit their teeth.

Another of Switzer's vivid memories of the trail was the trip down "Break-Neck Hill," about Mile 37, where he and his partners had to tie a large tree on behind their sleigh as a brake. Anyone not taking this simple precaution was liable to end up at the bottom of the hill with his neck and those of his animals in keeping with the name of this lethal hill.

Except for having to endure extremely cold temperatures at night, and also having to help road engineer E.H. McQuarrie and his crew cut several miles of trail through the bush, the Switzer party got through in good shape. Others were not nearly as lucky — especially those challenging the route during the spring and summer months when mud was belly deep to the tallest horses. Many families had to abandon household goods and farm machinery beside the trail, hopefully to be picked up the following winter when the muskeg froze over.

Many were led into hardship through blatantly false brochures and maps issued by promoters. In 1910 Frank Oliver, publisher of the Edmonton *Bulletin* and former Minister of the Interior in Ottawa, was advising prospective homesteaders to go into the Peace River Country where good land was available. Nothing was wrong with that advice except that some map-makers were publishing a map that showed a good automobile road all the

way from Winnipeg to Grande Prairie via Edson. Robert Cochrane, who farmed for many years near the Kleskun Hills northeast of Grande Prairie, received such a map before leaving Winnipeg and shipped his car and farm machinery by rail to the end of steel at Edson. Fortunately, he learned at Edmonton that the Edson Trail was not quite the boulevard the map described it to be and took the longer road into the Peace via Athabasca Landing, Grouard and the Smoky River crossing. He picked up his farm equipment later during the winter freeze-up. He was lucky but others, fooled by the brochures, paid dearly for their folly.

Ralph Otis Johnston, who emigrated to the Peace from Lacombe, told a Grande Prairie *Herald Tribune* reporter in 1966 how he thought the Edson Trail came to be. Settlers were flocking into the Peace by 1910 and a shorter route than the 500-mile safari over the Athabasca Trail was an imperative. After the Grand Trunk Pacific arrived at

(Below) A common street scene in Edson, showing a horse team and a bull team preparing for the long trek north, about 1912-13.
(Opposite page) Time out beside the Edson Trail, as this unidentified traveller of 1914 has a bite to eat.

(Top) *A typical stopping place on the Tony River on the Edson Trail. Most accommodation was rough and ready in an era when it was considered a sign of respectability when a man travelled with his own bedroll.*
(Center) *A bull team setting out for Grande Prairie along the Edson Trail.*
(Bottom) *In winter feed had to be taken along for the animals, as shown in this snowy scene at Edson about 1910.*

Edson, said Johnston, "We sent Henry Roberts, Harry Adair and O.H. 'Rutabaga' Johnson out that fall to find a way to Edson, end-of-steel. We should have gone to Whitecourt though — it would have been a better trail. We got a shorter route all right, but we sure got a rough one too." Nevertheless, the men chose the route and the Alberta government sent engineer A.H. McQuarrie and a large road crew to cut the trail, corduroy the worst stretches of muskeg, bridge some of the smaller streams, and locate ferries on the bigger rivers such as the Athabasca, Little Smoky and Big Smoky. By the fall of 1911 the road was "as ready as it would ever be."

Looking at it from the perspective of the northern end where it joined the old road that led from Grouard to Grande Prairie near Sturgeon Lake, according to Mr. Johnston, "It went pretty well south all the way except for about 6,000 turns along the route."

At first there were no stopping places and no winter feed for the oxen and horses. But as they invariably do along any newly opened route, regular road houses sprang up at various intervals. There was Shelherd's at Mile 15; Auger's at Mile 20; Mahaw's at 35 and Severson's at 53, the Athabasca River Crossing. Then there was Anderson's at the Berland or Baptiste River; Riches' at 78, Foster's at 90, Kimmerly's at Mile 100 and Smith's at the Waskehegan River. Between Sturgeon Lake and Grande Prairie there were a half dozen more, including Harper's and Goodwin's. None was in the luxury class, all being utilitarian in nature, but they provided a meal for man and beast and a place to roll out a bedroll.

By the summer of 1911 there was a stagecoach travelling over the Edson Trail and those who rode it never forgot their experience. J.B. Taft was the stage owner and had a contract to carry the mail. When the men cut the trail during the previous winter, they made some attempt to cut off the stumps at ground level, but those stumps seemingly grew a few inches each day the following summer as the passing traffic packed the earth down around them. Consequently, the stage ride constituted so much a round of endurance that most passengers preferred to walk along behind. Matt Parks, who drove the stage for J.B. Taft for a year, later liked to tell of his adventures while acting as carrier of the Royal Mail.

On one trip he picked up a sack of mail at Edson that was destined for Calais. Since he did not know the immediate whereabouts of that post office, he used the mail sack for a pillow and more or less forgot about it for some six weeks, until a later trip when he met a fellow who complained about the irregularity of the mail service. Questioned as to the name of his post office the fellow replied, "Calais." Needless to say Mr. Parks surrendered his pillow without going into a detailed explanation. On another trip, a young woman confided to Matt that,

some time before, she had been in an argument with her husband and had left him. But after working in Edmonton for the winter to earn some money for their homestead, she was on her way back to Grande Prairie to rejoin her spouse. Matt thought it strange that the husband was not around the homestead cabin where he dropped the woman off and that the cabin door was locked— unusual in the Peace at that time. However, at the lady's insistence, he pried the cabin door open and left her there, although he wondered what she would do for food as there seemed to be little in the house. During the course of a busy schedule he all but forgot the event until some time later he read in an Edmonton newspaper that the lady had been killed by her husband after returning to that city. Apparently she had tired of waiting for him at the homestead and had gone looking for him in the city. She found him all right, but had been shot for her troubles. The husband then turned the rifle on himself.

When his contract expired, Matt gave up driving the Edson Trail, but later helped bring a government water well drilling outfit that had been abandoned along the route. Though he managed to bring in the rig over a winter road without too much trouble, he later learned that 16 horses had been lost while hauling the machine to the point at which he had picked it up.

Until his death at Grande Prairie at the age of 92, William Hosker, known to oldtimers as "Wapiti Bill," and to his close associates as 'Pop', never tired of telling of his trip over the old Edson Trail. Although a successful innkeeper in his native Preston, England, the lure of free land brought Pop to the Canada in 1911. His first farm experience was gained after he reached the new land, first as a farmhand near London, Ontario, and later as a cowhand on a ranch near Calgary. But working for someone else held little appeal for him and in the summer of 1912 he bought a team of horses and a wagon, loaded up with settler's effects and headed up the Edson Trail. Years later he retained a vivid picture of that trip — the axle-deep mud, the steep hills and the mosquitoes and blackflies: "The closest place to Hell we'll likely see on this earth," was his observation.

Nevertheless, Pop Hosker found what he was looking for at the end of the trail on the banks of the Wapiti River, where he picked out his homestead. Four years later he sent for his wife and family. Mrs. Hosker and her two boys, Art and Harold, had a considerably better trip into the area, for they came in over the newly-built Edmonton, Dunvegan and British Columbia Railway.

The arrival of the ED&BC Railway at Grande Prairie in 1916 spelled the end of the old Edson Trail. Although those who had travelled it considered themselves a breed apart, no one was sorry to see it abandoned. ●

*(Left) The Legendary Sam Steele.
(Opposite page) A Blood Indian camp near Lethbridge.
This was a common scene to Steele and his men of the
NWMP. Most Indians respected the red-coated police-
men, Steele's biggest headache over the years being
the white whisky traders.*

THE LEGENDARY SAM STEELE

**Samuel Benfield Steele became a legend
in his own lifetime, and one of the very
few Canadians honored with a parade in
New York City. As Mounted Police
officer and soldier, he made history
for 30 incredible years.**

MANY of our history books give the impression
that the Canadian West of a century ago was a
drab place, totally lacking in colorful characters and
outstanding events that make up the history of our
southern neighbor. This is nonsense. We, too, had
Indian wars, gold rushes, and buckskin-clad
trappers. Furthermore, we had frontiersmen as
brave and bold as Kit Carson and Davy Crockett—
Jerry Potts and Gabriel Dumont to name only two.
True, we did not have blue-clad cavalry, but we did
have a more effective and certainly more respected
force — the North West Mounted Police. And one of
these policemen became a western legend in his
own lifetime; in fact, on a visit to New York, he was
honored with a parade — something unheard of for
a Canadian. This man was Samuel Benfield Steele.

Sergeant-Major, Chief Inspector, Superintendent— he was all these and more. He was one of
the main organizers who prepared the newly-
formed Mounted Police for their march into the
western plains in 1874, and one of the few to
witness the signing of Treaties Six and Seven by the
Cree and Blackfoot tribes. These treaties brought
peace to the prairies and allowed white settlers to
move in and take up farming.

When the Canadian Pacific Railroad was built
across the prairies and through the mountains to the
west coast, Sam Steele was there, curtailing the illicit
liquor trade, keeping strikes from getting out of

hand, and playing the role of policeman, magistrate and public relations officer. During the Riel Rebellion Sam formed a band of scouts to lead General Strange's Army in tracking down Chief Big Bear's rebels and helped bring the uprising to a quick close. In all, Steele spent more than 20 years on the prairies, chasing cattle rustlers, horse thieves, whisky traders and renegade whites and Indians. During this period there was an interlude when he and 75 men were sent to the East Kootenay district of British Columbia to defuse a potential uprising of Chief Isadore's Shuswap Indians. Then, when the 1898 stampede to the Klondike goldfields burst on the world, who should be sent north in command of the NWMP in the Yukon? Who else but Colonel Samuel Steele.

Sam was a big man with massive shoulders and chest. "Erect as a pine and quick as a cat," was the way his friend George Hope Johnson described him. He was born in Simcoe County, Ontario, in 1849, the fourth son of Captain Elmes Steele, who had had an illustrious career in the Royal Navy before emigrating to Canada.

Sam's youth was, in many ways, almost as exciting as his later career. Of it he wrote: "In those days every man and boy, and many girls and women, could shoot, swim and find their way through the forests, which were then trackless wilderness, and all men and boys could ride well. I

had the benefit of all this, and in winter could skate, play any game, wrestle and box..."

Although his life was saddened at age 11 by the loss of his mother, he nevertheless acquired a fine education from his father and from "a talented old English gentleman, Mr. Edwin Slee," whose wife taught him French. Riding and shooting, two skills which were later to serve him well, he learned from his half-brother, John, who was the top marksman of Simcoe County.

For centuries Steele's forefathers had been military people and it was natural for him to follow in their footsteps. In the mid-1860s, when he was 16, he joined the militia, hoping to quell the Fenians, the Irish rebels who were raiding Canada from the United States. As it turned out, Sam did not get into action against the rebels, but his stint with the militia was the catalyst that decided the direction his career would take.

Sam Steele was not the first man to join when the North West Mounted Police was formed in 1873. "That honor went to the fellow who enlisted me," he often joked. Nor was coming west with the force a new experience for him. He had already served in Manitoba with the Ontario Rifles during the first Riel-led rebellion in 1870. This tour of duty, plus previous and subsequent military service, helped when he asked to transfer to the NWMP. He went with the blessing of his commanding officer and was accepted with the rank of sergeant-major.

Men like Sam Steele and the new force were badly needed for, contrary to what most of us learned in school, we did have a wild and woolly West. In fact, from the late 1860s until 1874 when the Mounted Police arrived in what is now Alberta, total lawlessness reigned in the southern sector. American whisky traders had established forts with colorful names like Whoop-Up, Stand-Off and Slide Out, mostly in the southwest corner of the province within a 100-mile radius of modern Lethbridge. From these forts they impoverished the Indians by selling them rot-gut "firewater" in exchange for buffalo hides, horses and anything else of value. Even the independent Blackfoot seemed totally incapable of resisting the urge to drink and, when drinking, completely unable to control themselves. As a result, drunken orgies ended in countless killings, not only of Indian by Indian, but of Indian by white man.

To most of the traders an Indian was a worthless creature, fit only to be exploited. The trader sat behind the heavy oak door of his fort, dishing out whisky through an iron-barred window. One buffalo hide, worth $15 in Chicago, netted the redman one cupful of searing booze; a fine pony, a gallon. If the Indian became too obnoxious after being robbed of his hides and probably his pony and his wife, the trader had no compunction about shooting him. With no law to stop the trading, it was not surprising that the Blackfoot tribes, once the proudest and the richest, were soon impoverished with scarcely enough ponies to hunt buffalo.

This, then, was the situation on the prairies when on May 3, 1873, Prime Minister John A. Macdonald introduced the bill calling for the formation of the North West Mounted Police. Recruiting began in September, mostly in Ontario. Then 150-strong, including Sergeant-Major Steele, the force set out for Fort Garry, Manitoba, where they spent the winter.

That winter was a busy one for Steele since it was his job to instruct his men how to break and ride horses. Some of the horses had never been ridden and Sam spared neither man nor beast — not even, apparently, his own brother, Dick. One day, as Sam was putting the men through their paces, a partially broken horse threw Dick. Worse, it kicked him while he was down. This did not seem to bother Sam. "Someone catch that poor horse," he ordered. Then, almost as an after-thought, came another command. "And carry that awkward lout off the parade square."

The journey to the West in the summer of 1874 is surely one of the highlights in the history of the NWMP. Some 150 men who had trained in Toronto joined the Fort Garry contingent and all headed across the broad prairie.

"To a stranger," wrote Colonel George French, their first commissioner, "it would have appeared an astonishing cavalcade. Armed men and guns looked as though fighting was to be done — what could cows, calves, plows, harrows, mowing machines, etc., be for? But that little force had a double duty to perform — to fight if necessary, but in any case, to establish forts in the far west."

Everything required for self-sufficiency went along. Besides 274 Mounted Policemen, the "astonishing" cavalcade consisted of 310 horses, 20 Metis guides, two field guns, two mortars, 142 oxen, 93 cows and calves, 73 wagons and 114 Red River carts, plus an assortment of hay-making machines, plows and harrows. The force carried enough food for a year and farm equipment to ensure that, wherever they established forts, they could grow their own vegetables and grain.

As it turned out, there was no fighting on that epic journey other than the hectic struggle to move so cumbersome a body over so vast a distance. Sam Steele's group, A Division, commanded by Inspector W.D. Jarvis, broke off from the main force at Roche Perceein, Saskatchewan, south of modern Estevan, and headed for Fort Edmonton, while the major force pressed on to what is now southern Alberta.

It was a rough trip for animals and men. Both groups were baked by a relentless prairie sun, sickened by bad water from stinking sloughs, plagued by flies and mosquitoes and drenched by lashing thunderstorms. Ponies unused to working without a daily ration of oats grew thin on a strictly grass diet and many died, while Red River carts and wagons constantly broke down or got bogged in mud-holes and had to be pried loose. Consequently, progress was slow and summer heat had turned into the frosts of early winter when the disheveled caravan finally pulled into Fort Edmonton. According to an odometer carried by Inspector Jarvis, they had travelled 1,255 miles — a long trek for a party carrying its own supplies.

Steele was not long in getting into action. When the whisky traders heard an armed force was moving toward them, most of those in southern Alberta promptly left. But near Tail Creek, some 90 miles southeast of Edmonton, a half-dozen continued to operate. Inspector Jarvis, Steele, his brother Dick, and seven other policemen set out to run them out of the country. It took less than a week to round up the booze salesmen, confiscate their liquor, fine them each $150 and send them packing.

Steele's first Alberta stay turned out to be a rather short one. When the sternwheeler *Northcote* came chugging up the North Saskatchewan River in July of 1875 on her maiden voyage, she brought the first significant amount of mail A Division had received since leaving Manitoba. She also brought orders that Steele had been promoted to Chief Constable and that he should proceed to Manitoba to take over the Swan River post. Since A Division was then in the process of erecting a new home at Fort Saskat-

(Above) A drawing of Fort Macleod, established by the NWMP in 1874.
(Below) Two scenes of Fort Whoop-Up. The first shows the Interior of Square, while the second shows some Blood Indians outside the fort in 1870.

chewan, Sam would have preferred to stay to see it completed. But a policeman's duty was to go where orders told him to, so he said his goodbyes and prepared to head back east.

His trip to the new post was an exciting one: down the North Saskatchewan River on the *Northcote* to Pemmican Portage, then on to Fort Garry with a canoe-load of pious Indians. Of this experience Steele wrote: "Whenever they stopped for a meal all knelt to pray. The red-coated white kneeling in a circle of Indians, the wild surroundings of rock, forest and lake, and the deep tones of the praying pilot lending a solemnity to it all — it's something I will never forget."

His stay at Swan River was not much longer than his stop-over in Edmonton. In July, 1876, Lieutenant-Colonel James F. Macleod took over as commissioner from Colonel French and two weeks

later Sam's division set out to attend the Indian Treaties at Fort Carlton.

The quickness with which the Division hit the trail is a good example of the constant state of readiness the NWMP became noted for. At 6 a.m. on August 6, Macleod rode into Swan River with orders to move out at 9:30. It would be a safari of 1,150 miles and everything, including supplies for the following winter, had to go along. Preparations fell to the orderly room clerk, to the orderly sergeant and to Chief Constable Steele. By 8:45 everything was ready, including five horses that were shod that morning. At 9 a.m. they were on the road, a full half-hour ahead of schedule.

Before they left they learned that Swan River had been declared unfit for anything but an outpost. Fort Macleod was now the headquarters for the horsemen in scarlet.

Treaty Six with the Plains and Woods Crees took place at Fort Carlton, some 45 miles southwest of Prince Albert. (Also at Fort Pitt and later at Sounding Lake). A colorful throng of more than 2,000 Indians gathered there, the braves decked out in their most splendid paint and feathers. In exchange for reservations, money, farm machinery, medical care, schooling — in fact, for what one writer called more succinctly, "permanent welfare"— their chiefs signed away a huge chunk of their land. After the signings, Steele and D Division set out for Fort Macleod. On the way he learned from Colonel Macleod some of the details of what had happened in 1874 to the southern contingent of the force while Steele had been travelling with Inspector Jarvis to Edmonton. The setting for Fort Macleod, Colonel Macleod told Steele, was chosen by Jerry Potts, a half-Scot, half-Blood Indian scout.

Macleod told Steele how they had hired Potts as a guide in Fort Benton, Montana, while he and Colonel French were there for supplies and directions to Fort Whoop-Up. "Not only did Potts lead us directly to Whoop-Up," Macleod said, "he is still with us and is an invaluable scout and interpreter."

As yet unaware of the worth of his new guide, Macleod told Steele how he had not been sure he could believe Potts when he said that most of the whisky runners had pulled out when they heard the Mounted Police were coming and that Whoop-Up was likely deserted. Macleod expected a fight, but Potts was right— there was no one there but Dave Akers and a few Indian women. Akers invited Macleod in for a meal, one of the best he had had since leaving Manitoba.

When Macleod saw the inside of Fort Hamilton, or Whoop-Up as it was more commonly known, he was surprised that the owners, J.J. Healy and Alfred Hamilton, had not defended it. It was certainly built to withstand a considerable siege. Finished about 1872 at the confluence of the St. Mary's and Oldman Rivers, less than 10 miles from modern Lethbridge, it purportedly got its name from

I.G. Baker, then a prominent Fort Benton merchant. When his nephew, Alfred Hamilton, was pulling out with a load of supplies for the new post, Mr. Baker warned him: "Don't let the Indians whoop you up."

The fort was some 200 feet square, with two outer walls about 12 feet apart made of heavy logs, and braced across every 10 or 15 feet with log partitions which formed rooms for living quarters, storage, blacksmith shops and such, with doors and windows opening onto an inner square. The walls were roofed with heavy logs, loop-holed for rifles, and every chimney had iron bars across the top to prevent entrance from that direction. Heavy oak doors with windows through which trade goods were passed completed the structure. Had the traders decided to stay and fight, the dozen or so men employed there under Dave Akers could have withstood a lengthy siege even involving cannon and mortar fire.

Some of the troopers were disappointed to find the place all but deserted, for a good fight would have broken the tedium of the long march. Macleod's only disappointment was that the owners were asking $25,000 for the place, a much larger sum than he had at his disposal. It would have made an ideal headquarters, but he would have to look elsewhere. Turning to his new scout, whom he now knew he could trust, Macleod asked Potts to lead the way. Potts quickly complied. He led the foot-sore cavalcade to a location by what he called "De Old Man's River." It was a fine setting with good water and grass, and an ample supply of timber for building. "While my men were building Fort Macleod," the colonel told Steele, "Potts went out to explain to the Blackfoot, Blood and Peigan chiefs that the men of the force had come as friends."

He must have done a good job for, about a month later, Crowfoot of the Blackfoot, Red Crow of the Bloods, and Bull Head of the Peigans rode in to meet Colonel Macleod and the pow-wow went as smoothly as a gathering of old friends.

Because of the thorough briefing, Steele was familiar with the background of Fort Macleod when he arrived at the post in late October 1876. Serious crime was not prevalent— the coming of the main force two years before had quietened things. But life was never dull. Gambling remained legal until late 1877 and Sam and his men were often out all night settling arguments when some unlucky dude lost his poke. Prohibition had been declared throughout the North West, but booze was occasionally smuggled in from Fort Benton and other south-of-the-border points. It gave the red-coated policemen plenty of work, not only rounding up the bootleggers, but also looking out for their clients who were invariably in a fighting mood.

St. Patrick's Day, 1877, is a prime example. Steele was reading and thinking about going to bed when at midnight a wild-eyed Irishman burst in with the news: "There's a hell of a fight going on down to Trader Murphey's in the village!"

Steele promptly headed for the battle scene, enlisting Sergeant-Major Tuke and his men on the way. Outside the trader's cabin were half a dozen plainsmen spoiling for a fight. There was no time for formality. Tuke grabbed the nearest belligerent and shook him like a terrier shakes a rat, while Steele kicked in the door. Before the combatants knew what was happening, the police had subdued them, confiscated the liquor and arrested the trader. As they were leaving, Tuke spotted a foot protruding from under a pile of furs. It proved to belong to a constable named Paddy, a member of Tuke's troop. He, too, was hauled unceremoniously to the lock-up to go before the magistrate in the morning. And as Steele stated, "He met the fate of all in the force who sacrificed duty at the altar of Bacchus."

In September of 1877, Steele attended the signing of Treaty Seven with the Blackfoot Confederacy at Blackfoot Crossing on the Bow River, just south of the present village of Cluny. Like Treaty Six, it was an impressive show, with around 3,000 Indians attending, all dressed in their most colorful costumes. The Honorable David Laird, Lieutenant Governor of the North West Territories, and Colonel Macleod represented the Crown. Chief Crowfoot spoke for the Blackfoot, Blood, Peigan, Stoney and Sarcee tribes.

"While I speak be kind and patient," he said. "I have to speak for my people who are many, who rely on me to follow that course which will be best for them… We are children of the plains. It has been our home and the buffalo have been our food always. I hope you will look at the Blackfoot as your children and that you will always be kind and charitable to them. They all expect me to choose the right course for them, and I trust the Great Spirit to help them to be good people…

"The advice given me and my people has been very good. If the police had not come to this country where would we be now? Bad men and whisky were killing us so fast that very few of us would be left today. The Mounted Police have protected us as the feathers of the birds protect them from the frosts of winter… I am satisfied. I will sign the treaty."

Steele could not help wondering if Crowfoot or any of the others gathered there grasped the total implications of the treaty. How could anyone foresee what having to settle on reservations would do to a nomadic people who for centuries had roamed free over a vast land? But there was no time to ponder the question for there was an entire prairie to police.

PART II

Another of Sam's more memorable assignments also came in 1877 when he accompanied Commissioner Macleod to Fort Walsh in the Cypress

Hills, near the present Alberta-Saskatchewan boundary, to confer with Chief Sitting Bull. Sitting Bull had just brought his people into Canada after annihilating General George Custer and his 7th Cavalry at the Little Big Horn River in Montana. Sitting Bull hoped that in Canada his people would escape the wrath of the United States Army.

Steele was favorably impressed with General Terry and his escort of American infantry soldiers who came to Fort Walsh to try to persuade Chief Sitting Bull to return to the United States. Obviously Sitting Bull did not share Steele's admiration, for he refused to go back. He accused General Terry of lying and the American government of cheating and stealing Indian lands. It would be many more years before the Sioux would return to their homeland, but that is another story.

Meanwhile Steele was never short of work. Horse stealing had been an honorable tradition among the prairie Indians for nearly 150 years before the NWMP came, and just because the red-coated policemen frowned on the practice, it did not make it an evil thing in the eyes of most Indians. Consequently, Steele and his men were often out day and night trying to steer the culprits on a new course. As he wrote: "Parties had to be sent out at all hours looking for horse thieves; to make sudden raids on Indian camps to capture law breakers; to lie in ambush at far coulees or lonely fords to head off criminals making for the U.S. border with their plunder or trying to escape a warrant; or to intercept whisky outfits heading north from Montana to carry on their illicit trade..." Not surprisingly, Steele and his men were well-seasoned lawmen, tough but always fair. In 1884 they were sent across the Alberta-British Columbia border to police the Canadian Pacific Railway, which was then being pushed through the Rocky Mountains via the Kicking Horse Pass.

The Mounties needed to be tough, for some very rough characters were working on the line. Some of these men sold whisky, with the inevitable trouble that accompanied this trade. Moreover, the British Columbia government was not much help. The Mounted Police had jurisdiction over a strip of territory 10 miles on either side of the railway right-of-way, in which no liquor could be legally sold under the Federal Preservation of Peace Act. But there was nothing to prevent bars being built outside this strip. Worse, the British Columbia government did not want to be deprived of what it considered its legal right to revenue anywhere within the province and sold liquor licences to almost anyone who asked.

In Chief Inspector Steele, however, the boozers faced a formidable foe. There was little he could do to stop the bars from selling liquor, so he attacked the problem from another angle. Anyone under the influence of alcohol was introduced to the local lock-up and heavily fined. To go on a safe binge a worker had to walk at least 10 miles, and this distance was doubled when Steele persuaded the Dominion government to increase its domain to 20 miles either side of the railway. If Steele could help it, nothing was going to stop the CPR from going through.

Surprisingly, with all the tough characters following the construction gangs, there were only two killings during the time the Mounties policed the British Columbia section of the line. One of these took place near a roadside inn which was actually 22 miles south of Golden and well outside of Steele's territory. The other was at Kicking Horse Flats where a small community consisting mostly of saloons had sprung up.

At the Flats a group of American construction workers were gathered in the tent of a Negro barber. One of the men, a conductor and a Democrat, got into an argument with the barber who was a republican. Something the conductor said so angered the barber that he picked up one of his razors and began slashing at everyone in sight. Needless to say, he soon cleared the tent of all but the conductor and his friend, a burly brakeman, who were at the back of the tent and unable to get away. The barber then made a run at the conductor, trying to disembowel him with a couple of mighty swipes. Fortunately he succeeded only in slicing through a couple of layers of clothing. Before he could do any more damage, the brakeman drew a revolver and shot the barber dead.

Naturally, the brakeman was apprehended by Steele's men and brought to trial. But it was obviously a case of self-defence and the magistrate let the brakeman go.

Justice was not nearly as quickly administered when a Mr. Baird of Missoula, Montana, was shot on the trail three miles south of the stopping house known as the Hog Ranch and an estimated $5,000 belonging to the company he worked for stolen. As soon as Steele heard about the killing he sent two men in pursuit of the murderer. The constables quickly located the spot where the killer had ambushed Baird and trailed him to a Columbia River crossing, where they found his Winchester discarded in shallow water. Ironically, the Mounties apparently spent the night with the murderer at the Second Crossing, now Revelstoke, but did not recognize him as the description given them by Manuel Dainard, the murdered man's companion, in no way matched. Dainard, it seems, gave a false description, because "Bull Dog" Kelly, the murderer, had threatened to return and kill him if he talked.

This was one case when the Mounties did not get their man.

After Christmas, 1884, Steele moved his headquarters from Golden to Beaver River, then a mile from the end of the rails. In this area was located as unsavory a bunch of hooligans as could be found anywhere. They had set up a number of bars and

The remarkable Sam Steele, NWMP, who played a leading role in the taming of the Canadian West.

were preying on the construction workers by rolling any foolish enough to get drunk on their poisonous booze. Because the railway's chief engineer, James Ross, would not allow his trains to bring in food to this tough segment, they generally got their supplies by stealing them. Consequently the police had their hands full. Then, as if there were not trouble enough, the railroad workers went on strike.

All through February and March of 1885 dozens of workers complained to Steele that their pay was being held up and that they would strike if it did not soon come through. Sam tried to persuade them to be patient. "Your pay is guaranteed by the Canadian Government," he told them. It did no good. The workers were agitated by rowdies who had worked on the Northern Pacific Railway in the United States and, on April 1, they walked off the job.

In the meantime Steele had received a telegram from the Lieutenant-Governor of the North West Territories saying a rebellion, led by Louis Riel, had broken out in Saskatchewan. "Come out of the mountains at once and bring your men," the telegram said.

"Cannot come," replied Steele. "The workers have gone out on strike."

Next came an urgent wire from the Mayor of Calgary: "For God's sake come! There is danger of an attack by the Blackfeet!"

Again Steele replied: "Cannot come; wire the Lieutenant-Governor."

Steele expected trouble from the workers and it was not long in coming. A couple of days after the strike began, Sergeant William Fury and three constables had to hold off a large crowd of armed men, who were trying to stop a train-load of track-layers from working. Fortunately the Mounties met the mob, who were firing revolvers and raising a fearful uproar, at the mouth of the narrow Beaver River Canyon and were able to stand them off without anyone getting hurt. When the strikers saw that Fury and his men would not back down, they decided to call it a day and let the track-layers go to work.

During this time Steele had been incapacitated with a severe case of flu. And while Fury was engaging the strikers in the canyon, Constable Kerr had gone to the end of steel to purchase a bottle of medicine for his boss. On his way back he heard one of the troublemakers trying to incite a group of strikers to attack the Mounted Police barracks. He immediately tried to arrest the rabble-rouser, but suffered a severe pummelling from the strikers for his trouble, and was forced to leave without his intended prisoner. A few minutes later Kerr met Sergeant Fury, who brought the news to Steele. "It's a pity he attempted the arrest without enough help," said an unhappy Steele. "But what is done is done. Now we've got to take that man at all costs— we can't let the rest of the gang think they can play with us. Take whatever men you need, Fury, and bring that man in!"

Off went Fury, only to return a little later with a torn jacket. "The gang took the prisoner away from us." he told Steele.

"That is too bad," replied Steele a little sarcastically. "Now take your revolvers and shoot anyone who tries to interfere with the arrest!"

Fury was off again, this time taking with him Constables Fane, Craig and Walters. A few minutes later a shot rang out and George Hope Johnston, a federally appointed magistrate who acted as Steele's deputy and became Sam's close friend, intoned solemnly, "There's one of them gone to hell, Steele!"

The two men stepped to the office window to see Constables Craig and Walters dragging a man across the bridge that separated the police barracks from the shanty-town of Beaver River. The prisoner was kicking and cursing, and ably abetted by a woman dressed in red who was shrieking and calling the Mounties some very uncomplimentary names. Although very weak from his illness, Steele grabbed a rifle and ran out to help Fury and Fane, who were trying to keep the mob from crossing the bridge.

"Arrest that woman and bring her along!" he shouted to Fane, and to the menacing mob he gave a stern warning: "Hold it right there or we'll open fire!"

The mob answered with jeers and curses. "Look

at the bastard," said one. "His own deathbed makes no difference to him."

Sam may have looked as though he was not long for this world, but his stance indicated quite plainly that if he was to depart from it, he would be taking a few strikers with him. While he and his men covered the mob, Johnston read the Riot Act. Steele again warned them to back off or he and his men would open fire. By this time quite a number of well-armed town citizens had gathered to back up the police. It was all that was needed— the riot was over.

It turned out that the man Johnston thought had been sent to Hades was only wounded by Sergeant Fury. He was treated by CPR doctors, fined $100 by Magistrate Johnston and turned loose. Other strikers who were arrested were given the same light punishment. It was all that was necessary for, on April 7, the workers received their pay and the strike ended. That same day Steele left Fury to gather up the men and horses of the little detachment and follow when everything was ready. Steele was off for Calgary. By April 19, as a newly-appointed major in charge of a group of Mounted Police and hard-riding cowboys known as Steele's Scouts, he was heading north with the Alberta Field Force under Major General T. Bland Strange to help quell the Riel's uprising of Metis and Indians.

The primary target of Steele's Scouts was Chief Big Bear's band of Plains Crees. Big Bear's people, who were gathered at the Frog Lake Reserve some 150 miles northeast of Edmonton near what is now the Alberta-Saskatchewan border, had massacred nine white men who worked there and taken two white women prisoners. They had then moved on to Fort Pitt, driven out the Mounted Police detachment stationed there, torched the fort and captured all of the civilian residents. It would take a full chapter to tell all of Steele's exploits as he guided the Alberta Field Force in a relentless pursuit of Big Bear. Briefly, during the chase in which several pitched battles were fought and Sergeant William Fury wounded, Big Bear's band was gradually split up and most of his prisoners taken from him. Finally, on July 2, the chief was captured by Sergeant Smart and Constables Sullivan, Nicholson and Kerr. Meanwhile, General Frederick Middleton's army, which had been sent earlier from Ontario, had pretty well finished mopping up the rest of the rebellious forces. The North West Rebellion was over.

By a strange quirk of fate, General Middleton gained most of the credit for putting down the rebellion and was awarded a knighthood by Queen Victoria and $20,000 by the Canadian Government. General Strange, a retired British general who had left his ranch near the Blackfoot Reserve near Gleichen to lead the Alberta Field Force, and whose troops had been solely responsible for tracking down Big Bear's Army, was awarded little more than a pat on the back. The general, however, knew good work when he saw it and he mentioned Steele in dispatches. "Major Steele and his cavalry," he noted, "were the eyes, ears and feelers of the force, and their spirited pursuit of Big Bear crowned with success a long, weary march...."

The citizens of Calgary were equally appreciative of Steele's work and feted him at a banquet where they presented him with a valuable diamond ring. But Steele had no time to rest on his laurels. After a quick trip to Winnipeg, he was again off to British Columbia to resume duties as Commissioner of Police for the Canadian government. He was not too surprised to find that law and order had been well enforced during his absence by his old friend, George Johnston, and his federally appointed group of special constables—not that he had been given much help from the provincial magistrate who apparently did not like federal people butting into his territory. Consequently, an argument as to who had jurisdiction over what went on almost daily. It ended abruptly on November 7, 1885, however, when Donald A. Smith, later Lord Strathcona, drove the last spike at a spot now known as Craigellachie and the CPR was completed. In recognition of his service, Steele was invited to accompany a train-load of dignitaries on an excursion to the Pacific.

After that he returned to the mountains, but soon the Mounted Police, along with most of the railroad engineers and contractors, left in two long trains. Apparently few of the men enjoyed the confines of the towering Rockies, for when the trains emerged from the Bow River Pass onto the rolling prairies, there was a loud shout, "Hurrah, civilization at last!"

Steele, too, was happy to be back on his beloved plains. He was not, however, happy with some of the changes that had taken place since the arrival of the NWMP 11 years before. The buffalo herds that had seemed to be inexhaustible in 1874 were all but gone. The Indians were bemoaning the loss and the Metis buffalo hunters who, 10 years before, were a happy-go-lucky people with a plentiful supply of game, were now eking out a living gathering the bones of the once mighty herds and selling them for some $2 a ton to sugar factories in the United States. During the late 1880s and early '90s thousands of tons of buffalo bones were gathered and shipped out, leaving anyone who came later with the impression that the great hump-backed beasts must have been figments of overly active imaginations.

There were other things that irked Steele. While at Battleford during the trials of some of Big Bear's people, he learned that although many members of the NWMP had served more time putting down the Rebellion than had many army troops, they were not eligible when campaign medals were awarded in June of 1886. The Mounties did not get their medals until a full three years after the campaign.

Then there were the liquor laws. "Our powers under it," wrote Steele, "were so great— in fact so outrageous— that no self-respecting member of the corps, unless directly ordered, cared to exert them to the full extent." The police had the power to enter any private dwelling without a warrant, to confiscate any liquor found there and to arrest the occupants. "This state of affairs continued for some years, despite the fact that the judges quashed nearly every conviction brought before them," he claimed. He did not think that the law passed earlier to save the Indians from extinction should apply to the settlers now flocking in. "It was an insult to free people," he thought.

In January of 1887 Steele was transferred to Lethbridge, but did not stay there long. In May he received new orders. There was trouble with the Indians in the East Kootenay district of British Columbia and the few whites there feared for their lives. Steele's orders were explicit: Take Inspectors Wood and Huot and 75 men and straighten things out.

PART III

The situation in the Kootenays when Steele (since promoted to Superintendent) and his "D" Division arrived that summer was almost ludicrous. A squabble between Colonel James Baker, MPP for the district, and Chief Isadore and his tribe of Kootenay Shuswaps as to who owned a piece of land known as Joseph's Prairie, where Cranbrook now stands, was the reason for the emergency. Baker had bought the land from John and Robert Galbraith, two brothers who had obtained the property from the provincial government and established a ferry across the Kootenay River during the 1864 gold rush to Wild Horse Creek.

The trouble was that the British Columbia government could not adequately explain what right they had to sell the land, since it apparently belonged to Chief Isadore and his people. As long as the Galbraiths had owned the property, they allowed Isadore's people to live there undisturbed. But when Baker took over, he ordered Isadore to move, an action that naturally did not sit too well with the Indians.

Then there was a conflict between whites and Indians that was far more inflammatory. In the summer of 1884 two placer miners were murdered at Deadman's Creek on the Wild Horse-Golden Trail. Constable Anderson of the British Columbia Provincial Police, the only policeman in the East Kootenays, arrested an Indian named Kapula and locked him in the jail at Wild Horse, not far from where Fort Steele now stands. Isadore took exception to this action as he did not think Kapula guilty. He and several of his braves broke into the lock-up, set Kapula free and ordered Anderson out of the country.

At this time there were only about a dozen whites in the entire East Kootenay area and Isadore's action caused considerable apprehension among them.

They appealed for help and in January of 1887, Commissioner Lawrence Herchmer of the NWMP snow-shoed into the area from Fort Macleod to look the situation over. He learned that Isadore's tribe, horse-riding Indians numbering nearly 200, were well armed and could, with sufficient provocation, easily wipe out the handful of whites.

However, it was not until June, after a meeting between Herchmer, British Columbia Indian Affairs Minister I.W. Powell and Stipendiary Magistrate A.W. Vowell that British Columbia finally agreed to let the Mounted Police straighten things out. By then Steele and his men were already on the way, travelling by CPR to Golden, then down the Golden-Wild Horse trail. To aid in moving some of the supplies south from Golden, Steele hired a stern-wheel steamer, the *Duchess*, but, unfortunately, she sank with the loss of much valuable equipment.

After this misadventure, Steele hired the only other vessel on the upper Columbia River, an unbelievable creation called the *Cline*. *Paddle-wheels On The Frontier*, by British Columbia author Art Downs, gives the following description of her:

"She was the creation of 'a scatterbrained young Canadian' named Jack Hayes. Her lines were not unlike a sack of potatoes, the only difference between bow and stern was a paddlewheel at one end. But since her hull was originally a railway barge built of four-inch planks, her square design was understandable. She was sturdy enough, but her sturdiness was not all asset. As her owner admitted: 'It made her sit kinder heavy in the water'."

When Steele hired her she was on her second voyage of the summer. Unfortunately for the policeman, it was her last. Loaded with men and rations and forage for the horses, she sank near Spillamacheen, the officer's red jackets mingling with the oats to form a colorful pattern as they floated downstream.

With these mishaps and other delays it was August 1 by the time the Mounties reached Wild Horse. Finding a suitable spot for a headquarters took longer than Steele anticipated, but, finally, with the help of Robert Galbraith he chose some bench-land near Galbraith's ferry, and there his men erected Fort Steele.

Apparently the policemen had brought more than just their supplies with them. Somewhere along the way, possibly while camped at Golden for a month awaiting orders, some of them contracted mountain fever, a form of typhoid, and soon an epidemic was raging. An account of the consequences appeared in the book, *Sport and Life*, written by a venturesome Englishman by the name of W.A. Baillie-Grohman, who spent considerable time in the Kootenays during the 1880s. Two of Steele's men who were returning from a trip to the railroad at Golden were suddenly taken ill while stopping overnight at Grohman's sawmill, some 50 miles north of Fort Steele. Seeing that they were too sick

Chief Isadore and his council of Kootenai Indians at Fort Steele in 1896.

to ride, Grohman quickly dispatched a rider to inform Steele. A day later a sergeant arrived with a foam-flecked team and wagon to take the men home. The two constables looked terribly ill and Grohman was reluctant to let them go, but the sergeant insisted. Both were placed in the wagon on a layer of pine bows which hopefully would cushion the shock of the springless vehicle.

"It was raining heavily at the time," Grohman wrote, "and as the driver had forgotten to bring the wagon cover, the doctor's instructions to the sergeant to bring as much lumber as he could find room for were acted on, by lashing sort of a roof over the wagon-bed in which the sick men lay. Death is habitually taken in a lighter vein by western men than it is among more civilized surroundings where accidents are rare, but nevertheless the sergeant's reply when I asked for what purpose the inch boards were required at the fort must have seemed of great significance to the invalids lying there in plain hearing. 'Oh,' said the sergeant, 'the doc told me that if the men were looking bad, I should bring along enough lumber to bury them with, for they have more dead men than lumber at the fort, and whipsawing ain't healthy in this weather.'

"The sergeant wasn't far out; one of the men was dead, we heard, when the fort was reached, and the other 'used up the balance of the lumber' a day or two later, as the driver laconically wrote one of my men."

Despite Grohman's morbid report, Steele did not seem to think conditions in the Kootenays were any more or less difficult than in dozens of other places he had been stationed. His immediate concern was to get the fort built and to contact Chief Isadore and the two braves suspected of complicity in the murder of the two prospectors.

When the two Indians came in voluntarily, Steele could find no evidence that they knew anything about the murders and he laid no charge. Instead, he sent them back to their people with food and blankets for the journey. Before they left, Sam explained to Chief Isadore that the Mounties came as friends and that the Indians would receive the same fair treatment afforded the whites. The speech obviously impressed the stolid chief, as from this point on his attitude toward the whites improved.

During his year's stay in the East Kootenays, Steele found the Indians to be the most honest he had ever known, with crime rare among them. Undoubtedly one of the reasons was Chief Isadore's absolute power. Not even Crowfoot of the Blackfoot tribe ruled so supremely over his subjects.

Wrote Steele: "When Christmas came, the Indians, as was their custom, rode in a body to St.

Looking down Riverside Avenue in Fort Steele in 1898. The old North West Mounted Police jail is in the right foreground while the main part of the town is in the background.

Eugene Mission, where they took up quarters in their log houses, and for a whole week attended the church services. In the interval, Isadore and his four sheriffs seized all who had been guilty of any offence, such as drunkeness, gambling or theft. They were tied down hand and foot to a robe and soundly flogged, regardless of age or sex. By some means or other the chief knew the culprits, but in spite of the fact and the consequences of their folly, they never failed to show up and take their medicine...."

It took Sam most of a year to untangle the business of who really owned Joseph's Prairie. Colonel Baker claimed it since he had paid the Galbraiths for it, but Chief Isadore contended that the government had no right to sell it to the Galbraiths since it had belonged to his people for generations. He had no intention of vacating until his people were adequately paid.

It seemed a reasonable demand and after a visit in the spring of 1888 by Mr. Peter O'Reilly, Superintendent of Land and Indian Reserves for the Province of British Columbia, Sam finally negotiated a settlement for Isadore. The chief even apologized for accusing Baker "of grabbing all the land in the country" and said his people would not trespass again. Steele promised to have an irrigation ditch dug to Isadore's reserve, while the federal government promised to build an industrial school near the St. Eugene Roman Catholic Mission. Both promises

were fulfilled and there was no further trouble with the Kootenay Indians.

On June 16, 1888, Superintendent Steele received orders to move back to Fort Macleod. Before leaving he thought it would be good public relations to have his division hold its annual sports day and invite the Indians. The day was a complete success, with many of the Indians carrying off the prizes donated by some leading whites of the district. After it was over, Chief Isadore lined up his tribe to say goodbye to the scarlet-coated horsemen.

"I received him on some rising ground, accompanied by Colonel Baker, Mr. Galbraith and other leading white men," Steele remembered. "The chief addressed me on behalf of his people, speaking in the highest terms of the manly and moral behavior of the men of the division. He added that in the future if there was any cause for complaint, instead of taking the law into their own hands, they would visit Fort Macleod to obtain advice from the Great Mother's Red-Coats."

On August 7 the Mounties were off for Fort Macleod by way of the Crowsnest Pass. En route, Steele took note of the coal deposits in the Alberta section of the pass and reported them as accurately as he could. He should have been proud of that report, for it led to a coal mining industry that continues to this day.

For his work in the Kootenays Steele received high praise from Commissioner Herchmer in his

(Above) Major-General Sam Steele, in 1918. After an amazing career as police officer on the Canadian prairies and in the Yukon, Steele commanded Lord Strathcona's Horse during the Boer War.
(Below) Charcoal, Indian outlaw. The clothes were provided by the photographer, the large hat serving to hide the handcuffs. Charcoal was so weak that he was hanged sitting in a chair.

report to the Canadian government for the year 1888: "I will specially call your attention to the extremely able manner in which Supt. Steele managed matters in the Kootenay district of B.C., which I think will have a lasting impression on the Indians of that country. I propose, with your permission, as soon as the Crowsnest Pass is free of snow next June, to sent a patrol into Kootenay for a few weeks. The satisfactory passage of 'D' Division through that part of the north west reflects credit on Supt. Steele and all ranks of his command...."

No doubt Steele was pleased at the commissioner's report, but, as usual, he had little time in which to reflect on it. In December of 1888 he was placed in charge of the Fort Macleod district. Two divisions— roughly 150 men— were needed in the area since the original handful of ranchers was increasing day by day. As each new settler arrived, one of Steele's men would visit him and have him sign a "patrol" slip on which he was requested to list any complaint. With each homesteader still several miles from his nearest neighbor, the Mounted Police formed a link between them. At that time the scarlet-coated horsemen probably had a closer relationship with the people they served than that achieved by any force at any point in history.

One of the greatest summer problems in the district for Steele's men—other than the Indians surreptitiously substituting their rancher neighbor's beef herds for the now missing buffalo— were prairie fires. "The grass," said Steele, "became very dry, in fact turned into hay on the ground in August, and it was as nutritious as when it was green. But it would ignite as easily as tinder and many hard rides had to be made to detect the persons responsible." Any Mountie spotting smoke would ride directly to the spot and all able-bodied males within a 10-mile radius were supposed to turn out and help extinguish the blaze.

As often happens, there was also a humorous side to the prairie fires. Anyone detecting someone deliberately setting a fire was required to report the culprit to the nearest NWMP or magistrate. For this the informer was entitled to a $50 reward. An enterprising settler from the Pincher Creek district took full advantage of this provision while putting up hay for Steele.

"One of his men," claimed Steele, "while smoking set the prairie on fire, whereupon the contractor rode at full speed toward the village of Pincher Creek where there was a magistrate. On his way he met a Mounted Policeman riding toward the fire and, as he galloped by, called out, 'One of those men of mine has started a fire; all the hay will be burned; for the Lord's sake turn out as many men as you can to put it out'!"

By the time the contractor returned, the Mountie, with the help of the workers, had the fire extinguished. "Where in blazes did you go?" the irate policeman demanded.

"Oh," replied the contractor nonchalantly, "I've been to see the magistrate. It was like this: I laid a complaint against myself for starting a fire through my hired man. The magistrate fined me $100. But since I laid the complaint, I was entitled to the reward. Saved myself $50 you see."

The first photo shows the members of Sam Steele's detachment at the summit of Chilkoot Pass in the winter of 1898.
The bottom photo shows officers of Strathcona's Horse en route to South Africa in 1900. Under Steele's leadership this regiment, half of whom were cowboys from Alberta, played an important role in the Boer War.

In January of 1890 Steele took time off from his busy routine to head for Montreal, where he married Elizabeth Harwood. On his honeymoon in New York City he was feted by the police who knew of his reputation. Moreover, the New York fire department put on a parade of 60 firewagons for him and his new bride. It was indeed a high tribute to a Canadian by a city usually indifferent to foreigners, no matter how heroic or high their rank.

Before Steele returned to Fort Macleod he stopped off in Ottawa for a meeting with Prime Minister John A. Macdonald. Sir John quizzed Steele on the need for a railroad between Calgary and Edmonton, since there was a bill before the House on the matter. Sam's reply that a railroad certainly was needed had a positive stimulus on the Prime Minister. That same afternoon Macdonald rushed the bill through the House and the Calgary and Edmonton Railway Company began building the following summer.

During his career in the West, Sam Steele took part in many manhunts, with one of the biggest taking place in the fall of 1896. A Blood Indian variously named Charcoal, Dried Meat or Bad Young Man shot another Indian named Medicine Pipe Stem. Steele quickly dispatched Inspector Jarvis and a detachment of Mounties to the scene, the Cochrane Ranch, some 50 miles southwest of Fort Macleod. But by the time Jarvis and his men arrived, Charcoal had vamoosed to parts unknown.

Although Charcoal apparently never left the Macleod district, he led the NWMP on a long and tedious chase. Nearly 100 Mounted Police, a large but undetermined number of ranchers and cowboys, and around 75 Blood and Peigan Indians took part in the manhunt. Steele was severely criticized by bigotted district authorities and by biased eastern newspapers for arming and employing Indians. Sam chose to ignore them and it turned out his decision was a wise one.

Had Charcoal surrendered he probably would have only faced a charge of manslaughter since there were indications that medicine Pipe Stem had provoked his own murder by being too familiar with Charcoal's wife. Instead he chose to run and the result was tragic. Sergeant William Wilde— the same man who had accompanied Steele while policing the British Columbia section of the CPR and during the Riel Rebellion— spotted Charcoal on Beaver Creek not far from Pincher Creek. Wilde was riding a very fast horse and after a short chase overtook Bad Young Man. Wilde leaned over to haul the fugitive from the saddle, but Charcoal swung his rifle around and shot the sergeant in the chest. As Wilde lay where he fell, Charcoal dismounted and fired again. Then, with a fierce whoop he sprang onto Wilde's horse and rode off before the rest of the posse could overtake him. Since Wilde was one of the best liked men in the force, the manhunt resumed with a vengeance. Until the

sergeant's murder the Indians had been sympathetic to the fugitive and had been helping him with horses and food. Now they too were anxious to see Charcoal apprehended.

Many times the wily outlaw was almost captured, only to escape. Finally Steele's decision to employ Indians paid off. A young Blood brave with the unlikely name of Many Tail Feathers Around His Neck proved so adept at tracking the fugitive that Charcoal had no time to rest. Many Tail Feathers sighted Charcoal several times and even got close enough to fire at him once, although he missed. The fugitive then doubled back from the Waterton River to the Blood Reserve some 50 miles to the east.

There, as he attempted to get provisions and a fresh horse, he was overpowered by two Bloods, Left Hand and Bear's Back Bone. Both were cousins of the murderer who had promised Steele to capture him should the opportunity present itself.

"Charcoal was tried, found guilty and sentenced to hang," remembered Steele. "He died like a true warrior, singing his death song all the way to the scaffold."

That was the last big manhunt on the prairies for Steele. A little more than a year later he was on his way to the Yukon to police the great flood of humanity heading north. The famous rush to the Klondike was on!

A whole book could be written on Steele's exploits in the Yukon during the gold rush, but since this account is primarily concerned with his adventures in Alberta, his Yukon adventures do not belong here. Suffice it is to say that he was promoted to Commissioner of Police in the Yukon with the rank of Lieutenant-Colonel. Steele carried out his job so well that, unlike most gold rush towns, Dawson City was one of the most law-abiding places in Canada. Steele became known as "The Lion of the Yukon" for his iron rule, although the Yukon was by no means a funless place— except on Sunday when no one dared to so much as tend a fish net lest he be charged with contravening the Lord's Day Act.

Sam Steele served 19 months in the Yukon, leaving there on September 26, 1899, after being relieved by Superintendent A. Bowen-Perry. A week or so later he passed through Alberta on his way home to Montreal. Most thought that after a career such as his he would be content to take life easy for awhile. They were wrong. On March 17, 1900, he boarded the Ss. *Monteray* at Halifax as commander of a newly-recruited cavalry regiment, the Lord Strathcona Horse, about half of whom were cowboys from Alberta. They were on their way to South Africa and the Boer War.

Sam Steele was to become a Major-General and experience a new career as eventful and exciting as his more than a quarter-century in Western Canada with the North West Mounted Police. But that, too, is another story. ●

For 60 years, Dr. William Fairfield blazed one agricultural trail after another and did more for the farming industry in Southern Alberta than anyone else in the province's history.

Agricultural Trail Blazer:
W. H. FAIRFIELD

"ALMOST 60 years to the day after he landed here, Southern Alberta's best known pioneer and moving spirit in agricultural trail blazing died quietly about 10 p.m. Thursday night." Thus began an article in the March 24, 1961, issue of the *Lethbridge Herald* in its farewell message to agricultural scientist Doctor William Harmon Fairfield.

Obituaries tend generally to paint a rosier picture of a person than the facts of real life bear out. Such was not the case where Dr. Fairfield was concerned. In fact, the reverse is true. Dr. Fairfield has undoubtedly done more for the farming industry in Southern Alberta than anyone else in the history of the area. Just a few of his accomplishments include: he got alfalfa to grow in Southern Alberta where before his coming all attempts at growing it met with defeat; he persuaded farmers to grow windbreaks in a land where trees previously had grown only in river bottoms; he discovered the grey wooded soils of the Alberta and Saskatchewan parklands lacked sulphur and that when this ingredient was added, these soils would produce considerably more.

Three years before the *Lethbridge Herald* printed its farewell tribute to Dr. Fairfield, on July 20, 1958, *Herald* staff writer, Joe Halla, had covered an event held in Lethbridge where hundreds of outstanding citizens and many of Canada's foremost agricultural scientist gathered to honor Lethbridge's most noteworthy citizen. By then Dr. Fairfield had been retired for 13 years after serving from 1906 to 1945 as the superintendent of the federal government experimental farm at Lethbridge. At that event Dr. Fairfield was presented with a fellowship in the Agricultural Institute of Canada, the highest honor that organization can bestow upon a fellow member.

This was only one of many honors he had accumulated over the years. Two of the awards he cherished most were an honorary doctor's degree bestowed upon him by the University of Alberta in 1940 and the Order of the British Empire awarded him by King George VI in 1953. All his awards came because of his work in agriculture and for his great contribution to humanity in general.

William Fairfield, a jolly man whose hearty laugh was his trademark, was born in Titesville, Pennsylvania, in 1876. His roots in the New World go back considerably farther than that. His Fairfield ancestors came to America from England in 1630, some settling in Massachusetts, and William's direct ancestors taking up land in the Tennessee Valley of New York State in the same area where Franklin Delano Roosevelt, late president of the United States, was born.

The Fairfield family were caught in an untenable situation during the American War of Independence. Fiercely loyal to the British Crown, but at the same time having developed a deep affection for their adopted country, they waited until the war was over, then after great deliberation, joined hundreds of others in a migration to Canada. These were the people who became known as the United Empire Loyalists. The Fairfield family settled near Kingston, where they built of hewn logs what was believed to be the first two-storey house in what was to become the Province of Ontario. That house, known both as the "White House" and "Fairfield House," stands

(Above) *Seed grain specialists and train touring western Canada. W.H. Fairfield first on left, bottom row.*
(Below) *Lethbridge residents with Blood and Peigan Indians at the Lethbridge Fair, 1910. W.H. Fairfield, third from right in back row, agricultural trailblazer.*

today and was commemorated in October of 1958, when a plaque was unveiled by the Historic Sites Board of Ontario. That stately old home overlooks Lake Ontario, and is located on Collins Bay on the north side of Highway 33, 10 miles west of Kingston.

Although one branch of the Fairfield family still live in Ontario, the climate proved too humid for William's mother, who was afflicted with asthma, so his mother and father moved to Titesville, Pennsylvania, where William was born.

At Titesville Dr. Fairfield's father spent 15 years in the oil industry, then, in 1886, when William was 10 years old, headed West to Denver, Colorado, to try his hand at farming and cattle raising. Perhaps if the family had stayed in Pennsylvania, William would have become an oilman and undoubtedly would have done well in that field. Fortunately for agriculture, his family came West and in 1890 William enrolled in the Colorado State Agricultural College in Fort Collins. Four years later he graduated with a Bachelor of Science degree, and in another four years he had obtained a Master's degree, writing his thesis on seed germination and the effects of various alkali salts on soils. He obtained his Master's degree from the University of Wyoming while serving as an assistant professor of agriculture and horticulture, working in that capacity from 1895 until 1901. At the same time he was head of a small experimental station near Laramie. For an ordinary man it would have been a back-breaking schedule, but for William Fairfield it was easy, as he was working in a field he had grown to love.

It was at this time that word of the opening of the Canadian West to homesteaders began to trickle down to Wyoming. Perhaps it is not surprising that William began to take more than a passing interest, for stories of Canada, perhaps embellished somewhat by his parents, were still indelibly entrenched in his mind. In 1901 he decided to head north to Lethbridge and have a look for himself. He had heard that irrigation was playing a large role in the opening up of this new territory and to him the combination of cattle raising and irrigation was an intriguing challenge. His brother, Harry, proved more than willing to go along.

It was a decision neither would ever regret. According to *Lethbridge Herald* staff writer, Joe Halla, "The success of the Fairfield brothers was soon the talk of Southern Alberta." William Fairfield's farm on the southern outskirts of Lethbridge is now commemorated by a rustic sign erected by Alberta Historic Sites people beside Highway 5, which leads southwest to Cardston. It was on this farm that William was able to apply his vast store of knowledge of agriculture learned during his long tenure at the University of Wyoming and the results probably exceeded even his optimistic expectations.

One of his challenges was to get alfalfa to grow in the area. Charles Ora Card, leader of the Mormon movement from Utah to Southern Alberta and founder of Cardston, told William that for some reason, though his people had grown alfalfa successfully and in profusion in Utah, they were having absolutely no success growing it in Southern Alberta. An interesting challenge, thought Mr. Fairfield, and he immediately set out to solve it. His fertile mind began clicking. He remembered reading something in one of the many texts he had used over the years—something about alfalfa growing only on land that had successfully produced alfalfa before. Nitrogen-fixing bacteria—that was the key. As an experiment he imported a large bag of soil from an alfalfa field in Wyoming. The result, if it did not amaze him, certainly startled his neighbors. For the following year a field on his farm, that till then had only produced a sickly, spindly yield, when innoculated with the soil from Wyoming, produced a rich and bountiful crop of alfalfa.

Until this time Card had been having his doubts about farming in Southern Alberta, even with irrigation, for it was a well-known fact that successful farming required the nitrogen-fixing ability of a crop such as alfalfa. The Mormon leader had been thinking seriously of taking his people back to Utah but, thanks to Fairfield, there was no need for that. The Alberta Railway and Irrigation Company, who were busy extending irrigation ditches throughout the area, were so pleased with Fairfield's experiment that they started a demonstration farm to show the farmers how to farm successfully with irrigation and placed him in charge.

One of Fairfield's most visual experimental successes was with trees. When he found they would grow in profusion, he got farmers to plant windbreaks on their land. Until then the only trees from Lethbridge to Medicine Hat grew along river bottom land. Today every town and city in Southern Alberta has its tree-lined streets and tall windbreaks shelter almost every farmstead from horizon to horizon.

Another important discovery came at the Cheddarfield Illustration Station near Rocky Mountain House, which was then under his supervision. When he experimented with the grey wooded soil of the area and found they were sulphur deficient, he suggested that the farmers add this ingredient to their land; in doing so, they upped their crop yield as much as two-fold.

Dr. Fairfield was always a community leader as well as a leader in the agricultural field. During his illustrious career he was a member of the Lethbridge Exhibition Board. He served on the Committee of the Lethbridge Irrigation District, was honorary president of the Alberta Sugar Beet Growers, president of the Southern Alberta Sheep Growers Association and was a life member of the Lethbridge Chamber of Commerce. He retired with many honors in 1945 and passed away quietly at his Lethbridge home in March of 1961.

He was truly one of Alberta's great pioneers. ●

Although no longer "spring chickens," Will and Ellen Fryer joined the great exodus to the Canadian prairies. Despite their advanced years, they made a valiant attempt to wrest a living from the soil. But Grandpa Fryer had to admit that he was a better blacksmith than farmer.

HOMESTEADING IN ALBERTA

WHEN Will and Ellen Fryer, my Grandmother and Grandfather, came to Alberta in 1908, they were making a distinct break with their past for the second time in their lives. In 1880, Grandpa, a blacksmith by trade, and Grandma, a trained practical nurse and mid-wife, left their native England for Detroit, Michigan, where riches were supposed to abound. There they raised their family, two sons, as well as burying four other sons who died of ailments that probably would not be considered extremely serious in this modern age of 'miracle drugs.'

It is not likely that they would ever have considered leaving Detroit, for they had a good home, many friends and were reasonably well off. However, Grandpa was losing his health due to the smoke and noise in the foundry where he worked and Grandma had to battle her asthma each summer when the ragweed prevalent in the area began spewing its deadly pollen into the atmosphere. Since their two sons were fully grown and neither wanted to leave Detroit at the time, Grandpa

and Grandma left them behind. (Son John, my Dad, did follow them out later after homesteading in Montana, coming north in 1919 with Mother and two children, to take up land one-half mile to the west of Grandpa and Grandma's.) Moving away meant leaving family and friends and was not a decision lightly taken, but Grandpa and Grandma realized their health had to be their primary consideration. There was no ragweed in the Canadian West according to the brochure put out by the Canadian government. As for smoke and noise, the brochure said, rather poetically: "...the air is fresh and clear...the only sounds in summer are those of birds singing, cattle lowing, bees humming...."

Not being "spring chickens" anymore, they thought a few precautions were necessary. Therefore Grandma stayed in Detroit settling the estate while Grandpa went out to Edmonton looking for land. Strangely enough, even in 1908 homesteads were not as plentiful as Grandpa had been led to believe—at least not within a 50-mile radius of the city. However, he finally chose his homestead six-

and a half miles south of the hamlet of Carvel. Why he chose that quarter is speculative, but I always thought it was because he imagined there were more acres crammed into a quarter well contoured with hills than on a level one. To him the hilltops with their scanty vegetation made for easy clearing and breaking. Moreover, he wanted and got a place with lots of pot-holes to ensure the many cattle he hoped to raise always had plenty of water to drink. His hill and pot-hole paradise was located some 40 miles southwest of Edmonton.

Once Grandpa had made his choice of land, his next move was to locate some form of power— something to pull the wagon, plow and other farm implements purchased from a used machinery dealer. As the animals were to be the first he ever owned, he chose them with great care and deliberation. None of those flighty high-stepping, half-broken mustangs for him. He wanted something of

a more utilitarian nature. A very astute horsetrader had just the thing—at least he convinced Grandpa they were. They turned out to be two not-too-well-broken, very slow and decidedly ornery oxen. The dealer had probably been waiting for quite a time to find someone to take them off his hands as, even in 1908, oxen were fast being replaced by horses.

Anyway, with his oxen, his machinery and the deed to his homestead he set out to prepare his estate so that Grandma could join him before the ragweed season hit Detroit. He had a house to build, some feed to put up for his chargers and, if all went well, a little land to prepare for next spring's seeding.

He chose the highest hill on his land for his homesite. From there, like a king, he would be able to scan his whole domain. Besides, there were plenty of poplar trees nearby from which he could get logs for his cabin. But if Grandpa was a fine blacksmith, having spent his whole life at that trade, a carpenter he was not. The logs he chose were selected more for their proximity to the building site than for their straightness and matching dimensions. Consequently, the finished product was something less than symmetrical. Nevertheless, with a good amount of clay mixed with straw, he was able to plaster the cracks and make a reasonably weather-proof home. For a roof he hauled lumber from Stony Plain, which was then the end of steel of the

(Left) Building a sod house.
(Below) A sod house on the Prairies.

Homesteading on the Alberta frontier. Here, the author's grandparents Will and Ellen Fryer pose with their cantankerous team of oxen.

CNR. It was a two-day journey by oxen. Windows and doors from the same lumberyard completed the house.

Grandma was not very impressed with Grandpa's efforts when she arrived later that year. The log house still had no floor and she had some reservations about the length of her stay. She was even less enthusiastic about the large number of cattle that roamed unhindered over the unfenced landscape. And when she met a band of nomadic Indians while returning from a visit to the nearest neighbor who lived a mile away, visions of massacres and scalpings of the old Wild West flashed through her mind. To her great surprise and relief, the leader of the group, a tall, distinguished-looking fellow, rode up and said in near-perfect English, "Welcome to the West, Missus. Don't worry about my boys; they are just showing off a bit." They were indeed showing off, rearing their horses and dashing them up and down the trail, putting on a hard-riding show the like of which Grandma had never seen before.

With his cabin finished and Grandma there to do the cooking, Grandpa set about breaking some of his treeless hilltops. His skill in handling the oxen, however, was something less than proficient. Their ideas seldom coincided with Grandpa's. He never did learn to steer them where he wanted to go and the stubborn creatures liked lunch breaks far better than work. Grandma in later years used to get tears in her eyes as, laughing, she told us grandchildren how the oxen used to take plow, Grandpa and all into a nearby lake whenever the flies were bothering them or whenever they thought it was time for a drink. However, for a man unaccustomed as he was to farming, he managed to get a fair amount of work done that summer. Besides breaking a few acres, he put up hay enough for his animals, built a barn for them, purchased a cow, a couple of pigs and a few chickens, all of which he housed with the oxen.

During their first winter, the newly-built house kept the two pioneers warm, thanks to an ample nearby wood supply. But the following spring, when the frost came out of the ground, their home was on the move. High winds aided by the steep hill did

nothing to help the matter. When the house had slid almost five feet from its original location, Grandma had had enough. "I'm going back to Detroit," she told Grandpa. "While I'm selling the house there, perhaps you can anchor this place down a bit. I'm just not ready for this mobile living, Will!"

So Will put Ellen on the train for Detroit. He then disked and seeded his hilltop acres. Next, with the help of a neighbor, he tore down his unstable cabin and moved it to a new location near the wagon trail that zigzagged passed his homestead. Here it was sheltered by a heavy stand of poplar. If the logs were ill-fitting the first time they were assembled, on their second meeting they were even more mismatched. However, as before, with plenty of clay plaster and a few coats of whitewash, the walls were up to stay. This time Grandpa added a floor. The house, in fact, stood for over 60 years until some bird-brained vandal burned it down a couple of years ago and wiped out one of the district's few remaining landmarks.

It did not take Grandpa long to learn that he had made the big change in life too late to ever become a proficient farmer. But he never quit trying. Word soon spread that Grandma was a trained nurse and mid-wife and she soon had all the work she could handle. Between her and her good friend Rachel Deans, a registered nurse and zealous missionary worker, they helped bring most of the babies in the district into the world from about 1910 until well into the 1930s.

Grandpa, being a top-notch blacksmith, built a little shop on his farm, made his own tools and probably made as much from his trade as he did from farming. When the High Level Bridge was built in Edmonton in 1912, he rented out the farm to a neighbor and went working on the bridge instead. When the neighbor produced more grain from the farm than he ever had, Grandpa undoubtedly realized that he would always be a better blacksmith than farmer.

But he gave it his best effort, graduating to horses and then to a Fordson tractor as his means of power. If he had dreams of a big, mechanized farm, it never came to pass. He was 67 when, one hot summer day in 1927, he told Grandma he was not feeling very well and thought he would lie down. He was dead within a week. Complications of diabetes he never knew he had, the doctor claimed. Grandma was 83 when she passed away in 1945.

Since none of the grandchildren seemed cut out for farming, the homestead was later sold to a neighbor. It is now part of a highly mechanized farm, probably the kind that Grandpa had envisioned. A fine gravel road now passes by the farm. Though everyone in the area met hardship, especially during the Dirty Thirties, prosperity in the district is now more the rule than the exception.

I think if my grandparents could see that district now, they would both be very pleased. ●

(Far left) Peter Vasilievitch Verigin, the lordly spiritual leader of the Doukobors in Canada until 1924.
(Left) Anastasia Fedorouna Holooboff, more commonly known as Anastasia Lords. Spiritual leader of the Lordly Christian Community of Universal Brotherhood from 1924 until her death in 1965, she is buried in the cemetery of the village she founded two miles from Shouldice, Alberta, in 1926.
(Below) A black and white reproduction of a full-color painting depicting the "Burning of the Guns," by artist Terry McLean.

Fleeing from persecution in their native Russia, the Doukhobors settled in Alberta shortly after the turn of the century. But instead of peace and prosperity they encountered, in varying degrees, much of the persecution they had hoped to escape upon leaving Russia.

SPIRIT WRESTLERS

ALBERTA'S DOUKHOBORS

THERE is an Alberta Historic Sites sign erected on Highway 3 west of Cowley that honors the Doukhobors of Alberta. The sign is entitled "Toil And Peaceful Life," which is an apt description of the 3,000 or so Doukhobors who claim Alberta as their home. Had things turned out as originally planned, the Doukhobor population of Alberta could quite conceivably number closer to 20,000. For the entire group of 7,500 that emigrated from the Caucausus in Russia was originally scheduled to settle in the Beaverhill Lake area, some 40 miles east of Edmonton in what was then the North-West Territories.

But the year was 1898 and Frank Oliver, owner, editor and publisher of the Edmonton *Bulletin*, was also the Member of Parliament for the district. He was a strong advocate of opening and settling the West, but his concept of a good settler was one of British stock. He strongly opposed the coming of what he called "inferior" Doukhobors to the area. Consequently, although a two-man Doukhobor delegation had reconnoitered the Beaverhill Lake district and found it suitable for their needs, when the delegates returned to Ottawa to finalize the move, they were informed that there had been a change in plans and that their people were not wanted in Alberta. Instead they were allowed to choose land at Verigin, near Kamsack, and at Blaine Lake, some 50 miles north of Saskatoon, Saskatchewan.

According to Michael M. Verigin of Cowley, who acts as secretary for the United Doukhobors of Alberta (Cowley-Lundbreck), nearly 7,500 Doukhobors arrived at Halifax in January, 1899, and settled in Saskatchewan. It took another 16 years before the first Doukhobors settled in Alberta. They made their home in the Cowley-Lundbreck area in the southwest corner of the province. In the meantime they had encountered, in varying degrees, some of the persecution they had hoped to escape upon leaving Russia.

For people who, in the main, wanted only to live a peaceful communal life and worship God in the way they think is right, they have had a very turbulent existence. In their native Russia, according to Miss Liuba Verigin, daughter of Michael Verigin, in a term paper she wrote while attending Selkirk College in Castlegar, British Columbia, her people were given the name "Doukhobors" or "Spirit Wrestlers" around 1785 by Archbishop Ambrose of the Russian Orthodox Church. Wrote Miss Verigin: "The church was implying that the Doukhobors were wrestling against the Spirit of God. The Doukhobors accepted this name because they did fight, not against, but for and with the Spirit. Earlier they had been called 'Ikon-bortse' (icon wrestlers), for they went against the Russian Orthodox Church by their refusal to worship icons. Instead of bowing to church icons, the Doukhobors bow to each other, recognizing the Spirit of God which dwells in the human body."

Miss Verigin states that a sectarian movement developed in Russia around 300 years ago, which immediately came into conflict with the Russian Orthodox Church and the state. Their philosophy of communal living and vegetarianism could quite possibly have been overlooked by church and state, but when the Doukhobors professed, on Easter Sunday, 1895, that they were also pacifists, they were treading on Tzarist toes and their freedom was at best tenuous from that point on.

Said John J. Verigin, Honorary Chairman of the Union of Spiritual Communities of Christ (Orthodox Doukhobors), great-grandson of Peter the Lordly Verigin, in a speech given in Toronto in February, 1963: "They gave up the consumption of animal flesh as food, for they believed that the killing of animals brutalized the human sensibilities. They also gave up alcohol and tobacco for these are harmful to the body. They made a decisive stand against militarism and all forms of violence. In the summer of 1895 — June 29— they burned all the arms they had acquired (for bearing arms was) against their faith."

Persecution of the Doukhobors had been practised in Russia as early as the late 1600s, so when the opportunity came to emigrate to Canada they accepted it. Both Leo Tolstoy, the great Russian writer, and Elmer Maude of the Society of Friends (Quakers) in England, helped influence the Tzarist government to let them go, when, 7,500-strong, the Doukhobors arrived in Canada in January of 1899. Up until that time they were the largest aggregation of people to arrive as a group on Canadian shores. Land awaited them in Saskatchewan.

Theoretically, with Canada's supposed religious tolerance, and because the Canadian government had promised them military exemption, the Doukhobors should have been able to settle peace-

ably, develop their farming communes and live happily ever after. But it was not to be. In 1907 their old nemesis, the Honorable Frank Oliver, who had by then risen to Minister of the Interior in the Laurier cabinet, again made his opposition felt. He had been against the Doukhobors coming in the first place and now, in order to shoo them back to Russia or to any country other than Canada, he clamored for an act that would force them to swear allegiance to the Crown in order to gain title to their homesteads. Says Michael Verigin: "This the Doukhobors refused to do, saying it was against their faith, of which the government was aware, and they lost their lands.

"To avoid the oath of allegiance, the Doukhobours bought land in British Columbia from private owners and moved to that province, leaving only a small group at Verigin. In B.C. they settled at Brilliant and Grand Forks in the West Kootenays." They made the big move in 1908.

During that time Peter The Lordly Verigin was the leader of the Doukhobors who then called themselves the Christian Community of Universal Brotherhood. He travelled back and forth between British Columbia and Saskatchewan communities, acting as both administrator and spiritual leader. It was not until three years later that the first Doukhobors arrived in Alberta— not to stay but to plow land with oxen in 1911 for the Canadian Wheat Lands Limited in the Suffield area, and, in 1912, to help build the McGregor Dam near Brooks.

"During their history," Michael Verigin says, "the Doukhobors were always farmers and were so in Saskatchewan. But in B.C. they were forced to become fruit growers and loggers. For their logging operations they needed horses, and being vegetarians, a diet consisting of fruit, vegetables and dishes made from flour. Consequently, it was necessary to import, that is, have flour and horses shipped in from Verigin, a distance of around 1,000 miles."

In order to cut down on the long haul, Peter The Lordly Verigin, spiritual leader of the Communal Doukhobors, decided to look for land closer to the British Columbia communities and in 1915 bought land near Lundbreck, Alberta. States Michael Verigin, "Peter Verigin then asked my grandfather, Semeon Ivanovitch Verigin, to pick the men that he would need to colonize the land in Alberta."

Semeon Ivanovitch, who was at that time living in Brilliant, British Columbia, gathered his group together and moved to Alberta to settle nine miles north of Lundbreck. In her term paper Liuba Verigin wrote: "He took with him a blacksmith, steam engineers, carpenters and other workmen to start a colony in the area." Thus began the first Doukhobor commune or village in Alberta. It comprised about 50 people and was named "Bogatoi Rodnik," which translates to "Rich Spring" in English.

"In 1916 and 1917," said Michael Verigin, "we bought more land around Cowley and soon had over 12,000 acres." In rapid succession his people erected several more communal villages to accomodate the 300 people who arrived from British Columbia by 1917 and built a grain elevator at Cowley and an elevator and large flour mill at Lundbreck. At the same time the sturdy Doukhobor farmers were raising horses and grain on their land and shipping the surplus to their brethren in British Columbia in exchange for fruit and lumber.

For the next seven years Peter The Lordly visited the Alberta communes at regular intervals and directed operations personally while there. His office was a house built for him at Cowley which also served as his home during his stays in Alberta. Each commune elected its own leader to direct work while he was away, counselling his other Doukhobor settlements in British Columbia and Saskatchewan. In their first years in Alberta the Doukhobors bought a store building in Cowley and turned it into a prayer home for the area. During this period in Alberta at least, the Doukhobors were living the kind of life they had always hoped for. But dark clouds loomed on the horizon.

Ever since their arrival in Canada the Christian Community of Universal Brotherhood had been well aware that many of their English-speaking neighbors resented their coming; they did not understand the Doukhobor language nor their way of life. And because of lack of understanding, they saw the Doukhobors as a threat to their own way of life. Cries of, "They will buy up all the good land; they will not fight for their country; they won't vote or take part in community activities; they will or won't do this, that or the other thing," were as familiar to the Doukhobors then as they are today to another communal group, the Hutterites. Some farmers fear that the Hutterites will eventually take over most of the good farming land, forcing their neighbors from their lands. The fact that the Hutterites own perhaps two percent of the farm land seems not to matter. Like the Doukhobors, the Hutterites come from peasant stock, farmers for countless generations, and are therefore good at what they do. Perhaps it is their proficiency in farming that breeds jealousy in the hearts of some of their less efficient farming neighbors.

Whether it was a plot by persons wishing to harm the whole Doukhobor movement or some maniacal person with a strong grudge, working on his own, may never be known, but, on October 29, 1924, someone planted a time bomb on the train on which Peter The Lordly Verigin was riding. As the train approached Grand Forks late at night, his coach was torn asunder by a terrific dynamite blast that killed nine other persons besides the Doukhobor leader. The saddened Doukhobors returned the shattered body of Peter The Lordly to his home at Brilliant then, with some 7,000 weeping mourners in

(Top) Miss Anastasia Lords with village children before the newly-built prayer house in 1929.
A group of Doukhobor men and women from the village of Bogatoi Rodnik.

attendance, laid their leader to rest on a hill overlooking the village. His nephew, Larion Verigin, gave the following eulogy:

"Peter The Lordly was born in the Holy Spirit and descended to us as Christ-Saviour from the Heavenly Father for the salvation of our souls. He possessed in the beginning of his life as lamb of God, meekness and kindness. He relied during his life upon the will of the Almighty Father. The Heavenly Father has always been with him. He never feared any enemies...and was calling his people to peaceful life and brotherhood, as children of one father —God...

"The spirit of courage has outlived all misfortunes ...and as great shepherd he has not left us. He came to us in the year of 1902 and opened to us his superior holy mind, which assembled us and our descendents into the Christian Community of Universal Brotherhood life. Blessed be his name forever. He stretched a brotherly hand to us in Christ's name so as to establish God's kingdom on the earth for the salvation of our souls.

"God rest our dear benefactor's soul, Peter Lordly. Let our faith multiply in his holy mission and let there be peace on earth and good will towards men...

"Glory to God!"

With that the Doukhobors buried their leader and sent word to his son, Peter Petrovitch Verigin, who was living in Russia, to come to Canada and take over as leader.

Although the Alberta Doukhobors accepted their new leader, Miss Anastasia Holoboff of Brilliant, known as Anastasia Lords, did not. Anastasia, whom Michael Verigin describes as "a very dedicated person and a close companion of the late leader," believed that she had been tutored for the position of Spiritual Leader. Consequently, she broke away from the main body and in 1926 brought a group of some 26 families to Shouldice, Alberta, to start a new commune. This she named "The Lordly Christian Commune of Universal Brotherhood," independent from all other groups of Doukhobors, including those in Alberta. Wrote Liuba Verigin of that move:

"The group established itself east of Arrowwood, near Shouldice, where they erected a large prayer home and houses which were built in like pattern. The ruins of those buildings can be seen to this day. The community eventually grew to 165 people."

Anastasia's colony considerably increased the communal Doukhobor movement in Alberta for a time, but it was not long before a shortage of land, crop failures and various other factors caused members to drift away to find work elsewhere. By 1942 the colony had ceased to exist, although Anastasia and a few of her followers remained at Shouldice until she passed away in November of 1965. Anastasia Lords is buried in the village cemetery at Shouldice where, for many years a nearby railway siding and water tank bore the name 'Anastasia' in her honor.

What drought and shortage of land did to break up Anastasia's communal group, the Great Depression and a number of trust companies succeeded in doing to the rest of the Alberta Doukhobor communals. The part played by the trust companies is still a sore point with the Doukhobors, as Michael Verigin explains:

"The hard times during the Depression also affected the Doukhobor Communes and in 1937, when the Christian Community of Universal Brotherhood in the three provinces had only a remaining debt of money borrowed equalling four percent of the total value of community property, or $319,276.00, the Sun Life Assurance Company and National Trust Company began foreclosure proceedings and in 1938 the Christian Community of Universal Brotherhood Ltd. came to an end in B.C., Saskatchewan, and here in Alberta, too. In 1939 we here in Alberta were offered our land back to be farmed privately, and about 200 Doukhobors accepted the offer, but close to 100 moved away to B.C. Those of us who stayed, farmed out land on a crop-share basis, making payments to the National Trust Company for 10 years until the loan was paid off."

Although two-thirds of the Doukhobors stayed and paid off their farms, the trust company foreclosures effectively finished their communal movement.

"Today very few Doukhobors remain as farmers in the Cowley-Lundbreck and Shouldice districts," Michael Verigin states. The younger generation has left for the cities where they have become teachers, lawyers, doctors, nurses and joined the ranks of the work-a-day world. The elders have either passed away or moved into retirement in B.C., the Crowsnest Pass and Calgary. We who remain here still gather for worship at our prayer homes in Lundbreck, where our cemetery is also located. We are registered as the United Doukhobors of Alberta, Cowley-Lundbreck, the cemetery at Shouldice as the Lordly Christian Community of Universal Brotherhood, and a prayer home nearby at Mossleigh as the Doukhobors of Mossleigh and District."

Wrote Liuba Verigin: "The Doukhobors centers for worship are simple structures called 'Prayer Homes.' When the brethren gather for 'sobrania' (worship), the first act upon crossing the threshold is to give the ritual greeting: 'Glory to God.' The brethren seated in parallel rows respond: '(We) Praise and thank God for his Grace.' Again a greeting is given: 'Christ is Risen!' and the response is: 'In the righteous Christ is Risen!'

"At the head of the parallel rows of brethren... is a small table with a crocheted cloth. Both are made in the community and serve as a place to set the symbols of the Doukhobor faith: bread, salt and water.

"These elements have a rich symbolic meaning in the history of the religion. Bread, salt and water are the primary symbols of the faith. They represent life, hospitality and love to all mankind."

Today one wonders if early government officials who saw something sinister in the Doukhobor movement would have felt the same way had they taken time to learn what the movement was really about. In a small way the present Alberta government has made amends for some of the wrongs done to the Doukhobors by earlier regimes by erecting a Historical Sites sign at Cowley honoring these people. That sign is appreciated, for as Michael Verigin states:

"We are thankful and grateful to the Alberta government for honoring the Doukhobor people in Canada with such a sign." Hopefully this story, too, will help to give a better understanding of Alberta's Doukhobors who, on the whole, are a fine and decent people who want only to live, work and worship in peace. ●

DEAD MAN AT THE PUMP

"Oh, that poor stiff," said one of the lumberjacks, "he got himself killed this morning. We were taking him to the coroner. . . ." But the lumberjacks had not counted on their friend's return from the dead!

IF yesterday's criterion of death were still being used, many persons living and enjoying good health today might long since have been relegated to their final resting place. How many are there among us who have not heard of at least one person who was presumed dead—through drowning, asphyxiation, or from any of a variety of sicknesses or accidents—only to be revived through the miracle of modern medical science?

Not many years ago if a doctor could find no pulse or evidence of respiration, that was it—he would immediately pronounce death. Nowadays if he or she were to pronounce death on these criteria, he might conceivably find himself charged with criminal negligence or, at the very least, called before a board of his peers and severely reprimanded.

Death need not necessarily follow because breathing had ceased or even if the heart has stopped. Many a fireman or first-aider can attest to having revived victims of various accidents whose pulse and breathing were absent, simply by the prompt and vigorous application of the proper first-aid measures.

But even without the help of prompt first-aid or the intervention of contemporary medical science, there have been numerous examples of seemingly miraculous and spontaneous revivals from death. Many, if not most of us, have heard of at least one of these incidents. I doubt, however, if anyone has heard of a stranger case than that of "the dead man at the pump." This was the case of a lumberjack who was presumed dead—for over 12 hours—only to revive miraculously and recuperate fully in spite of severe frostbite and terrible injuries inflicted by a falling tree.

I first heard this story as a boy and had it further verified later when I ran across an article by William Spindler while browsing through a September, 1945, issue of the long-defunct *Alberta Folklore Quarterly*.

A few years before the First World War Spindler was hauling freight for a lumberman whose mill was located some 70 miles southwest of Edmonton. One cold winter night, half-frozen and his horses exhausted from pulling a heavy load all day over powder-dry snow, he pulled into a stopping place about halfway between the mill and Edmonton. He unhitched his team and was preparing them for the night when he thought he heard the pump handle rattle in the stable yard. Thinking it must be another freighter pulling in, he fed and bedded down his horses, then stopped by the pump to see who was there.

Even before his lantern illuminated the pump, Mr. Spindler heard what sounded like moaning. As he moved closer the lantern glow revealed the source of the moaning. With one hand on the pump handle and barely able to stand was a man whose head and upper torso were encased in a mass of frozen and clotted blood. One arm dangled uselessly by his side and further examination revealed that both of his feet were frozen. Spindler grabbed the injured man just as he began to collapse.

When a shout failed to bring anyone from the house, Spindler rolled the badly injured man into a blanket, then ran for help. Besides the stopping house owner, his wife and grown son, two men sat at the large kitchen table. "Who is that man outside?" Spindler shouted.

"Oh, that poor stiff," answered one of the men, "he got himself killed this morning. Tree fell on him. We was taking him to the coroner in Edmonton."

The two men, both lumberjacks, refused to believe their compatriot was still alive. Uneducated and superstitious, they were afraid to go near the injured man. Finally, however, Spindler persuaded them to help him bring the poor fellow into the house, where he was washed and bandaged and given a few drops of hot broth.

Their belated attentions helped, for the man not only survived the 25-mile sleigh ride to Stony Plain, where Dr. Oatway looked him over, he also survived the additional 20-mile ride into Edmonton, where he spent several months in the hospital.

A few years later Spindler again met the fellow, who was then operating a streetcar on the newly-built Edmonton Street Railway. The former lumberjack, whose name he never did learn, recognized Spindler and pulled off his cap to reveal a large white scar on his head. The hospital had obviously done a good job of patching up his mangled head, broken arm and frozen feet.

Too good, perhaps, as, although Spindler had no concrete proof, he believed that the "dead man at the pump" went overseas with the Canadian Army during the First World War and is one of those to whom we pay homage on November 11. ●

Jerry Potts, The "dead shot and plainsman without parallel."

JERRY POTTS

FRONTIER SCOUT

Jerry Potts has been termed Canada's own Davy Crockett. Although a considerably homelier version that the legendary American folk-hero, Potts established himself as an indispensable guide to the North West Mounted Police.

IN every era and in every area there is generally one man who stands out like a beacon among his contemporaries. One such person was Jerry Potts, who proved an invaluable guide and interpreter to the North West Mounted Police when they arrived in what is now southern Alberta over 100 years ago. Old Jerry, as he became affectionately known, has often been mentioned as Canada's counterpart of that famous American frontiersman, Davy Crockett. Though Potts was no match for Crockett in looks, physique or oratory, the comparison is not that exaggerated. Jerry was a small man, slim, a bit stoop-shouldered, bowlegged and rather homely to boot. Moreover, he never used two words when a grunt would suffice. But his fighting prowess certainly matched Crockett's, and in his uncanny ability to find his way over trackless plains, Old Jerry was a man unsurpassed.

That famous North West Mounted Policeman, Colonel Sam Steele, in his book, *My Forty Years In Canada*, summarized Potts' amazing sense of direction when he wrote: "He was the man who trained the best scouts in the force, and in the early days when the prairie was a trackless waste, there were very few expeditions of importance that were not guided by him or the men he taught the craft of the plains. As a scout and a guide I have never met his equal; he had none in either the North West or in the States to the south. Many such men have been described in story and their feats related around a campfire, but none whom I have known or of whom I have read equalled him. In the heat of summer, or in the depth of winter, in rain or in shine, with him as

Peigan half-breed Jerry Potts, centre, participated in the battle against the Crees. It was Potts who noticed the enemy attempting to withdraw. At his signal, the Peigans and Blackfoot warriors charged on horseback, forcing the Crees into the river. As many as 300 of their number are thought to have fallen in the last great Indian battle of the plains.

guide one was certain to arrive at his destination. It did not matter whether he had been over the country before—it was all the same to Jerry Potts—although he never looked at a map or compass."

As often happened with colorful men during the frontier era, a host of myths arose around Jerry Potts, especially about his early life. But thanks to years of research by historian Hugh A. Dempsey of the Glenbow-Alberta Institute in Calgary, many of them have been cleared up. Although the fiction perpetrated by early writers made for exciting reading, the facts dug up by Dempsey's dogged work prove that Potts' life was colorful and eventful enough without embellishment.

He was born at Fort McKenzie in Montana about 1840, the only son of Andrew Potts, a Scotsman employed by the American Fur Trade Company, and Namo-Pisi, an Indian woman from the Black Elk band of the Blood tribe. Jerry apparently never got to know his father, for while he was still very young, one of his father's employees, a French Canadian named Mercereau, threw a trouble-making Peigan brave named Ah-Pah, or One White Eye, out of the trading post. That night Ah-Pah returned to the post seeking revenge. Assuming that Mercereau was still on duty, Ah-Pah knocked loudly on the window of the closed gate. When it was opened, he shoved the muzzle of his rifle through and fired. But instead of Mercereau, he killed Andrew Potts.

Mr. Potts had always been kind and fair to the Peigans and they were enraged at the senseless killing. They promptly avenged the death of their friend by executing Ah-Pah, but young Jerry was left without a father.

Jerry spent the next five years of his life as the adopted son of Alexander Harvey, one of the most notorious characters ever to frequent the upper reaches of the Missouri River. Harvey's motto was "Never forgive or forget." Around 1843 he sought revenge on a band of Blackfoot warriors by firing a cannon into their midst. His reason? An unknown person—perhaps a Blackfoot, but perhaps not—had murdered a Negro employee of his. Harvey reckoned that the 13 Indians he killed would just about make up for the loss of his helper.

Fortunately for Jerry, his adopted father was later run out of the country by irate citizens, who could no longer stomach his excesses. Then Andrew Dawson, a kindly Scotsman known as the "last king of the Missouri River," took the boy into custody. Under his new father's tutelage, Jerry was well prepared for life on the frontier. Dawson not only taught Jerry to speak English and five Indian dialects, but also briefed him in the intricacies of the fur trade and taught him how to get along in both white and Indian societies. Somewhere along the way, Jerry acquired a taste for liquor and for fighting. The former undoubtedly shortened his life, but the latter made it possible for him to survive as long as he did.

A prime example of his fighting ability occurred when he was about 20 and camped with a band of Blood and Peigan Indians in Montana. One day he set out alone to hunt buffalo. He was riding along Shonkin Creek after crossing the Missouri River when suddenly he found himself surrounded by seven warriors from the Crow tribe. Four carried rifles, while the other three were armed with bows and arrows. Feigning friendship, the Crows used sign language to invite Potts to come with them to visit their chief, who was camped a few miles away. Being outnumbered, there seemed little Jerry could do but tag along.

Luckily, one of the dialects he had learned from his father was Crow. Since his companions did not know this, they spoke freely of how they planned to dispatch their young guest at the first opportunity. Alerted, Potts unobtrusively dropped behind, and the second he heard the click of a rifle being cocked, he sprang from his horse and opened fire. The four Crow riflemen were taken completely by surprise and missed with their first shot. Before they could reload their clumsy muzzle loaders, they were dropped from their ponies by a deadly hail from Potts' six-shooter. Scared witless, the three bowmen took off for home at full gallop.

Later that day Potts gathered a large party of his Blood and Peigan friends and that night raided the Crow camp to teach them a lesson they would never forget. When the battle ended, dozens of Crow warriors lay dead and the rest of the tribe was fleeing in terror.

Then there was the time when Jerry was leading George Steele, who later became Indian agent for the Blackfoot tribe in Montana, and a companion on a prospecting trip. Suddenly a war party of nearly 200 Sioux came whooping out of a coulee. Potts and his companions fled as fast as their ponies could carry them, but the Sioux had superior horses and were rapidly gaining ground. Ever inventive, Potts saw the need of new strategy. At his command the three men whirled their horses and headed back toward the Sioux. The Sioux were so surprised by this turn of events that the tactic worked. Before the Indians could react, the trio had passed through their ranks and barricaded themselves in a log cabin a mile or so along the coulee from which the Sioux had emerged. When the Indians attacked, Potts had his two companions load the rifles and handguns, while he lay down such a barrage that the Sioux soon had to retreat after leaving a dozen of their men behind, wounded or dead. Unfortunately, during the fight the trio's horses high-tailed it for quieter grounds.

Potts knew from experience that after nightfall the Sioux would attack and try to burn them out. He waited till dusk, then wrapped himself in a blanket like an Indian brave, made a broad circle, and casually strolled into the Sioux camp from the rear. Then, without the Indians realizing what was happening, he stole three of their best horses and led them back to the cabin. As he and his two companions vanished safely into the night, Potts couldn't resist the opportunity of letting go with a wild war-whoop of defiance.

Stories like these get around and Potts soon earned the reputation of a man not to be trifled with. His reputation was further enhanced in the 1860s by his capers with a longtime friend, George Star. When Potts and Star had a few drinks they delighted in showing off by trimming each other's moustaches at long range with their six-shooters. Time after time Star and Potts survived this questionable sport with scarcely a trickle of blood, bringing their superstitious Blackfoot friends to the belief that both surely must have supernatural powers.

Chance involved Potts in the last big battle between Indian tribes held on Canadian soil. In 1870 Jerry and George Star were employed as buffalo hunters at Fort Whoop-Up (south of modern Lethbridge at the confluence of the St. Mary's and Oldman Rivers) when a group of some 800 Crees and Assiniboines led by Chiefs Piapot, Little Pine, Big Bear and Little Mountain decided to take advantage of a smallpox epidemic that had decimated their traditional enemies, the Blackfoot, Blood and Peigan tribes, by raiding their land. The Cree-Assiniboine alliance struck at night on October 24 and killed some women and children, as well as the brother of Chief Red Crow of the Bloods. Two bands of Bloods put up a stubborn resistance and sent for help to a large group of Peigans who were camped to the south. When the Peigans got word of the fight they formed a war party of nearly 200. Armed with new repeating rifles, they headed for the battle scene, picking up Potts and Star on the way.

Potts was elected leader. After some preliminary manoeuvres, he hit the Crees and Assiniboines in a frontal attack that took them by surprise and drove them back across the Oldman River (then known as the Belly) where the city of Lethbridge now stands. Nearly 300 Crees and Assiniboines died that day while Blood and Peigan losses were less than 50. It was a complete victory for the Bloods and Peigans and Jerry Potts was proclaimed their hero. He had not escaped completely unscathed, however. A Cree musket fired at point-blank range had knocked him flat and left a powder burn on his left ear. But the fact that he never got more seriously hurt made the already awed Indians more certain than ever that he must be some kind of god.

Jerry Potts never did things by halves—not even when it came to marriage. When his first wife, Mary, a Crow Indian, left him to return to her people, he married two sisters, Panther Woman and Spotted Killer, daughters of Peigan Chief Sitting-In-The-Middle. When the two sisters died during the 1869-70 smallpox epidemic, he married another Crow woman with the unlikely name of Long Time Lying Down. Though most of his many children died at an early age, at least two sons survived, Joe and Charlie. Their descendants in southern Alberta and Montana carry on the proud blood lines of the formidable little frontiersman.

The deaths of his father, wives and children were only part of the tragic events that haunted Potts throughout most of his life. In 1872 he learned that his half-brother, No Chief, and his mother had been killed by a whisky-crazed group of the Many Children band of the Bloods. Jerry was working as a horse wrangler at Fort Kipp north of modern Lethbridge when he got the news. Not the type to forgive and forget, he inquired around until he found out who had killed his mother. Two months later, when the Many Children band were camped near Fort Kipp, he followed the killer, ironically known as Good Young Man, when he and a brave named Morning Writing left camp on a hunting trip. Potts overtook the two and fatally shot Good Young Man when he tried to escape. Morning Writing put up no resistance and Jerry let him go unharmed.

With his mother's death avenged, but sickened by the way whisky traders were debauching the Plains Indians with their rot-gut booze, Potts quit his job and returned to Montana. It was two years before he returned to Canada, this time in the employ of the North West Mounted Police.

It was a lucky day for the red-coated policemen to find Jerry Potts when they came west in 1874. They were heading for the most notorious of the southern

William B. Pocklington, Blood Indian agent, with Indian chiefs, 1886. L-R: Standing—One Spot, (minor chief, Bloods); Red Crow, (head chief of Bloods); Dave Mills, (half Negro interpreter); E.R. Cowan. Seated—Willaim B. Pocklington.

Alberta whisky forts, Whoop-Up, but when they reached the Sweetgrass Hills on the Alberta-Montana border, they were lost. Fortunately, Colonel George French and his second-in-command, Major (later Colonel) James F. Macleod, decided to take a jaunt down to Fort Benton, Montana for supplies. There they were persuaded to hire Jerry Potts, who not only led them to their destination, but remained with the force until his death in 1896.

"He won the confidence of all ranks the first day out," Sam Steele later wrote of the little scout. The second morning Jerry took his place at the head of the long column and at noon they found him dressing out a fat buffalo cow he had shot. Later that day he led the foot-sore Mounted Policemen to the clearest, sweetest, coldest water they had tasted since leaving Manitoba four months before. "To those new to such life, he appeared to know everything," Steele wrote.

The pony policemen soon learned that their new guide was a man of few words. Thinking they must be nearing their destination, Fort Whoop-Up, after four long days of marching from the Montana border, one of the officers asked: "What do you suppose is beyond that next hill, Jerry?"

"Nudder damn hill," was Potts' laconic reply.

Later, asked the probable reason for the bullet-riddled body of an Indian lying beside the trail, Jerry's answer was a simple, "Drunk." Sadly his explanation was all too correct. Before the scarlet-coated horsemen arrived in what is now southern Alberta, hundreds of Indians died in fights brought on by drinking the poisonous liquor sold them by unscrupulous whisky traders.

Modern Blackfoot spokesmen often claim that the Mounted Police missed the essence of old-time chieftains' speeches because of their laconic interpreter. True, Jerry Potts may have left out most of the flowery adjectives, but he did get down to the meat. Like the time in the early 1880s after most of the buffalo had vanished from the plains and a hungry band of Peigans came to NWMP headquarters at Fort Macleod. Their chief spent a good half hour explaining their needs. Potts boiled it down quickly. "Dey want grub," he told a startled Colonel Macleod.

Another time several prominent chiefs of the Blackfoot Confederacy (Bloods, Peigans and Blackfoot) rode into the fort. Each spent at least a quarter

(Top NWMP scouts at Macleod in the 1880s. Jerry Potts is second from left in back row.
(Bottom) In an earlier battle between the Blackfoot and the Cree, the heroic missionary Father Albert Lacombe had attempted to stop the fighting. Instead, he was hit by a Cree bullet. Long afterward, he recalled the frenzied sounds of Indian battle: "...The groans of the dying, the yelling of the warriors, the harangues of the chiefs, and the noise of dogs and horses, all mingled, formed a kind of hell."

hour telling Macleod how pleased they were that the Mounted Police had chased the whisky traders back to Montana. Potts summarized it in five words: "Dey damn glad you're here."

Early in 1875 Potts proved to his NWMP employers what an amazing scout they had acquired. In February he went with Captain L.M.F. Crozier and 10 men to track down some American whisky peddlers operating in the Bow River area, south of modern Calgary. The weather turned bitterly cold, but did not prevent Jerry from leading the Mounties to the whisky camp north of the Highwood River. There they arrested the traders, but not before a blizzard blew up and cut visibility to less than 50 yards and obliterated the trail.

"We couldn't be guided by the wind," said Sergeant W.D. Antrobus later, "because it didn't blow five minutes at a time from one direction." It didn't seem to bother Jerry Potts. Though visibility gradually diminished to 30 yards, he led the group unerringly to a sheltered spot on the Highwood River where they camped to wait out the storm."

In March of that same year he again demonstrated his uncanny ability to find his way regardless of weather conditions. This time he was guiding Colonel Macleod and three men to Helena, Montana, to pick up the payroll, when another visibility-obliterating blizzard struck. For two days the party waited out the storm in a sheltered coulee, but their food ran out and they either had to move or starve. It was all routine to Jerry. Though all but he lost their directions five minutes after breaking camp, he guided them unfalteringly to Rocky Springs, Montana, where there was both food and shelter. Only when they had thoroughly thawed themselves before a roaring campstove did Colonel Macleod learn that Potts had been snowblind throughout most of the journey.

Although he was an invaluable scout and intepreter, Potts was by no means the perfect employee. He loved to drink and it got him into trouble now and then. On one occasion he went with two constables to intercept two whisky traders who were reportedly bringing a load of booze from Fort Benton along the Whoop-Up Trail. As the peddlers crossed into Canada, Jerry and the two Mounties were there to greet them. They were arrested, handcuffed and placed in the back of the wagon with their booze. Potts then climbed into the wagon to drive the horses while the two Mounties rode on ahead. Trouble was, it was a long, slow trip and, halfway back to Fort Macleod, Jerry got thirsty. By the time he and the traders reached the fort, they had drunk all the evidence.

"On another occasion Potts had to be tied up until he slept off a particularly fiery drunk," Hugh A. Dempsey noted in his booklet, *Jerry Potts, Plainsman*, "and once he almost shot a member of the force whom he mistook for an old enemy. One policeman observed that Potts had 'an unquen-

chable thirst which a camel might have envied. He drank whiskey when he could get it. If he could not get it, he would take Jamaica ginger, or essence of lemon, or Perry Davis's Pain Killer, or even red ink'."

His virtues, however, far outweighed his vices. His ability to get along in both Indian and white societies certainly paved the way when the NWMP moved into the West. And had it not been for Potts, who rode countless miles and held pow-wow after pow-wow with Blackfoot, Blood, Peigan and Stoney chiefs, explaining why it was best they not become involved when the North West Rebellion broke out in 1885, the history of the settling of the West might well have been written in blood instead of ink.

Though Potts was a little man, he was tough enough to challenge all comers and to sleep out on the prairie on the coldest night wrapped only in a blanket. But he did have some flaws in his make-up. One was a superstitious nature inherited from his Indian mother. Another was lung trouble that bothered him throughout much of his life and, combined with his love of whisky, was to cause his death.

His superstition, however, did have a humorous side. Early in the 1890s he and his friend, Constable Tom Clarke, went duck hunting. During the hunt Clarke fired at some low flying ducks and was startled to see his partner fall to the ground. Sure he had killed the little scout, Clarke rushed over to find Potts sitting up and rubbing the side of his head. "Something hit me on the head and knocked my damn block off," he moaned.

Fortunately, the only damage was a single shotgun pellet lodged in Jerry's ear, which he insisted upon leaving there as his good luck "medicine." Forever after, when he had had a few drinks he told everyone his story. Finally Constable John Clancy got tired of hearing it. One night as a few friends had gathered in Clancy's cabin and were passing around a bottle of whisky, Jerry began telling of his experience for perhaps the fiftieth time. Clancy waited patiently until Potts was done, then asked to see the scar. Before Jerry knew what was happening, Clancy extracted the pellet with his pocket knife.

Jerry took losing his good luck charm as an ill omen and so it proved. A few months later—July 14, 1896—he began hemorrhaging from the lungs after a long drinking bout. He died a few hours later and was buried in the NWMP cemetery with full military honors.

"Jerry Potts is dead..." said a news item in the *Fort Macleod Gazette*: "To the Mounties he was an unfailing guide, a faithful interpreter and a true and loyal go-between. 'Faithful and true' is the character he leaves behind...."

It was a simple but fitting tribute to a magnificent frontier scout. ●

MARTIN NORDEGG
PIONEER COAL DEVELOPER

A liar, an imposter, a charlatan, it was said of Martin Nordegg when he claimed to have found rich coal deposits on the eastern slopes of the Rockies. Yet Nordegg defied the experts by founding one of the greatest coal producers in the province and the town that bore his name.

ACCORDING to Professor Potonie of the Berlin Academy of Mining, who wrote the book, *The Origin Of Coal*, a classic for its time, there was no coal where mining promoter Martin Nordegg found vast seams in 1907. Coal simply did not form in the Cretaceous rock that make up the Rocky Mountains. Therefore the sample that Nordegg had just brought back to Germany could not possibly be from there. Eminent professors do not make mistakes. Consequently, claimed the professor, Martin Nordegg was a liar, an impostor, a charlatan— nothing more than a rascal and not a very nice fellow to boot.

Though dumbfounded, Nordegg was not deterred. In 1906 he had sailed to Canada, sponsored by a large German development corporation, to find exploitable minerals. After many months of combing the wilds of Northern Ontario with little success, he headed out to Alberta and spent the summer of 1907 with guide and pack-train, wandering the eastern slope of the Rockies. There he found exploitable minerals in profusion— at least three vast coal fields— one along the Kananaskis River, one on the Brazeau and yet another along the Big Horn River. Now he was in Germany, trying to raise something like $5 million to develop a mine, build a town and construct a railway to haul the coal away. It was an incredible sum that caused George W. Buexenstein, president of the Deutches Canada Syndicate, who had sponsored Nordegg's trip to Canada, to blink and turn pale. The president was used to dealing in vast sums, but $5 million to develop a mine 5,000 miles away seemed a bit overwhelming even to him.

But Martin Nordegg knew the coal was there. All that was needed were the finances to develop it and

(Opposite page top) Nordegg around 1914. Note mine tipple.
(Bottom) The main street of Nordegg, showing the Bank of Commerce on the right. In January of 1955 the famous mine was closed down. Since then some of the original buildings have been used as a minimum security prison.
(Above) Martin Nordegg, founder of the coal mining town.

he was not about to let anyone, not even the most eminent of professors, spoil things for him. He sent a telegram off to Ottawa and the answer confirmed that there were indeed vast reservoirs of coal along the Alberta foothills. Moreover, Nordegg again travelled to Canada and persuaded government officials in Ottawa to send an invitation to Professor Potonie to come see for himself the coal fields of the Rockies. The Professor accepted the invitation, travelled with Nordegg to the nearest coal field Nordegg had staked— along the Kananaskis River west of Calgary— conceded that coal did indeed form in Cretaceous rock and admitted: "I will simply have to rewrite my book."

The fact that Martin Nordegg was concerned with coal in Alberta in the first place came about mostly by chance. Born in Selesia, Germany, in 1868, he was a graduate of Charlottenburg Technical College where he studied engineering and photochemistry. After a short hitch in the German army, and an unhappy marriage that produced a daughter and ended in divorce, between 1895 and 1905 he seems to have spent more years outside Germany, working in England and Ireland as a photographer. He came to Canada because of a chance meeting with Colonel Onesiphore Talbot, a Member of the Canadian Parliament who was visiting Germany to learn something about technical development. After a visit to the photochemical laboratory in Berlin where Nordegg worked, Colonel Talbot persuaded Nordegg to come to Canada where opportunities were boundless. Nordegg was convinced and it did not take him long to obtain $60,000 in financial backing, a passport and passage on a ship sailing from Hamburg.

Nordegg's philosophy seems to have been: the best way to start a new life in a new country is not at the bottom, but at the top. Whatever, when he arrived in Ottawa, where he met his friend, Colonel Talbot, he ensconced himself in the finest hotel in town, the Russell House. On the first evening of his stay he succeeded in getting himself introduced to Prime Minister Wilfred Laurier. The Prime Minister in turn steered Nordegg to the Minister of Mines, William Templeton, who thought, as a good Easterner should, that the best place for Nordegg to invest money was in the East— specifically in the mining area of Northern Ontario and more specifically in the great nickel field around Sudbury or in the new cobalt-silver field around Cobalt. Consequently, Nordegg spent considerable time during the summer of 1906 and the winter of 1906-07 in tramping the rocky terrain of the northern Ontario bush, obtaining considerable experience and a surfeit of mosquito bites in the summer and frostbite in winter, but finding no claims of great value.

Back in Ottawa, however, he learned from the Minister of Mines of the vast coal fields in Alberta. Not surprisingly, in the summer of 1907 he headed west. There he staked or had others stake great coal fields in the Kananaskis, Brazeau and Big Horn River basins.

Before going to Alberta himself, however, he was tempted to venture into a completely different field. While staying at Ottawa's Russell House he read in the newspapers of various coal surveys then underway, particularly those of government surveyor George M. Dawson of Yukon fame (Dawson City is named for him). At this time, he chanced to meet and have a few drinks with none other than Guglielmo Marconi, the man who was to send the first radio message across the Atlantic. Nordegg and Marconi became good friends and Marconi asked Nordegg to join him in his radio development venture. However, when one of Nordegg's government friends suggested that Marconi was, to put it in modern terms, "some kind of a nut," Nordegg declined the offer— and by so doing probably turned down the greatest opportunity of his lifetime to achieve fame and fortune.

Nordegg, of course, did gain fame, although to a lesser degree than he would have had he joined Marconi; he undoubtedly would have done well in any field he chose. But his destiny was linked with the Alberta foothills. In May of 1907, at Morley, west of Calgary, he met Factor Stuart Kidd of the Hudson's Bay Company store. Kidd in turn introduced him to Tom Lusk, then one of the best, and the best-known packers and outfitters in the country. Lusk was a Texan who some dozen years before was reported to have come to Alberta one jump ahead of a sheriff's posse—something about a gunfight in Texas where a man was killed, which Lusk neither confirmed nor denied. In his memoirs, *The Nordegg Papers*, later compiled into a book entitled *The Possibilities Of Canada Are Truly Great* by T.D. Regehr, Nordegg described Tom Lusk as follows:

"He spent his life in Texas and came north only a dozen years ago... He wore a Stetson hat, and a red bandana decorated his neck. His silver spurs on his high Strathcona boots tinkled like bells. His leather belt was studded with silver nails. He looked like a figure from a Wild West show."

Though Tom Lusk apparently never drew a sober breath while preparing for the prospecting trip, he was all business on the trail and proved to be every bit as good as people claimed he was. He led Nordegg to a fine coalfield at Kananaskis, then on north to the Brazeau and Big Horn area, where Dominion Land Surveyor, D.B. Dowling, whom Nordegg had borrowed from the Canadian Government, was busy staking suitable coalfields. Oddly enough, although Dowling and Nordegg staked enough coal in the Nordegg-Brazeau area to last a century, it was neither of these fields that eventually became the site of Nordegg's mine and town, but a field he accidentally discovered himself in the fall of 1910 while riding out from Rocky

Mountain House to see how his men were doing at the other claims.

By then Nordegg had obtained financing in Europe and formed the Brazeau Coal Company Limited in partnership with William Mackenzie and Donald Mann, the builders of the Canadian Northern Railway, now Canadian National. Mackenzie and Mann were to build a railway into the mine and buy all the coal Nordegg produced. Between 1907 and 1910, Nordegg had made many trips across the Atlantic obtaining European capital and had met many of Europe's most prominent businessmen; he even had a short meeting with Kaiser Wilhelm, the German Emperor.

Nordegg, as vice president and general manager of the Brazeau Coal Company, took on the job of opening the mine and building the town. He was to have 100,000 tons of coal dug and waiting by the time the first CNR locomotive arrived on the site. Total financing to cover the cost of the mine, town and railway had skyrocketed from the original estimate of $5 million to a total of $9.5 million. Mackenzie and Mann were surprised and pleased when Nordegg, good as his word, actually had the 100,000 tons of coal waiting when the first Canadian Northern train reached the site in 1914.

The town that was to bear his name was Nordegg's pet project of the entire enterprise. He wanted it to be a model town and it was. That is, it was but for a few minor details. He wanted all the miner's cottages to have baths, but encountered stiff opposition from some of his building engineers. Since many of the miners had never even seen a bathroom, let alone used one, the engineers saw no

(Top) A ghost town for eight years, Nordegg got a new lease on life in 1963 when some of its buildings were taken over by the Alberta Government for a Correctionql Institute.
(Bottom) Another view of Nordegg in its heyday.

need to install such extravagant plumbing. Nordegg insisted and finally reached a compromise: the larger five-room cottages would have baths, but the four-room houses would be built without. It turned out that the builders were more familiar with the wants and needs of the miners than Nordegg. For when the town was built and the miners and their families settled in, Nordegg, upon inspecting the cottages, was flabbergasted to find that more than one family used the bathtub for a coal storage bin and the toilet for a convenient bath for the baby. So much for his new-fangled ideas!

Another problem with his model town came about because of the nature of the terrain on which the town was built. Since the land was on a slope and because the miner's cottages took up the space below the railway tracks, the mine officials, despite a strong argument from Nordegg, insisted upon having their homes built on higher ground on the opposite side of the tracks. This, claimed Nordegg, created "a caste system of superior men and even more superior women," above the tracks. During the early years no argument put forth by Nordegg could convince the wives of mine officals that they should mix in any social function with the miners and their wives living on the other side of the tracks. Since the schoolmarms also lived below the tracks, they too were considered somewhat inferior. During Nordegg's tenure the only exception made was that of the wife of the station-master, who lived on the upper floor of the railway station which was located in lower town. The exception was only granted after her sister, who was married to the manager of the company store and lived in upper town, threatened to invite all the ladies from lower town to a tea party given in honor of her sister. The upper-crust ladies held a conference and finally decided to allow the station mistress and the school teachers into their group. But that is as far as they would go. They did, however, allow the residents of lower town to use their tennis court and curling rink on certain days and certain hours. But, during those hours, no woman from upper town ever showed up at the rink or court lest she become contaminated by the working classes.

Although Nordegg was proud of his town, which grew to a population of 3,500 people at its peak, and produced 10 million tons of coal over the years, he did not get to live there very long. The First World War broke out in 1914 and, although he remained as mine manager until well into 1915, when reports began to reach town of some of the miners' relatives and friends being killed in France, the previously friendly attitude of some of the Nordegg people began to turn against Martin Nordegg, who by then was considered an enemy alien. Consequently, Nordegg spent most of the war years living in New York, although Canadian immigration officials did give him a special pass to allow him to cross into Canada whenever he wished. However, during the war years the company was gradually taken out of his hands by Mackenzie and Mann, the Canadian Bank of Commerce and by Lazard Brothers, all of whom were trying to get control of the company from the Deutches Canada Syndicate. Then, in 1918, the custodian of Enemy Property assumed control of the Brazeau Coal Company to ensure that German investors did not benefit from the company while they were at war with Canada.

Despite all the under-handed efforts of Canadian and British interests in trying to gain control of the company while Nordegg, as an enemy alien, was more or less helpless to fight back, he did manage to regain control after the war and to sell the shares at a profit to the German investors. In order to regain control, he had to take out Canadian citizenship papers. He could have taken them out during the war, but he thought that doing so was the coward's way out. He loved Canada but he did not wish to forsake his homeland at a critical time.

With the company disposed of, Nordegg was free to carry out two of his fondest wishes: "To roam the world to my liking and assist mankind. And I carried both through." He did that and more. In the immediate postwar years, he devoted his time to raising money in the United States to help restore war-devastated Europe. Then, for many years, he helped Thomas Mulvey, Secretary of State with the Mackenzie King government, with the countless other problems that developed during the postwar period. He also remarried, this time to a Canadian woman who was his faithful companion until his death in Ottawa in 1948 at the age of 79.

The town that Nordegg built lived on until 1955. By then the railways had all switched, or were switching, to cheaper, cleaner burning diesel fuel. Coal was no longer needed.

It was a sad day in January of 1955 when officials of Brazeau Collieries Ltd. told the remaining 130 miners that the mine was closing. The previous summer, 230 miners had received the same gloomy news. Miners in the over-50 age group, many of whom had spent all their working years in the Nordegg mines, were the last to go. That was small consolation for them, for most knew no other way of life and many felt they were too old to start anew. By the summer of 1955, except for a handful of care-takers, the town was deserted. And so it remained until 1963, when the Alberta Government took over some of the buildings for a minimum security prison.

It is interesting to speculate whether Martin Nordegg would have allowed the town he had worked so strenuously to build to meet such an ignominious fate? Since coal was phased out in favor of cheaper and cleaner burning fuel oil and natural gas, he probably would have had no other choice but to close his town and let his people go. But one thing seems obvious— he would not have closed shop without one gigantic fight. ●

Daugherty was foreever complaining about the Peace River country and promising to sell out. When he continued to dawdle, his impatient wife decided to hasten his departure with poison.

THE DAUGHERTY MURDER CASE

MOST must be aware that the Peace River Country was settled by as fine a bunch of pioneers as could be found anywhere. Consequently, violent crime was minimal. Unfortunately, a few unsavory characters did manage to filter in. The Daugherty's of Hythe were one such couple. Although hardly to his credit, about the worst crime Daugherty could be accused of was that of not being satisfied with the country. He was forever telling people he wanted to sell his farm and move out.

But this sacrilege was nothing compared to the crime with which Mrs. Daugherty was finally charged. It was hardly a secret in the early 1920s that the Daughertys were not on the best of terms—in short, they hated each other. Had Daugherty kept his promise to sell out, conceivably they might have split the proceeds and gone their separate ways. When he procrastinated too long, Mrs. Daugherty decided to hasten things along a bit by lacing her husband's food with poison.

Daugherty refused to die, however. But Mrs. D. was a determined woman. She forthwith pushed her groaning husband down the cellar steps, dispatched him with a bullet in the head from his own .30-.30 rifle, then quickly buried him right where he lay.

The murder was not committed spontaneously, so to speak, but with considerable premeditation. Prior to feeding her old man the arsenic cocktail, Mrs. D. had written several letters to herself to which she signed her husband's name. These she mailed to a friend with orders to have them sent back to her at weekly intervals. Naturally neighbors eventually noticed that Daugherty was missing, but it was not until three months had elapsed that someone thought to notify the police.

Shown the letters, the police seemed quite satisfied that Daugherty was merely on a trip as Mrs. D. claimed. But when Constable John Sullivan was posted to Grande Prairie district, he was not at all sure. A handsome young member of the Alberta Provincial Police, Sullivan stood over six feet in height and had a way about him that some women found irresistible. When he learned that the Daugherty property was for sale, he dressed in civilian clothes and went calling, pretending he was looking for farm land.

Mrs. Daugherty was taken with the constable's good looks and immediately fell in love with him. She invited him to share her abode while the land sale was being consummated. Sullivan went along with the arrangement, even insisting it become a permanent one. He told her, however, that he could not meet her price for the land, but said he knew a fellow who could. But, said Sullivan, the man would not consider buying the land without the husband's signature.

This turn of events set Mrs. D. back only temporarily, when she begged Sullivan to help her forge the necessary signature. Now Sullivan knew his suspicions had been well-founded. He refused to help forge the document, but kept her hopes high by telling her of the fancy places he planned to take her after the sale. Mrs. Daugherty could contain herself no longer. "If I told you Daugherty was dead, would you help forge his name?" she asked.

"Sure," said Sullivan, upon which Mrs. D. opened the cellar door to show where Daugherty was buried. Cool as could be, Sullivan helped forge the signature. Next morning he took the document into Grande Prairie, then returned the next day in uniform with two other policemen to help him make the arrest. It was a wise move, for Mrs. Daugherty roughed up all three before being subdued. When it was all over she was supposed to have said: "In spite of all this, I still love you, Sullivan."

By some strange quirk of fate, Mrs. D. was never convicted of murder. She was released on the grounds that she killed her husband in self-defense. But justice prevailed, nevertheless. A year or so later she was arrested and convicted in Vancouver on a narcotics charge. She spent most of the rest of her life in jail. ●

(Opposite page) Once into the Yukon fortune hunters could travel by boat for the remaining distance to Dawson City. Here, a scow shoots the rapids of Miles Canyon.

(Right) Another route to the gold fields was by way of the Chilkoot and White Passes. Here, scows loaded with livestock cross Lake Bennett, on whose shores cities of canvas appeared overnight.

THE KLONDIKE TRAIL

The "All-Canadian Route," this overland nightmare was billed by its promoters. It may have been the shortest route on the map but, like the infamous Chilkoot Trail, the route from Edmonton was a killer of man and beast.

TWENTY-odd miles west of the thriving Peace River Country city of Grande Prairie stands the boarded-up remains of an old single-room schoolhouse. Named Klondike Trail School, it stands beside one of the many trails taken by the goldseekers who headed overland from Edmonton to find their fortune in the famous gold camps of the Yukon. Who were these people, where did they hail from and why did they choose the overland route to the Klondike when the sea route up the west coast of British Columbia and across the White or Chilkoot Passes was obviously so much easier?

In answer to the first question it need only be said that they were ordinary young men (and women), people with a strong feeling for adventure. They undoubtedly hoped to hit a big strike in the gold fields, but were probably no more "gold hungry" than the average person. They were, however, more willing than most to face hardship and to take risks in an attempt to find their fortune.

Where did they come from? From many places— the British Isles, Australia, South Africa, although by far the biggest majority came from the United States and Canada.

Why did they choose the Edmonton route (also known as the 'All-Canadian Route' and the 'Back-Door Route')? Some claim it was because they were misled by unscrupulous promoters and businessmen anxious to make a fast buck. Historians like James MacGregor heartily disagree. Actually, it seems more likely that potential gold-seekers simply got out

a map of Canada and discovered that Edmonton was the closest place to the Klondike that could be reached by railroad. Thus they chose it as their starting point. Others, like T. Milvain, who floated down the Athabasca-Mackenzie River system, then went over the Richardson Mountains to the Klondike, took that route because he was told that the route from Skagway over the Chilkoot Pass was terribly dangerous.

In fact, the Edmonton *Bulletin* did not begin touting Edmonton as the logical spot to begin a trek to the Yukon until after the town council, the Board of Trade and the editor of the *Bulletin*, Frank Oliver, began getting inquiries from potential prospectors from many areas. But once they saw the possibilities of making Edmonton the gateway to the Klondike, enterprising businessmen began stocking every conceivable item a man would need on a hike that would take him a year or more to accomplish. There is no denying, however, that, once bitten by the bug, the *Bulletin* editor and the Board of Trade tried to oversell the "All Canadian" route. Nevertheless, it was the gold-seekers themselves who initiated the route and the onus was on them to get through, turn back, or die in the attempt.

Actually there were two routes from Edmonton— the land route and the water route. All started out by land, with those taking the water route building boats or rafts at either Athabasca or Peace River Landing, before following either the Athabasca or Peace River to the mighty Mackenzie, thence

THE DEAD HORSE TRAIL. J.M.B.

(Above) Perhaps the most infamous chapter of the entire Klondike saga was that of the terrible mistreatment of pack horses. These bodies were but a handful of the thousands of animals who were ridden to death or left to starve when they could go no farther. Many were said to have committed suicide by leaping over the cliffs, preferring this fate to continued torture from their owners.
(Opposite page) With the gold miner went the forerunners of civilization. Here, a Canadian Bank of Commerce party heads for Dawson City to serve the miners.

downstream to either the mouth of the Peel River or the Rat River in the Mackenzie Delta. From there they went up either river, crossed over the Richardson Mountains till they hit the headwaters of the Porcupine, then floated down the Porcupine to the Yukon river, where they would catch the first sternwheel steamboat heading upriver to Dawson City and the gold fields. There was an alternate to this water route, such as going down the Mackenzie to the mouth of the Liard River, up the Liard to its headwaters, overland to Frances Lake, then down the Pelly and Yukon Rivers to Dawson City. None of these routes was easy by any stretch of the imagination and many drowned or died of scurvy or starvation before they reached halfway. But all were infinitely easier than the all-land trail, which is the topic of this chapter.

Although a handful of early-birds started from Edmonton during the summer and fall of 1897, by far the majority did not leave until that winter or early in the spring of 1898. Consequently, during the winter there were prospector's camps scattered all over town, swelling the population from 1,700 to probably four times that number. They were an exuberant lot and all cafes, hotels and mercantile establishments enjoyed a booming business as the Klondike-bound hopefuls prepared for their long journey.

Never did the gold-seekers portray more inventiveness than when choosing their means of transportation. Some preferred pack-horses, others dog teams, yet others horse or ox-drawn sleighs, wagons or Red River carts. But Charles Smith of Houston, Texas, showed the most imagination of all when he started out from Edmonton with a horse-drawn conveyance that utilized whisky barrels for wheels. Since he would have to cross muskeg and many rivers and streams, he assumed that whisky barrels would prove more practical than conventional wheels. Although, when he was about halfway to St. Albert, the hoops came off the barrels and his 'wheels' disintegrated, there can be no condemnation of his ingenuity.

The All-Canadian route started out as one trail, but did not remain that way for long. Most of the trails rejoined near what is now Watson Lake, Yukon Territory, but, between St. Albert and that point, they fanned out and criss-crossed like so many rabbit tracks in the snow. Interestingly, a trail which was axed out by a group of NWMP led by Inspector J.D. Moodie and paid for by the Canadian Government, followed the Rocky Mountain Trench northwest from Fort St. John, British Columbia, and apparently was used by no more than 50 people.

The Chalmer's Trail from Edmonton to Peace River Crossing and later known as the Klondike Trail, however, was used extensively. When, in the summer of 1897, the government of what was still known as the North West Territories realized that the rush to the Klondike from Edmonton was real, they decided to open a road. They hired a well-known guide, outfitter and woodsman named Dan Noyes to take care of packing, and T.W. Chalmers as engineer to map out the trail. On September 9, 1897, they set out with 10 horses pulling five two-wheeled carts. According to Chalmer's report they followed a fairly good road to Lac La Nonne. From there to the Athabasca River it was clearly marked but needed some work. They crossed the Athabasca River in canvas boats they carried with them, then began cutting a trail to Fort Assiniboine. Since they were now moving through heavy bush, they

decided to abandon their carts and use pack horses to carry their supplies.

With six axemen hacking down trees and clearing deadfalls, Chalmers pushed a wagon trail to Fort Assiniboine, then on to Lesser Slave Lake (present-day Grouard) and finally on to Peace River Crossing, where the town of Peace River now stands. Unfortunately, long before he could complete the wagon trail— in fact, while his men were still hacking through the heavy bush in the Swan Hills— the first major group of Klondike-bound hopefuls overtook and passed him. The government, however, was making travel somewhat easier for the gold-seekers by installing ferries on the Pembina and Athabasca Rivers, at the narrows on Lesser Slave Lake leading to Slave Lake Settlement and, during the summer of 1898, at Peace River Crossing.

No part of the Klondike Trail was easy going. But even after the work done by Chalmers, the part that proved the toughest and caused at least 100 men to turn back, was the first 350 or so miles to Peace River Crossing. Perhaps the best way to describe some of the hardships on this section is to refer to an account of one of the men who experienced them, Frank Walker of Fort Saskatchewan. He set out from Edmonton on March 8, 1898, leading a party consisting of his brother Albert, W. Hepburn, John Reid and several others. In an article that appeared in the Winter, 1959, issue of the *Alberta Historical Review* entitled "Overland Trail To The Klondike" he wrote:

"One of the most heartbreaking hills which tried all the skills and ingenuity even of the oldtimers who were on the trail, was at the crossing on the north side of the Athabasca River, near old Fort Assini-boine. The hill was a very long one and a great deal of the difficulty was experienced by the tenderfeet in handling the horses up this grade. The hillside was littered with broken boxes, smashed sleighs and harness, and practically every tree on the lower side of the grade was blazed and the owners of the outfits gave vent to their feelings in epitaphs upon the trees. At the very top of the hill on a rotten tree had been nailed a piece of board, with a hand pointing in each direction. The one in the direction of the Klondike had written underneath 'To Dawson City 2433½ miles' and otherneath the other hand said 'To Home Sweet Home.' Our party stood and laughed....

"The journey from Athabasca to the Swan Hills was practically uneventful, but at the Swan Hills became simply awful... I never could understand why the man who chose this route should ever pick such a terrible one....

"Passing along the south shore of Lesser Slave Lake, we commenced to find dead horses in abundance, the majority of course dying for lack of feed...."

An estimated 4,000 horses died along the route, mostly due to ignorance on the part of their owners, some of whom knew next to nothing about caring for the poor mistreated beasts. But those who realized the hazards they would face and prepared for them, surmounted most of the obstacles. For instance, Dr. H.L. McInnis of Edmonton set out on March 24, 1898. But, rather than following Chalmer's treacherous trail, he headed for Athabasca Landing. Two men travelled with him and, with 22 horses pulling sleighs loaded with hay, they easily got through to Lesser Slave Lake settlement. There he bought more hay from the Hudson's Bay Company and went on to Peace

River Crossing, where he arrived on April 11 with the horses fat and healthy.

For the ignorant it was another story. For them not only the trail to Peace River Crossing, but the trails from there to the Klondike were all terrible— hell for both man and beast. From the Crossing to Dunvegan there was a well-used wagon road on the north side of the Peace River all the way to Dunvegan. From there on, however, the trails were nebulous and often it was every man for himself. Some of the men, the exact number of which is unknown, crossed the river and followed the trail that led past the school mentioned at the start of the story. After crossing the Grande Prairie where travelling was reasonably easy, then through bush country most of the way from present Hythe to the Peace River, they eventually arrived at Fort St. John. Most of the trekkers, however, kept to the north side of the Peace from Dunvegan, staying well north of the river. They, too headed for Fort St. John. There were a number, however, who took a

(Right) An Edmonton party preparing to head for the Klondike in December of 1897. Although the map showed this to be the shortest route to the fabled Yukon — as the crow flies — in actual fact it was the worst for man and beast.
(Below) Riverboats at Dawson City at the height of the Klondike gold rush. This was the easiest way to travel — for those who made it as far as the Yukon River. Many of those who attempted to go overland from Edmonton did not.

completely different route by following a trail blazed by W.P. Taylor, an Edmontonian hired by the town council. His route took a more easterly direction, heading for Fort Nelson. It was a fair trail in winter, but since there were many streams and patches of muskeg to cross, something else again in the summer.

Probably the best way to give a picture of the route from Peace River Crossing to Fort St. John on the north side of the river is to let a man who travelled it tell the story. Joe McDonald, in his day a well-known frontiersman, guided the C.P. Braithwaite party from Edmonton to Fort St. John. When he arrived there he had an argument with his

employer and decided to return to Edmonton. He told the Edmonton *Bulletin* about part of his trip:

"From the Crossing (Peace River) to Dunvegan is a well beaten trail, but to follow it into Dunvegan is to make an unnecessary detour of about 30 miles in and back. By following the trail halfway to Dunvegan, at a place called Old Woman's Lake, a fairly well beaten trail made lately by travellers leads in a westerly direction. By travelling on this trail for six to eight miles and a mile beyond Island Lake, a big trail cut out like a surveyor's line can be seen due north. By taking notice they will see a trail just there running to the left which they will follow and just at the top of a little hill as they pass through some poplar, they will see "OK" marked in pencil on a blazed trail. This is the trail to follow to Fort St. John...."

For those going by way of Fort St. John, some 300 all told, it depended to a large extent on what they had in mind, the exact route they took or the speed they travelled. For some, getting to the Klondike was not very important. They hoped to find their bonanza along the way and panned every likely looking stream they came to. Quite a number reached Fort St. John in the fall of 1897 and many

more the following winter. It was a good place to spend the winter, for 12 miles upriver on Bear Flats there was ample feed for their horses.

The following spring, many started up the Halfway River, then crossed over the Laurier Pass to Fort Grahame on the Finlay River. From there they continued up the Finlay to the mouth of the Fox River, followed it to its headwaters, then crossed over the Sifton Pass and followed the Kechika River to its confluence with the Liard. They followed the Liard to Lower Post near the British Columbia-Yukon border and from there most struck northwest to the Pelly River, where they built rafts and took life easy as they floated downstream to the Yukon River at Fort Selkirk and down the great Yukon to Dawson City and the Klondike.

Not all followed this exact route and by no means all reached the Yukon. Maybe half of those going by way of Fort St. John turned back, while others, after reaching Fort Grahame, followed the Finlay to the mouth of the Ingineca River and on to the gold fields at Omineca.

It is easy enough to follow these routes on a map. But for those making the long safari, very little of the route made for easy travel. Cold and scurvy faced

Most notorious of the trails to the Klondike was that by way of the Chilkoot Pass. But the "All Canadian" route from Edmonton was also a killer, as more than one luckless adventurer learned too late.

the men in winter, while starvation threatened both man and beast. In the summer swollen streams, mud, mosquitoes and voracious flies took their toll. Nor were those the only enemies. Many of the gold-seekers were Americans who considered the only good Indian a dead Indian. The grassland near Fort St. John at Bear Flats and along the Halfway River was the traditional grazing ground for Beaver Indian ponies. Consequently, when the Klondikers moved their horses in without permission, Beaver braves were angry. When one group of Americans shot five of the Beaver's prize stallions and destroyed several laboriously built bear traps when their horses blundered into them, the Beavers were enraged. Barney Maurice, a High Prairie merchant in later years, who was at Fort St. John when the Beavers sought revenge, told what happened:

"In Fort St. John there was an Indian scare... On the top of the hill at Fort St. John there were about 75 buggies, wagons and Red River carts left by the miners. About 250 Indians put the whole works down the hill and I could see afterwards broken wagons and equipment for about 600 feet down. All the white men with the exception of a doctor, myself and my partner left at night. We had to stay but the Indians didn't do us any harm."

None of the land routes was any picnic to travel, but perhaps the least terrible of these was the one blazed by W.P. Taylor. He set out in February of 1898, mushing a team of seven dogs, and following the Chalmer's Trail as far as it went at the time— Deer Mountain in the Swan Hills — arrived at Grouard in a week. There he hired an Indian guide and persuaded Harry Garbett, an Englishman who later settled at Moberly Lake in British Columbia, to accompany him. They headed for Peace River Crossing and arrived there on March 17, St. Patrick's Day.

From the Crossing they headed northwest toward Fort Nelson, nearly 300 miles away. Along the way the group passed Cardinal Lake, crossed the headwaters of the Notikewin and Mud Rivers and reached the upper Chinchaga River on March 25. When the snow began melting as they neared the Fontas River, the men unloaded the toboggans, packed the supplies on the backs of the dogs and carried on. They followed the Fontas to the Sikanni Chief River, then struck over high ground until they intersected an Indian trail and followed it to Fort Nelson, arriving on April 8.

From Fort Nelson the Taylor party followed the Muskwa River about 50 miles, when they turned north over a divide until they hit the Toad River, then followed the Toad to its junction with the Liard at Toad River Post. They crossed the Liard about four miles downstream at the mouth of the Grayling River. There, Taylor left Garbett and his Indian guide to hunt, while he hired another guide from a band of Indians camped near the Grayling and pressed on. They trekked up the Grayling, crossed

over to the headwaters of the Crow, followed it to the headwaters of the Beaver, then crossed the Rock, Coal and Hyland Rivers and reached Francis Lake on May 19. Taylor then pressed on west until he reached the Pelly River where he and his guide built a raft and floated downstream about 50 miles. When he saw traces along the bank of at least one party of Klondikers having passed that way, and knowing the Pelly flowed into the Yukon and that the rest of the journey to Dawson City was a simple matter of floating downstream, on May 21 he turned around and headed back for Edmonton.

When going home, instead of heading for Peace River Crossing from Fort Nelson, Taylor took a trail that brought him to Fort St. John. This, he claimed, made for somewhat easier travel. At Fort St. John he built a raft and floated down the Peace to Peace River Crossing, where he arrived on July 15. From there it took only eight days to reach his home in Lac Ste. Anne, about 40 miles west of Edmonton, and he got there with six of his seven dogs alive and healthy.

Altogether Taylor covered 2,200 miles in 157 days, or approximately 14 miles a day. Of course, none of the 150 or so Klondikers who followed his trail could expect to travel that fast, for they were loaded down with enough supplies to last them a year— roughly a ton each. Nevertheless, Taylor proved that by travelling light the trip could be made in less than four months, rather than the 18 or so months it took most of those lucky enough to get through.

"The White Pass and Yukon Railway, heading from Skagway, Alaska to Lake Bennett, some 40 miles away, wrung the neck of Edmonton's All-Canadian routes to the Yukon," wrote James MacGregor in *Klondike Rush Through Edmonton*. And a good thing it did. For when the prospectors could make a leisurely trip up the British Columbia coast by boat from Vancouver to Skagway and then take a train over the White Pass to Lake Bennett, where they could build a boat or board a stern-wheel steamer and float down to the Klondike, there seemed little reason to break their backs tramping the Klondike Trail.

But before the WP&Y was built in 1898, about 1,560 people, including 20 women and four children, started out from Edmonton. Of these approximately 775 tried the land trails and 785 the water route. Approximately 565 reached the gold fields by water, while only 160 made it by land. Some 70 died on the way, at least two of whom were babies born on the trail.

Records show approximately how many started out, how many got through and how many died along the way. But, strangely, there seems to be no record of how many if any—struck it rich. Probably very few hit the jackpot, for, by the time they staggered into the gold fields, the great Klondike gold rush was already over. ●

Thomas Woolsey

Pioneer Missionary

*Although his physical stature seemed to render him
totally unsuited to a life on the prairie frontier,
Rev. Thomas Woolsey was a giant among men.*

THERE seems to be considerable controversy as to the nature of the Reverend Thomas Woolsey, pioneer missionary who devoted nine years of his life serving the Indians of what is now central Alberta. The Reverend John McDougall saw Mr. Woolsey as a man whose physical stature, or lack of it, rendered him totally unsuited to a life on the frontier. In his book *Saddle, Sled And Snowshoe*, McDougall claimed that Woolsey, even after spending almost a decade in the West, "could get lost in a 10 acre field." John did not see Mr. Woolsey as much of a dog driver either, for he wrote: "He could not run or even walk at a quick pace, so had to sit wedged in his carriole from start to finish between camps, while I kept his train on the road ahead of mine; for if he upset, which he often did, he could not right himself and I had to run ahead and fix him up." However, John did say of Woolsey that "He was always genial and kindly and a devoted servant of God."

Peter Erasmus, who also served with Thomas Woolsey for several years, agreed with McDougall on the latter point, but rated Woolsey's suitability for frontier life much higher than did John McDougall. It seems that McDougall may not have known that for some time prior to the time in 1862 when, as an 18-year-old he came West to help his missionary father establish Victoria Mission, Reverend Woolsey had been critically ill and had not completely recovered. Nor did he fully recover during the two years that John McDougall knew him.

According to Erasmus, whose autobiography (as told to Henry Thompson in 1925), was published as a book in 1976 by the Glenbow-Alberta Institute *Buffalo Days And Nights*, edited by Dr. Irene M. Spry), Woolsey was a good horseman and, although he may not have been a great dog driver, he was a man whom even the most vicious dogs saw as their friend. Erasmus, who was born in the Red River Settlement of Manitoba in 1833 and trained as minister for two years before accepting a position as interpreter for Missionary Woolsey in 1855, probably would have agreed that Woolsey could "get lost in a 10 acre field." But he would not have agreed that Woolsey was unsuited for the rigors of the frontier. In fact when he came West to join Woolsey at Fort Pitt, Erasmus was surprised, when shaking hands upon being introduced to his new employer, to find that Woolsey had an extremely strong grip for a man of small stature. As Erasmus stated: "He surprised me with the boundless energy he appeared to have. We sometimes rode long distances, spending long days and sometimes staying up late at night."

It was not until later when he became ill, undoubtedly from overwork, too much exposure to winter temperatures, and from too little food while administering to the Indians, that he finally lost his vigor. In fact he became critically ill in the winter of 1861-62 and possibly would have died had not an Indian medicine man prescribed some potent medicine which, when administered by Erasmus,

Fort Edmonton, where Rev. T. Woolsey spent several years.

helped Woolsey recuperate from a fit of chills and fever that had rendered him delirious. Woolsey never did recover completely and undoubtedly this led to the conflicting evaluations of his stamina by McDougall and Erasmus.

Reverend Woolsey was by no means the first missionary to work in this region. He was preceded by several, including the Reverend Robert Rundle and his helper layman Benjamin Sinclair of the Methodists, and Fathers Jean Baptiste Thibault, Joseph Bourassa and Albert Lacombe of the Roman Catholic Church. But when Thomas Woolsey arrived at Fort Edmodnton in 1855, he was met with more enthusiasm than he had any right to anticipate. Both his Methodist predecessors, Reverend Robert Rundle and Benjamin Sinclair, had served the area to the best of their ability, Rundle from his arrival in 1840 until a broken arm, improperly set, forced him to return to England in 1848, and Sinclair for the next two years, until hostile Indians murdered some of his people and forced him to abandon the mission he had established for Reverend Rundle at Pigeon Lake. But for the next five years there had been no Pro-

testant missionary in the area, and the Indians who had been converted by Rundle and Sinclair were certain they had been deserted— permanently.

Obviously Robert Rundle had done marvellous work among the Crees and the Stoneys during his eight-year tenure and had impressed them immensely, for Woolsey wrote in his report (now in the Glenbow files) of his approach to Edmonton: "Met with two persons from Edmonton who assured us that the Indians were anxiously awaiting the arrival of a missionary among them and stated that 30 camps of Sioux (Stoneys and/or Assiniboines) were desirous of hearing the herald of salvation, who would teach them the words of the Great Spirit."

At Fort Pitt, Woolsey met Benjamin Sinclair who had come down from Lac La Biche after hearing that Missionary Woolsey was on his way from the East. (Sinclair had gone to Lac La Biche and established a mission there after being driven from the Pigeon Lake Mission.) Of this meeting Woolsey wrote: "Language fails to describe the joyous manner in which he, (Sinclair) received us. He said he had done his best to preserve Mr. Rundle's Indians

from going over to the Romanists...and that the Indians had been expecting a missionary for seven years and that some of them had oft times wept when they thought that they might never again hear the herald of the cross."

He knew the Indians were expecting him but he had no reason to expect the kind of welcome he received at Fort Edmonton. Whether it was primarily to meet the Hudson's Bay Company supply boats with which Woolsey was travelling, or to meet Reverend Woolsey himself is not quite clear. Nevertheless something like 400 Crees were gathered and met his York boat as the oarsmen propelled it to the dock just below the old trading post. "Judging from my garment that the long looked for missionary had come," he wrote, "the countenances of many brightened up. By means of an interpreter I made myself known, which spread like electricity among them, and one continuous hand shake with certain expressions of joy at once bespoke of the delight they felt on seeing me for whom they had long waited."

The Indians' long wait paid off for, as John McDougall wrote in *Saddle, Sled And Snowshoe,* "Mr. Woolsey was kept busy holding meetings,

attending councils, visiting the sick, acting as doctor and surgeon, magistrate and judge; for who else had these people to turn to but the missionary?"Peter Erasmus claimed that Mr. Woolsey never seemed to acquire much of a grasp of the Cree language, but he nevertheless managed to get his message across: "I was called upon to sit out long afternoons and evenings interpreting the words between teacher and his interested listeners," Erasmus remembered. "He did not actually use a program of church services but carried on conversations much the same way they do today in Sunday Schools. He read passages from the Bible and explained the meaning. At first it was hard to get them to ask questions, but after a few visits... they appeared to enjoy the informal talks with their minister... There were very few who did not give him respect and an intensive (sic) hearing...."

Thomas Woolsey was born in Lincolnshire, England, in 1818 and served the Methodist Church in one capacity or another for some 15 years before coming to Canada in the early 1850s. He completed his studies for the ministry and was ordained at London, Ontario, in 1855. One of Woolsey's most noteworthy classmates was Henry Bird Steinhauer, the first man of Indian blood to be ordained in the Methodist Church and the great grandfather of Ralph Steinhauer, the first man of Indian extraction to become lieutenant-governor of any Canadian province. Reverend Woolsey's first posting after his ordination at London was to Fort Edmonton. He was accompanied on his journey West by classmate Henry Bird Steinhauer as far as Fort Pitt. Possibly Woolsey himself chose Edmonton after hearing about the place from the Reverend Robert Rundle, who was his brother-in-law. Woolsey spent the winter of 1855-56 around Fort Edmonton. In the spring of 1856, accompanied by Reverend Steinhauer and interpreter Peter Erasmus, he visited the abandoned mission at Pigeon Lake to see if it could be restored. Of that visit Erasmus said:

"Early in the spring of 1857 (actually 1856) as planned, Rev. Mr. Woolsey and I moved to Pigeon Lake. The Indians had gone a few weeks earlier… We found the buildings in bad state of repair, the roofs caved in and the doors hanging from rotten leather hinges. The chimney had to be torn down and rebuilt. We had a canvas tent along so we could be protected while this was being done. Early the first morning I started to work, tearing the roof off the house. I was just nicely started when a number of young men came with their tools and offered their help, but I told them the minister could not pay for their help. They just laughed and said they had been ordered to help by their chief; pay was no concern of theirs. This kindly act was typical of their way with the minister. They were generous and careful to see we had all the food we could use. In fact we had so many offers that we had to refuse for fear of wasting food."

Although Reverend Woolsey, at the insistence of the Indians, spent much of the next three years at Pigeon Lake, the place was not a success for the simple reason that Blackfoot raiding parties often invaded the area, harassing Woolsey's Crees and Stoneys. Consequently when the mission did not turn out as planned, Woolsey moved to Smoking Lake (present-day Smoky Lake) and set up a mission there. He made that his base until visited in late 1862 by the Reverend George McDougall, a long-time missionary from Ontario who had established missions in northern Ontario and at Norway House on the north end of Lake Manitoba. Mr. McDougall had just recently been appointed Superintendent of Methodists Missions in the West and was traveling with his 18-year-old son John on a tour of inspection. On Reverend McDougall's advice, Woolsey moved south to the north bank of the North Saskatchewan River, a spot George McDougall thought much better suited, since it was on the river and the main travel route of the West, while Smoky Lake was far off the beaten track. While George McDougall returned to Norway House to fetch his wife and children, Reverend Woolsey, with the help of John McDougall, moved south and began building a new mission which was named Victoria. The place was later renamed Pakan after Chief Pakan of the Crees when, after post offices were established in the West, the name Victoria was often confused with the British Columbia capital. Woolsey remained at Victoria until he returned to eastern Canada in 1864.

When the McDougalls visited Woolsey at Smoky Lake, he had as a guest none other than the notorious "Mr. O'B." (Eugene Francis O'Beirne), who apparently had been dumped there by some Edmonton-bound traders, who had been coerced into taking him along by the Hudson's Bay Company people at either Fort Pitt or Fort Carlton. At first Mr. Woolsey had enjoyed the company of the old fraud, for Mr. O'B. was an educated man and could be quite charming when he chose. But by the time the McDougall's arrived the welcome had worn thin, as Mr. O'B. began to show his true colors. Consequently, when John McDougall made a trip by dog team to Edmonton in the spring of 1863, Reverend Woolsey begged John to take O'B. along. Wrote John McDougall in *Saddle, Sled And Snowshoe:*

"The snow had almost disappeared and the first ducks and geese were beginning to arrive, when suddenly one evening Mr. Steinhauer and Peter Erasmus (Erasmus had quit Woolsey's employ sometime before to work for Rev. Steinhauer) arrived, en route to Edmonton (from White Fish Lake); Mr. Woolsey took me to one side and said: 'John, I am about tired of Mr. O'B. Could you not take him to Edmonton and leave him there? You might join this party now going.'"

On that trip O'B. insisted on riding the carriole rather than walking. Since the party did most of its travelling on river ice which was flooded by the spring run-off, in some places the dogs virtually had to swim, when the carriole would float and almost capsize in the water. Inevitably the water began to soak through the sled and finally to soak Mr. O'B. Wrote John McDougall: "He blamed me for it and presently began to curse me roundly, declaring I was doing it on purpose. All this time I was wading in the water and keeping the sled from upsetting." When O'B. began to curse, John no longer felt obligated to keep the sled upright, dumped O'B. into the overflow and calmly went on his way.

A few days later while nearing Edmonton, McDougall extracted an apology from his obnoxious passenger by simply letting the sled slide sideways until it was about to upset into open water, which was running deep. Then, as O'B. begged for mercy, McDougall stopped the dogs and threatened to let the carriole tip into the river unless O'B. apologized. Wrote McDougall: "And Mr. O'B. in most abject terms did make an apology. Then slackening the line a little, I let the sled flop up and down in the current and finally accepted his apology on

Pioneer prairie missionary Rev. Thomas Woolsey, 1818-1894.

condition that he would behave himself in the future. My dogs quickly pulled him out of the peril and we went on…" Needless to say, McDougall had no more trouble with O'B. on that trip. O'B., as outlined in the chapter, "The Amazing Mr. O'B.", hung around Fort Edmonton making a nuisance of himself until later that summer when he managed to attach himself to the Lord Milton and Dr. Cheadle party which was en route to the Cariboo gold fields.

Probably one of Reverend Woolsey's most satisfying achievements while at Smoky Lake and Victoria was helping to convert to Christianity the great chief of the Crees, Maskepetoon. Under Woolsey's tutelage Maskepetoon learned to read the syllabic script invented earlier by Reverend James Evans, Methodist missionary of Indian extraction who served in northern Ontario. Chief Maskepetoon, one of Grant McEwan's *Fifty Mighty Men*, had been a mighty warrior with many scalps to his credit until instructed in Christianity by the Reverend Robert Rundle. When Thomas Woolsey met the chief, he spent many hours with him, presented him with a *New Testament* which was written in syllabic and taught him to read it. Maskepetoon reportedly read two chapters a day from his Bible and as a result completed his philosophical transition from that of the war path to that of peace. For the rest of his life Maskepetoon spent his time trying to convey that message to others. Tragically, he was on a mission of peace to the Blackfoot some years later when he was murdered by a Blackfoot warrior.

Though John McDougall often chuckled at Woolsey's inability to find his way on the roadless frontier and once stated, "He will always depend on others," he nevertheless learned to love and respect the older man as Peter Erasmus had done while he was guide and interpreter to the dedicated missionary. McDougall, however, probably did not completely grasp just how much Woolsey had accomplished until the summer of 1863 when, after George McDougall and his family had arrived at Victoria, father and son left Woolsey in charge while they went on a buffalo hunt many miles to the south. Somewhere south of the North Saskatchewan River, the McDougalls met Maskepetoon, who, with some of his people, accompanied them to buffalo country. On the way they kept meeting parties of Indians, whom Maskepetoon would introduce to the McDougalls.

"Presently," wrote John McDougall, "I saw an old Indian of singular appearance approaching and I said to Maskepetoon, 'Who is that?' But when he saw who it was he did not reply, but turned the other way, which I thought strange. The old man came up to my side of the wagon and said: 'I am glad to see you, white man.' So we shook hands; and he made as if he would shake hands with the man beside me, for I knew he did not recognize Maskepetoon — not expecting to see him in my wagon, going this way. The chief still kept his face turned away. I saw, however, that after shaking my hand, the old man would also shake hands with my companion, so I nudged Maskepetoon and said, 'This man wants to shake hands with you.' Then the chief, as if jerking himself from under a weight or strain, turned and gave his hand to the old fellow, who, on recognizing him, grasped his hand and uttered the Indian form of thanksgiving, doing this in solemn earnest.

"It was some time before Maskepetoon spoke to me again: 'John, that man killed my son and I have often longed to kill him; but because I wanted to embrace the Christian religion, I have with great effort kept from avenging my son's murder. I have never spoken with him or shaken hands with him until now… It was a hard thing to do, but it is done, and he need fear no longer as far as I am concerned'." Woolsey had not preached in vain.

While John was on a trip to Fort Garry (Winnipeg) to obtain some needed supplies and farm animals during the summer of 1864, Reverend Woolsey left Victoria. But because he travelled east by river, while McDougall returned west by the old Winnipeg, Fort Carlton, Edmonton Trail, their paths failed to cross. John McDougall had grown very fond of the older man: "I missed the genial, kindly presence of my old friend, Mr. Woolsey. He returned to Ontario, following the route down the river in one of the Hudson's Bay Company boats and thus I had failed to meet him. Nine years on the Saskatchewan, from 1855 to 1864, in Hudson's Bay fort, in Indian lodge, beside many a campfire,

Rev. John McDougal, guide, interpreter and "roustabout" to Rev. Woolsey from 1862 until 1864.

he preached the gospel of a loving saviour. In his work he had undergone untold hardships, always and everywhere handicapped by physical infirmities. Transplanted from the City of London, England into the wildness and wilderness of the far West; having no experience or knowledge of the conditions of frontier life in a new country; with no knowledge of the language of the Indians— indeed I venture to say he had seldom seen an Indian—in the presence of the physical difficulties which were as legend everywhere around him in his new field, he was altogether dependent on those around him. This, too, in a country where the horseman and the hunter...were tried to the utmost. If upon such men as these there was constant strain and great hardship, what must have been the experience of Mr. Woolsey, arriving here fresh from the comforts of English life?

"For nearly a decade this devoted servant of God had journeyed incessantly through the length and breadth of the Upper Saskatchewan and among the foothills of the Rockies. He had alternately shivered and sweltered, starved and feasted. When freezing he was given a campfire in the frozen snow and colder air to thaw him. When scalding in the burning heat of a long midsummer day on the treeless plains, he had to refresh himself with a cup of tepid water in which an ordinary sight might behold extra-ordinary life. When starving even he, notwith-standing his Sabbatarianism, was forced to trail on in quest of food."

Peter Erasmus remembered one of those occasions while working for Mr. Woolsey when, "For some reason or other larger game— moose, elk and deer— upon which we depended for most of our meat supplies were getting scarce in the region. Greater distances had to be traveled to obtain game, which consequently was hard on the horses..." Woolsey also wrote of that quest for food: "June 4— In consequence of a scarity of pro-visions, we proceed to the plains. June 5— We are subsisting principally upon wild plants and the inner bark of trees. 'The Lord is my shepherd, I shall not want.' June 6— Three fine moose were killed this morning'." His marvellous faith had not let him down.

John McDougall told of the time when Reverend Woolsey was heading for Rocky Mountain House with a French Canadian guide and dog driver when they ran out of food. Under ordinary circumstances Woolsey would not have considered travelling that day, for it happened to be a Sunday, even though not travelling would have meant going hungry. But when his not-as-religious guide said, "Well, Mr. Woolsey, you can stop here and pray; but I am going on to the Fort and eat," Woolsey thought possibly the Lord would forgive him this one trans-gression and decided, albeit reluctantly, to climb into the carriole and go on to the fort where he could both eat and pray. There were times when even a man as devout as Woolsey had to bend a few of the rules in order to survive on the frontier.

To survive generally meant feast or famine. As John McDougall wrote: "He might sup and dine and breakfast for days on fish, another time on rabbits, another period on eggs in all stages of incubation; for a change he would pass from eggs to moulting ducks, and for days these would be his diet. Then would come longer intervals of buffalo diet…"

Both McDougall and Erasmus told of how Woolsey mastered the Syllabic system invented by James Evans. Wrote McDougall: "It was curious to listen to him reading a chapter in the Cree Testament to a group of Indians, himself not understanding 10 words in the chapter, while his hearers were grasping every word. Scores are those in heaven whom he taught to read the words of the Blessed Master…and graduates of his travelling college are scattered all through this western country today."

Strangely, although Peter Erasmus seemed to have been more impressed with Woolsey at their first meeting, it was John McDougall who was most deeply effected when Woolsey left the country. For while Erasmus only mentions that his former employer had left the country, John McDougall wrote: "I have been Mr. Woolsey's interpreter, guide and general 'roust-about' for the past two years and now that he has gone into a far country… I feel a strange melancholy." It had taken some time for Woolsey to make an impression on young John McDougall, but when he did make his imprint it was a deep one.

In the May 9, 1959, issue of the Edmonton *Journal*, "Oldtimer" wrote a short story of Thomas Woolsey's life. In his final paragraph he stated: "When he left the Edmonton district in 1864, Thomas Woolsey embarked on a year-long trip that took him to England. Upon his return to Canada he took posts at Farnham, Quebec and Ontario points before retiring in 1885. He died nine years later in Toronto, 39 years after answering his call to Canada."

Unlike some of his fellow missionaries Thomas Woolsey did not gain great fame and consequently is not known to many, other than those concerned with early church history in the West. But at least two of the mission sites where he served will not be forgotten. These are the Pigeon Lake Mission that he restored, and the Victoria Mission which he helped Reverend George McDougall and his son John to establish. Both are marked by Alberta Historic Sites cairns, that at Pigeon Lake bearing the heading, "Rundle Mission." Located at the north end of Pigeon Lake, it is one of the most popular picnic sites in the province. Victoria Mission, some six miles south of the town of Smoky Lake, has been partially restored and is visited by many historically-minded people.

The man who was ordained with Thomas

A cairn erected to honor the memory of Rev. George and John McDougal and their assistants.

Woolsey and travelled with him to the West— Henry Bird Steinhauer, the first Objibway Indian to become an ordained minister— likewise has not gained the fame that is, perhaps, due him. His first posting in the West was Lac La Biche, where he spent some time at the mission opened by Benjamin Sinclair, the lay preacher who helped Robert Rundle establish the mission at Pigeon Lake. Since Steinhauer hoped to teach his people how to farm, the swampy bush country around Lac La Biche did not suit his purpose so he decided to move to the White Fish Lake area and start a mission there. Obviously this area was more to his liking, for he remained there for almost 30 years, until his death in 1884. His name is honored by a cairn erected by the Alberta Historic Sites not far from the town of Spedden.

If Henry Bird Steinhauer did not gain the fame he perhaps deserves, one of his descendants certainly has. Ralph Steinhauer, long-time farmer in the Saddle Lake district, ensured the family name would be enshrined for all time when, in 1974, he became Lieutenant-Governor of the Province of Alberta. He was the first Indian person of any tribe to be so honored. Perhaps it was only fitting that a Steinhauer should be chosen, not only on Ralph's own merits, but also on the merits of an illustrious great grandfather.

The Reverend Gerald Hutchinson, in an article entitled "Early Wesleyan Missions," which appeared in the Autumn, 1958, issue of the *Alberta Historical Review*, gave the following description of the Reverend Steinhauer's work:

"Mr. Steinhauer lived his first years as an illiterate pagan, having no background or experience of the culture of (white) civilization. Yet he moved to the top of the field of Christian scholarship, receiving top honors in College and then further proved his capacity by teaching from the age of 14 until his death. He moved among people who were illiterate and pagan, moved to a new site, drew the people to him and established a settled, cultured agricultural community which continues today."

It would surely have been a great day for both Thomas Woolsey and his compatriot Henry Bird Steinhauer had they lived to see Henry's great grandson take the oath of allegiance as Ralph Steinhauer proudly stepped forward to become Lieutenant-Governor of Alberta.　　●

(Right) The monument and final resting place of the legendary Twelve-Foot Davis, overlooking the town of Peace River. Knowing that Davis had professed a desire to be buried on the hill overlooking Peace River Crossing, his old friend "Peace River" Jim Cornwall had his remains reinterred on this beautiful spot. His original headstone, a poplar stump, bore the following epitaph: "Pathfinder, pioneer, miner and trader, he was every man's friend and never locked his cabin door."
(Below) Catholic Mission, Dunvegan 1920.

TWELVE-FOOT DAVIS

Davis was a giant in spirit if not in stature. Although he could neither read nor write he knew something about calculating and, upon measuring two rich gold claims, proved that they were wider than they should be and staked the 12-foot-wide strip between them.

READ almost any book relating to the history of the Peace River Country, particularly to the final 20 years of the 19th century, and the name Twelve-Foot Davis is almost sure to appear. Who was this early pioneer whose name has become a legend in the North?

Needless to say, he was not a man 12-feet-tall. The fact of the matter is, he was a short man, stocky, and very strong. For when he freighted supplies on British Columbia rivers before coming to Alberta, he would carry a 200-pound pack across a portage — twice the load he expected any of his helpers to handle. He was born in Vermont in 1820, but little is known of his youth other than that he apparently never attended school and never learned to read or write. He must have served some time as a pastry

Hudson's Bay Trading Post, Fort Vermilion.

cook in his early years, for he knew how to bake a delicious pumpkin pie. Later, when he had a trading post at Fort Dunvegan, "Davis' Punkin Pies" baked from pumpkins raised in the mission garden there were known and praised the length of the Peace River.

Davis' first adventure of note occurred when he was 29, when, along with the other "49-ers," he journeyed to the California gold fields. Although his luck was no better than modest, he acquired a good knowledge of mining that was to serve him well when he moved up to the Fraser River during the famous Cariboo gold rush of the late 1850s and early '60s. He acquired a small fortune at Williams Creek although he was far from the first to stake a claim there.

That claim gave him more than fortune— it gave him the nickname "Twelve-Foot" that remained with him for life. Though illiterate, he obviously knew something about calculating. It seemed to him that two claims in the richest gold-bearing area were improperly staked. He followed his hunch, measured them, found they were wider than they should be, and immediately staked claim to a 12-foot wide strip left between the two claims. From this unusual claim he extracted upwards of $12,000— some claim it was closer to $20,000— and ever after was known as Twelve-Foot Davis.

From the Cariboo diggings Davis soon moved north and was among the first to stake a claim along the Omineca River. However, he was beginning to tire of mining and decided to try his hand at trading. Before long he had a string of trading posts along the Peace River from just above the Peace River Canyon, somewhere near the present Bennett Dam above Hudson's Hope, to Fort Vermilion, 500 miles downstream. He soon became known, loved and respected for his honesty and fair dealing with everyone, regardless of race or color. About the only man who ever had a disparaging word to say against him was Fletcher Bredin, trader, homesteader and parliamentarian, who claimed that Davis "was the dirtiest son-of-a-gun I ever met." Unbathed and uncouth, Mr. Davis undoubtedly was, but he more than made up for it through his kindness and generosity.

It was not long before travellers along the Peace River knew that the doors of Twelve-Foot Davis' cabins were never locked. Moreover, he always left a good supply of grub and extra blankets to be used by anyone who came along. He never kept books, but he did not need to as his memory never failed him. One story has been recorded of a Beaver Indian trapper leaving his furs to be exchanged for supplies Davis was to bring back from either Edmonton or Quesnel (he got his supplies from Quesnel originally and later from Edmonton) on his next trip out. However, the trapper died before Davis returned and it was not until 10 years later that his son came to trade at one of Davis' posts. On learning who the young Indian was, Davis told him he owed his father money for some skins and paid the astonished young fellow on the spot.

No man of the Peace River Country had more friends than Twelve-Foot Davis and even his rivals in trade, the men of the Hudson's Bay Company, grudgingly admitted that he was a fair competitor. Asked in his old age how he explained his abundance of friends, he gave this simple reply: "Maybe it's 'cause them fellers all needs smiles and all needs grub. I allus keep a good stock of both. When they stop at my place I just smiles at 'em and feeds 'em."

Although, as far as anyone knows, he never worked on a farm, Davis saw the potential of the Peace River area as farming country and seldom missed an opportunity to convince anyone who would listen to him. He saw the first of the farmers arrive: the Lawrences at Fort Vermilion, about 1885, and Reverend Gough Brick and his sons Allie and Fred at the Shaftesbury Settlement near Peace River Crossing, a year or so later, as well as missionary farmers like the Reverand Alfred Garrioch at Dunvegan and Shaftesbury. But the real farming era of the Peace did not begin until a few years after his death.

Twelve-Foot Davis died at Lesser Slave Lake (Grouard) while returning from Edmonton to his post at Fort Vermilion. By then he was almost blind, his legs crippled from too many years of moving freight in the cold waters of the Peace and Fraser Rivers. During his final days in the Catholic Mission hospital at Grouard one of the nursing nuns asked him, since he professed to no formal religion, if he was afraid to die. His answer was something like: "No, Ma'am. I ain't never kilt nobody; I never cheated nobody; like the good Lord wants, I allus tried to help fellers and be their friend. I know I ain't lived perfect, but I think the Lord understands. No Mam, I ain't afraid to die."

He passed away in 1900 and was buried at Grouard. But his old friend and fellow trader, "Peace River" Jim Cornwall, knowing that Davis had professed a strong wish to be buried on the hill overlooking Peace River Crossing, where the Smoky, Peace and Hart Rivers meet, obtained permission to exhume the remains and re-inter them on this beautiful spot. On the headstone that Cornwall had made for his friend and carved like a poplar stump is the following epitaph:

H F DAVIS

Born in Vermont, 1820
Died at Slave Lake, 1893 (sic)
Pathfinder, Pioneer,
Miner and Trader
He Was Every Man's Friend
And Never Locked
His Cabin Door

Grouard stopping place in 1905.

A notorious practical joker, storyteller and confidence man, he once sold a bootlegger his own booze. Sometimes his jokes backfired and Baldy Red found himself before a magistrate.

BALDY RED
PEACE RIVER PRANKSTER

WHEN George Yeoman passed away at Hythe in 1943 the Peace River Country bade farewell to one of its most colorful pioneers and certainly its most prodigious prankster. Like Topsy, stories about Baldy Red, as he was more commonly known, just 'growed' so that it is difficult to separate fact from fiction. But it is a well-known fact that Baldy liked nothing better than to pull one of his outrageous pranks, and no one was immune. Not even the various members of the police with whom he carried on a mild feud throughout much of his life in the Peace River Country.

Baldy derived his sobriquet from a fringe of sandy hair that ringed a shiny bald scalp. Dates are hard to come by but it is known he was born in Mount Forest, Ontario, and moved to Manitoba when he was five or six years old. He lived at Portage La Paririe until he was 15 or 16 and there are rumors that he taught school in Manitoba for a few years. Teaching did not appeal to him very much and around 1905 he came West, following the construction crews that were building the Grand Trunk Pacific Railway, now the Canadian National, through Saskatchewan and Alberta to the Pacific Coast via the Yellowhead Pass. Somewhere along the line he tired of that job also and headed north, first settling at Lesser Slave Lake, later renamed Grouard, where he diversified his activities by freighting, farming and bootlegging.

He was always a great story teller and liked to tell about the time during the First World War when he went overseas. "Yes sir!" he would say to anyone who would listen, "I went over there with a shipload of horses. Went up to London while I was there and do you know, wherever I went-Hyde Park, Piccadilly, Soho—all those places, people would come up to me and say, 'Hey, Baldy, how did you get over here?'" Modesty was not one of most outstanding characteristics. Neither was absolute honesty.

Take the time when he was operating a livery barn at Grouard. According to one story, a fellow buying foxes to stock a fur farm wandered into the area one fall and asked if he could rent a stall in Baldy's barn to keep a pair of foxes while he was out in the district making further purchases.

"Sure," agreed Baldy, "but I'm not guaranteeing their safety. Those creatures are pretty handy at escaping from most any kind of pen."

Sure enough, a couple of days later the foxes dug a hole through the floor of the pen and escaped. Baldy immediately informed the owner of his loss. However, when, as semi-domesticated foxes apparently sometimes do, the pair returned to their pen through the hole by which they had escaped, Baldy did not exactly shout the message to the world. Instead he blocked their escape route, lined the pen with chicken wire to prevent further escapes, then sold the buyer his own foxes when he came back the following spring on another buying trip.

Baldy liked to tell the story of how he sold a Peace River Crossing bootlegger his own booze. Baldy claims he located the cache of booze in a creek bank a few miles from the Crossing while camping there overnight on one of his freighting trips. He removed all labels and other identifying marks from the bottles, then took the illicit hootch into town with him and sold it to the man who had cached it.

As often as not Baldy's pranks backfired on him. Like the time he was hauled into court for stealing a cow. Baldy solemnly swore to the judge that it was purely a matter of misunderstanding. "It was getting dark and I stumbled over this rope lying on the road," Baldy explained. "So I picked it up, took it home and put it in the barn. How was I supposed to know there was a cow tied to the other end of it?" Somehow the judge was skeptical of the story and gave Baldy the alternative of paying a $200 fine or spending six months in the pokey. There are conflicting reports as to whether he paid his fine or took the alternative. However, either that time or in some subsequent escapade, he spent a term in the Fort Saskatchewan jail. While enroute to prison he travelled with a man named Demick from Peace River, who was doing time for stealing a watch.

Ever the prankster, Baldy kept needling his travelling companion by asking, "What time is it, Demick?"

Finally Demick could take it no longer and retaliated: "Milking time, you SOB."

Historian and long-time superintendent of the Beaverlodge Experimental Farm, E. Clifford Stacey, tells of Baldy Red running a stage from Smith to Grouard when the Edmonton, Dunvegan and British Columbia Railway was being built to the Peace River Country. "He kept four horses at Stony Point for changing," Mr. Stacy said. "The fare was $20.00. The enterprise was probably not profitable as his horses were plagued with hoof rot and swamp fever."

In the book *Beaverlodge To The Rockies* which Mr. Stacey edited, two oldtimers tell of coming into the Peace to take homesteads at Beaverlodge with a boxcar-load of horses and machinery. They obtained their supplies and loaded them onto the car, then waited for the train to take them to the end of steel, which was then Smith on the Athabasca River. Wrote Stacey:

"While waiting for the train to leave the Edmonton station, they happened to meet a hungry, forlorn chap who, appearing penniless, was looking for a way to get to Smith. Understanding the predicament of being destitute and finding the man friendly and compatible, Percy and Will offered him a ride in their boxcar. They shared their food and even a bottle of rum with the fellow during the journey. The destination of Smith was reached in the middle of the night when all were sleeping. The next morning Percy and Will awoke to the smell of bacon and eggs and coffee.

"Imagine their surprise at their penniless travelling companion able to provide such a banquet. Meanwhile the RCMP were combing the boxcars in search of whisky, going through contents such as flour and sugar sacks with large bayonets. Beyond Smith was Indian Territory and no alcohol could be taken into it to be sold to the Indians, although enough for personal medicinal purposes was allowed the settlers. Our daring friend told Percy and William that during the night friends had removed a load of whisky from a false bottom in the boxcar and were now well into the Peace River Country with it. Percy and Will were angry and shocked as, had the whisky been discovered in their car, they would have been jailed or deported. This fellow turned out to be the notorious Peace River Country bootlegger 'Baldy Red.' They never did know his real name." Since Baldy bought his booze for about a dollar a bottle in Edmonton and sold it in the Peace for as much as 10, he could afford to take a few risks.

He was probably still laughing about using a couple of homesteaders to his advantage when he pulled off what he considered his all-time prize joke. This time the Mounted Police were the victims. The way he told it, he pulled up in front of the police barracks in Peace River town one evening with a wagonload of booze covered with a tarpaulin. Spotting the NCO in charge, a relative newcomer to the Peace, Baldy jumped from his wagon and marched boldly up to the officer of the law. "I've a wagonload of government stuff," he said, truthfully enough, although he hinted that it was explosives, caps and all. "I wonder if I might persuade you fellows to keep an eye on it for me overnight. There's so darn many crooks around these days and I wouldn't want any of that stuff to get stolen."

So all night the unsuspecting policemen kept a watchful vigil on Baldy's booze, providing him with a story he never tired of telling.

Then there are a dozen different versions of the story of his escaping the police by insisting that he drive a skittish team into Grouard for a couple of Catholic nuns, while they drove his quieter team into the settlement. What the nuns did not know was that the police were waiting at Grouard to intercept Baldy as they had been tipped off that he was bringing in another load of his illicit booze. Naturally the police did not search the vehicle driven by the nuns. The story soon expanded to include a lawyer friend and the Reverend Forbes at Grande Prairie. Certainly Baldy Red did nothing to stop the story from becoming a legend.

This story, like many others, perhaps tends to paint Baldy as too much of a scoundrel. Certainly he was no saint, but he did have another side to his nature besides that of a prankster and bootlegger. On more than one occasion he helped people who were down and out and refused to acknowledge his good deed let alone accept payment. One grateful Peace River Country housewife told of Baldy escorting her husband out to Edmonton for medical treatment. She expected a bill of at least $100 for the services, but when she pressed him for a bill he at first told her to forget it, then after a little more deliberation said, "When you get to the city again, send me back a nice new necktie. I always liked fancy ties and a guy never seems to be able to find them in the Peace." The lady avowed that it was as good as done.

There is little doubt that Baldy mellowed as he grew older and there are even rumors that he taught a Sunday School class for a time in his later years. But nothing should be surprising when it came to Baldy Red. Prankster he was, and a shameless liar to boot. But he was one of the Peace River Country's best story tellers and certainly its most famous bootlegger. He has long since passed from the scene as have most of those who were the butt of his jokes. And with them has passed much of the humor and color of Peace River pioneer days. ●

WON'T SOMEBODY HELP POOR CARL?

He had been born with a silver spoon in his mouth; he was brilliant and had two university degrees. Yet he spent much of his life in a one-room log cabin on the banks of the North Saskatchewan River. What was the tragic secret of Carl Groskopff?

BY all standards Carl Groskopff should have been eminently well prepared for life. His father had seen to that. Herr Groskopff of the once proud Free City of Danzig was wealthy by all reckoning. His flour mills flourished throughout Europe, reaching their greatest prominence before the outbreak of the First World War.

Moreover, Herr Groskopff was a practical man. He realized that even the most prosperous of businesses could be destroyed by war and political upheaval and did his best to prepare his six children for life by insisting that each obtain a college education.

Carl was no exception. He attended at least two universities, emerging with training in architecture from the University of Danzig and a degree in chemistry, apparently from the University of Berlin. His father had quite obviously done his share; the rest was up to Carl.

With this background, why did Carl spend many years of his life as a homesteader, living alone in a one-room log cabin on the banks of the North Saskatchewan River? His problem began during the First World War when he was recruited into the German Army, given a commission and put in charge of a hospital supply unit stationed near the Russian Front.

Sometime during his college career Carl acquired a taste for lavish spending. His father, believing it was high time Carl learned self-sufficiency, told him there would be no more allowance. He would have to make do with his officer's pay.

It seems that if Carl had not inherited his father's good commonsense, he did inherit some of Herr Groskopff's business ability. Carl soon realised that abundant hospital alcohol could easily be diluted, bottled and turned into ready cash by selling it to an eager civilian and military market.

For a time Carl continued to live lavishly; even more so than he had on the allowance from his father. Needless to say, it was not long before military authorities began to realize that there was a lot more alcohol passing through the depot than seemed reasonable. To assure that it was being used for external purposes only, they began mixing a poisonous blue dye into the otherwise pure grain alcohol.

Carl met challenge with ingenuity. He put his extensive knowledge of chemistry to work, analyzed the dye-poison and devised a means of extracting it. His sales soon regained their previous lucrative rate.

Unfortunately for Carl, a jaundiced-eyed colonel uncovered the illicit trade. After a brief court-martial and a shorter incarceration, Carl was unceremoniously discharged from the army.

By the time he obtained his freedom the war was over. Though he heartily-disapproved of Carl's unorthodox behaviour, his father had not entirely given up hope. Many countries were clamoring for flour mills based on the Groskopff patent. Carl was given an opportunity to redeem himself. Off he went to design mills and teach the Groskopff milling formula. His tour included several countries in Europe, the United States and Mexico.

According to Carl: "You could enter any of zose flour mills dressed in a dark suit, tour ze whole plant and come out an hour or so later wizzout a trace of flour dust showing."

Obviously the mills he designed were successful for lavish praise poured in from most every country he visited. It seemed that Herr Groskopff's faith in his son was justified. Indeed, Carl would have gone on to even greater success except for his nemesis: alcohol.

After each project he would celebrate and each succeeding celebration grew progressively longer until the completion of a job in Europe, when he realized he would have to take drastic measures lest he end up on some skid road a common drunk. Maybe a trip to Canada would help, he thought. There must be many opportunities there to design flour mills or work as a chemist. Possibly in a new environment he could straighten himself out. So, about 1928, with his family's blessing, he emigrated to Canada.

Unfortunately, if his environment changed, Carl did not. A series of parties in various cities across Canada ended in one tremendous session in Edmonton. He was nursing a hangover big enough to down an elephant when someone mentioned that there were still a few homesteads available within a 50-mile radius of Edmonton. A few days previously he had received word from his father not to bother returning to Danzig until he made some progress toward sobriety. Could a homestead be the cure he was looking for? Carl asked himself.

Hoping for the best, Carl found a piece of land in a quiet, heavily-wooded area along the bank of the North Saskatchewan about 50 miles southwest of Edmonton. With money earned by working for a district farmer clearing land and from lumber cut from his wooded acres, he built a log cabin, bought a few horses and pigs and spent the next few years clearing land, logging and trying to wrest a living from his homestead. Possibly he would have succeeded but for the Depression.

When, during the Dirty Thirties, hog prices dropped to almost nothing and grain was also worthless, Carl, like thousands of others, saw his very existence threatened. He decided then to turn to his knowledge of chemistry for survival. Besides, he had an all-consuming thirst that would no longer be denied.

To his credit, some claim that he spent considerable time trying to find work as a chemist or architect, but when he found none he decided to try another tack. Using the last of his cash, he invested in some copper tubing and other paraphernalia for a 'still,' a barrel of molasses (for his hogs, of course) and an assortment of jugs and bottles. A few days of tinkering and he was in business. Soon he was turning his worthless grain into easily marketed alcohol. The mash mixed with some of the poorer quality grain made his hogs the fattest and happiest for miles around.

Inevitably his illicit activities brought down the ire of some of his more temperate neighbors. Soon the Royal Canadian Mounted came calling and Carl found himself languishing in jail.

Of course a man cannot be incarcerated forever—even for so heinous a crime as depriving the government of its justly due liquor tax. He served his term and was released. Meanwhile, the high quality of his moonshine had become known to many and was even more in demand than before his compulsory stay in the 'iron bar' hotel. Rumor had it that, according to provincial laboratory tests, that Carl's elixir was as pure as anything sold at the government liquor store—and considerably stronger and cheaper.

Once the constabulary was aware of Carl's illegal liquor making proclivities, they kept him under periodic surveillance. For several years there was a constant battle of wits—the Mounties attempting to catch Carl at his moonshining and bootlegging, and Carl to see that they didn't. Carl considered it an achievement of considerable magnitude if he could make his living from his still and have enough money left over to pay his fine if caught, so that he would not have to end up in jail. To him a sojourn in jail was only slightly less traumatic than a trip to the gallows. If he made enough from his 'work' to pay his fine and have enough left over to set up a new still, so much the better.

Ingenious were the methods he used to conceal his operations. Tunnelling was a favorite tactic. He built tunnels from under a false stall in his barn, from under woodpiles, from under haystacks, or from halfway down the riverbank. All led to underground stills. More than once he set up his hootch factory on the far bank of the river, crossing over at night by rowboat to escape detection.

Of course even with all his painstaking methods, he was bound to slip up once in a while. On one occasion he left a gallon of his booze, ready for delivery, in a gunny sack in his cabin while he slipped over to his neighbor's place to see if he wanted anything from town. While he was away the Mounties made a surprise call.

Finding the moonshine but not Carl, they left a young constable in charge of the hootch while the other two went searching for the missing man. They found him at the neighbor's and returned for their fellow officer and the incriminating evidence.

As they neared Carl's cabin they were startled by a series of wild shouts augmented by some painfully off-key singing emanating from within. Thoroughly puzzled, the two policemen flung open the door. There on the floor sat their fellow officer, the crock of moonshine cradled between his knees.

The urge to sample had proved too overpowering for the intemperate fellow. One sip led to another, and several others led to intoxication. Carl and the wayward officer were unceremoniously handcuffed together for the car ride back to town.

On another occaion Carl had a gallon of his fiery hootch in a haystack, where he was sure it would be safe until he was ready to deliver it to waiting customers in town. He could not understand how it was that the Mounties on their next visit headed right to that haystack and the incriminating evidence. As he was being hustled off for the inevitable incarceration and ensuing trial Carl could not curb his curiousity. "How come you fellows knew just where to look for the moonshine?" he asked the Mountie in charge. The policeman only smiled, but as they breasted the hill overlooking Carl's homestead, he stopped the car, took out a pair of binoculars and handed them to Carl. One look revealed the secret. The haystack looked identical to two others in the meadow except for a patch where Carl had concealed his liquor. From the top of the hill that spot stood out like a red flag tied to a pole.

The methods Carl employed in selling his produce were as numerous and as devious as those he used in hiding his stills. One was his broken wheel caper. To make a trip into town seem necessary and proper, he would sometimes remove and disassemble a wheel from his horse-drawn democrat and place it in the back of his car with a couple of kerosene cans. Then he would prop the axle up with a long pole and drive into town, obviously to replenish his kerosene supply and have repairs made to his democrat.

On arriving at the village blacksmith shop, wheel and kerosene cans were quickly removed. Leaving the wheel for "repair," he carried on through the back door of the shop to make deliveries of his potent hootch to eagerly awaiting customers from the supposedly empty containers.

Sometimes he would use a more direct approach. He would drive boldly into town with a jug of his illegal liquor on the seat beside him for all to see. His theory was: "No one suspects I would be so bold and foolish as to bring moonshine into town in broad daylight for all to see. Of course, if I tried to sneak down a back alley, immediately I would be caught."

Towards the end of the Depression, Carl, like most other people, gradually became more affluent. Eventually he retired his horses to pasture and purchased a dilapidated old truck. One evening as he was returning from town after delivering a load of grain and, presumably, a load of booze to his regular customers, he had evidently been sampling some of his own wares and was slightly tipsy. In attempting to cut a corner too sharply, a back wheel of his truck dropped over the shoulder and over he went, landing upside down in the ditch. His feet became thoroughly entangled in the controls and he was stuck fast. Meanwhile, gasoline from a ruptured line began trickling over him, soaking him profusely.

It was getting dark by the time a neighbor found him. Not realizing Carl was in the truck, nor knowing the fuel line had ruptured, the Good Samaritan struck a match for a better look. Seeing the flaming match and with his mind somewhat befuddled from drink, Carl became thoroughly alarmed and it was then he was supposed to have moaned: "Won't somebody help poor Carl?"

Fortunately the leaking gasoline was somewhat less volatile than Carl's booze or his truck could well have become his crematorium.

When Carl was sober, anyone talking with him could not help but realize he had a brilliant mind and a ready wit. Many times, especially during the Second World War, people approached him to ask if he would offer his services to the government or some munitions or chemical factory. "Why waste your time on a little unproductive farm when you could be so much more useful in a laboratory?" his friends often asked. It was no secret that Carl had an intense hatred of Hitler and Naziism, which was further intensified when his home city of Danzig fell to Hitler's advancing army. For many years Carl had no way of knowing the fate of his family.

Carl always considered these proposals seriously. Then a look of wistful sadness would cloud his face. Once he said: "Zat would never work out. Just when I was doing a good job and people were beginning to depend on me, I would have to have a drink. One drink would lead to many more. When somebody needed me most, I would probably let zem down. Zat has been ze story of my life."

As he grew older, Carl gradually began staying sober for longer periods. He eventually sold his farm and moved into town and presumably gave up his illegal activities. Of course he never managed to lick his old enemy completely but he did go back to architecture for awhile, designing schools until he retired. Upon retirement, however, he did not simply live out his years and pass unobstrusively from the scene. Nothing ever seemed to happen quite that way with him.

Sometime after the Second World War rumors began floating around that the Groskopff family had somehow managed to conceal a considerable fortune from the Nazis and the Russians who later occupied Danzig. That fortune was reportedly deposited in Swiss banks, some in Carl's name.

When, in 1962, neighbors realized that they had not seen Carl for a day or two, they went to investigate. The found him in his cabin—dead. Death by natural causes was the coroner's verdict.

The story should end there except for rumors that persist. Although Carl was found in his cabin, the door was locked from the outside, or so some claim. And though he was supposed to have withdrawn his inheritance, no trace was ever found.

Hearsay? Most likely.

But the controversy that surrounded Carl in life will probably persist in death until all those who knew him have likewise passed into the world beyond. ●

THE DAY TURTLE

On April 29, 1903, Turtle Mountain came tumbling down on the unsuspecting town of Frank. Seventy-six men, women and children died in this tragic disaster.

TELEGRAPH keys clacked but the messages were garbled. Something terrible had happened at the coal mining town of Frank in the Alberta section of the Crowsnest Pass, but exactly what, was not very clear. All that could be determined from the various messages arriving at telegraph stations across the nation that fateful morning of April 29, 1903, was that there had been a terrible disaster. But whether it had been an explosion in the mine, as one report stated, or an earthquake, as another report claimed, no one could be certain. Even the newspaper reporters who arrived by train the following morning were not sure what had happened. All that seemed clear was that a great chunk of Turtle Mountain had tumbled down and obliterated the coal mine entrance near the foot of the mountain, covered the valley and a couple of ranches to a depth of hundreds of feet with rock debris, blocked the Crowsnest River, and swept up and across the valley to knock out part of the village of Frank.

Actually, to this day rumors persist that, besides the official count of 76 killed, another 50 men lost their lives that morning. They were construction men, so the rumor states, who were camped on the recreation ground which was buried under hundreds of tons of rock and mud. Actually the "official" count of 76 was based on those reported missing. No one will ever know the exact number killed. The only exact figure is that of the 12 bodies actually recovered.

Had white men heeded an Indian warning, the Frank Slide disaster would never have happened. It was well-known that the Indians called Turtle Mountain "The Mountain that Walks," and that they would never camp near its foot. Unfortunately, white men seldom paid much attention to native beliefs, dismissing them as superstition. Consequently, when Henry Pelletier of Blairmore discovered a good coal seam near the base of Turtle Mountain in 1900, he was more concerned with its commercial potential than with any Indian legend

MOUNTAIN FELL

(Right) Rescued miners being taken to town by wagon, Turtle Mountain in background. (Below) This grim scene shows the damage to a row of miner's houses the morning after the disastrous Frank slide. Only the ruptured roof of the Alexander Leitch home shows to the right.

that it might be unstable. He staked a claim which he sold to Samuel W. Gebo, who obtained his financial backing from H.L. Frank, a Butte, Montana entrepreneur who believed in doing things with the utmost flair.

According to Frank Anderson, in *The Frank Slide Story*, Gebo began developing the mine in the spring of 1901. The main adit was about 30 feet above river level at the point where Goat and Turtle Mountains "nearly touched toes." The Canadian Pacific Railway ran a spur line to the mine tipple after constructing a bridge over the Crowsnest River (or Old Man River, as it was then called). On the flats west of Gold Creek the coal company erected 25 cottages, a boarding house for single men, and office buildings. That done, the two partners, under the title of the Canadian-American Coal Company, tried to attract businesses to their town, topping off their campaign by throwing a great opening extravaganza on September 10, 1901.

The CPR got into the act by running a special passenger train in from Lethbridge with round-trip tickets costing $2.25 from Lethbridge, $1.40 from Macleod and a mere six bits from Pincher Creek. H.L. Frank missed the train that was to bring him from Spokane but, in his usual flamboyant style, hired a locomotive and caught up to his train at Moyie, British Columbia. Some 1,400 people showed up for that blow-out in Frank. Included were Fred Haultain, Premier of the Northwest Territories, and Clifford Sifton, Minister of the Interior in Prime Minister Wilfred Laurier's cabinet. Everyone gorged to stupefaction on a huge dinner that was climaxed by two tons of fruit and ice cream brought in from Spokane. There were races (before the fete, as no one could have run afterwards), baseball and football games, and tours of the cottages and the mine, which had already been dug 1,200 feet into the mountain. Everything that could be done in a single day to make the place appear attractive to the potential miner and businessman was done, and all with the utmost extravagance.

And attract people it did. By 1903 Frank had a population of 600 and was still growing. It had its own electricity and water, a two-storey school, four hotels and 12 business establishments. Business lots sold for $400 to $600, while residential lots went for $250 and up. Frank seemed destined for booming prosperity.

And then the mountain fell! Not entirely without warning, either. Besides the Indian legend of "The Mountain That Walked," there were grim signs in the mine itself that something was amiss. On more than one occasion timbering crews found splintered props and other indications that the underground strata must have shifted. Possibly someone guessed the cause and voiced an opinion that all was not well. If so, his warnings were promptly ignored. The company was shooting for a daily output of 1,000 tons a day, and trying to reach that goal by using only one shift, with a night shift to do the timbering. It was an easy digging as far as mines go, with 10- to 12-foot seams which mostly sloped slightly uphill. Once the coal was loosened it practically slid down to the mine entrance. Foolishly, good mining practice was often ignored and the subsequent board of inquiry concluded that the mine definitely contributed to the great slide.

Murphy's Law— that which states that if anything can go wrong it will— soon took effect. Late April of 1903 was what Westerners call an unseasonably warm spring. These happen perhaps one year in three when April temperatures soar to 25 or so degrees Celcius. But, due to short memories, or perhaps because it is easier to remember unduly cold springs than warm ones, hot weather in April is "unseasonable." The Frank baseball club had already held its first practice on April 28 but, as is inevitable in the mountains, it was downright chilly by the early morning of the 29th. Engineer Ben Murgatroyd was shunting cars of coal from the mine tipple to the siding on the main line that morning. It was nearing 4:10 a.m. and still dark.

Suddenly the veteran of mountain railroading sensed that something was wrong. He perhaps felt, rather than heard, rocks breaking loose high up the mountain side. He was rolling his train slowly toward the bridge crossing the Crowsnest River with his two brakemen, Bill Lowes and Sid Choquette, walking alongside, when he abruptly ordered them to climb aboard. At the same time, he yanked the throttle back— and none too soon. Just as the puffing locomotive pulled its load across the river, the bridge was smashed from its moorings and flung aside like a feather in a windstorm by a tremendous blast of cold air, followed by a cascade of limestone rock plummeting down the mountain. Some 90 million tons of rock broke loose in one great slab, then broke into countless pieces great and small as it bounded and tumbled down the mountain and across the valley, crushing and burying everything in its path.

More by luck than good planning, the town had been built beyond the main path of the tumbling mountain side, or the death toll would have been much greater than it was. As it was, at least 76 lives were snuffed out that fateful morning, the powerhouse crushed and its operator killed, the mine entrance swept away and the air shaft blocked, the railway mainline buried and the river blocked. All buildings in the path of the avalanche were either splintered to matchwood or buried with their occupants. But it was not until daylight, when the dust began to settle, that the full extent of the damage was known. There undoubtedly would have been a further disaster had not the two brakemen, Lowes and Choquette, after their miraculous escape, realized that the famous passenger train, the 'Spokane Flyer,' was due from Lethbridge in 20 minutes. If it was not stopped it

More wrecked houses at Frank after the slide.

would pile into the slide that buried the CPR tracks. Despite their knowing that great boulders were still tumbling down the mountainside and that they could be crushed, the two men set out in the dark and the dust to crawl and stumble over the great jumble of limestone to the spot where the tracks emerged from the rubble. Just in time, they raced along the tracks to flag down the oncoming train. They were later commended for their effort and each awarded $25.

Although it seemed impossible that anyone caught in the path of the slide could still be alive, there were survivors. Sam and Lucy Ennis and their four children somehow escaped although their home was demolished. When the rescuers freed the family, along with James Warrington, Mrs. Ennis' brother, who had been sleeping in a room at the back of the house, they found an unexpected house guest: Mrs. John Watkins, who had been sound asleep in her home next door to the Ennis', had somehow been flung from her bed and into the Ennis home when her home was crushed. She was suffering from shock and internal injuries and was bleeding from dozens of rock splinters, but she lived to tell of her escape. Her two teenage children likewise escaped, as did a younger daughter named Fernie. Altogether 23 people emerged from the

rubble. But the most miraculous escape had to be that of baby Marion Leitch, who was flung several hundreds yards from her crib on the upper floor of her parent's home, only to land safely on some bales of hay.

At first there seemed to be no possible hope that any of the miners who had gone underground could have survived, for it seemed certain that if they had not been crushed by the collapse of the mine shafts when the mountain began to tumble, they would surely have suffocated because the mine entrance and air shafts were blocked. As it turned out, only three miners, A. Tashigan, Alex Clark and Fred Farrington, who had been eating their lunch at the mine entrance, were killed. The other 17 were deeper in the mine and still alive, although the people of Frank had no way of knowing.

Soon after word of the disaster, albeit garbled, began to be relayed via telegraph across the nation, the CPR sent in a special train to aid the stricken community. William M. Pearce, Inspector of Mines, rushed from Calgary and Inspector Davidson of the NWMP hastened from Pincher Creek with a sergeant and a constable. They were quickly followed by Inspector Douglas and 10 men from Calgary, and Inspector P.C.H. Primrose and 25 Mounties from Macleod. Inspector Primrose took

Rebuilding the mine entrance after the disaster.

charge of the situation to see that there was no looting. By the morning of April 30, correspondents from major newspapers had arrived. Some of the stories they dispatched over the telegraph and telephone wires were more the product of vivid imagination than of fact, however. Medical teams also arrived, but when they found that Dr. Malcolmson and his nurse, Miss Grassick, had the situation well in hand, they returned to their own jurisdictions.

Meanwhile, the trapped miners had realized that if there was to be any rescue, they would have to pull it off by themselves. When they felt the earth move, followed by a blast of hot air racing down the tunnels, all dropped their tools where they had been working in various parts of the mine and headed for the entrance, suspecting an explosion or cave-in. The jumble of rock, timber and other debris some 150 or so feet from where the entrance should have been confirmed that something terrible had happened. Although they were not sure what, of one thing they could be certain: they were trapped. Some panicked before cooler heads took charge. One of the men, probably shift foreman Joe Chapman, started giving orders. As the air shafts were sealed off, there was not much time. Whatever they could do to help themselves, they had to do quickly. Someone then remembered that one of the seams of coal outcropped higher up on the mountain face. Maybe, just maybe, they could dig through to the outside before their air gave out.

It was a close race. The river, dammed up by the slide, was rapidly filling the lower shafts of the mine and helping deplete the oxygen supply. Consequently, efforts to dig a tunnel big enough to crawl through were slowed as the oxygen supply diminished and the miners tired. Some could no longer gather sufficient strength to do more than sit back and rest. Then, suddenly, Dan McKenzie's pick broke through and sunlight and fresh air streamed into the mine. A few more hefty whacks and they were free. Only when they had crawled through their narrow escape tunnel and sat gulping fresh air high on the mountainside did they realize what had happened and what a narrow escape they had had. Far below them lay a huge slab of the mountain, broken into a million pieces and spread in a great fan across the valley floor. Had it broken off deeper, they, too, would have been carried along with the cascading limestone.

Strangely, the town of Frank did not die, although most of its residents moved out for a time. Premier Haultain arrived on a special train to receive a report on the damage to the town and the condition of the mountain. After nine days, although fissures had opened up high on the mountain, they appeared to have stablized and there seemed to be no further immediate danger to the town. Premier Haultain then pronounced that the people could return to those homes still standing. Thanks to Inspector Primrose and his troops, there had been no looting. Most of the people returned to their homes and their businesses, the mine reopened and remained in operation until 1913. It closed for a time after changing hands, then shut down for good after a second devastating explosion in 1917.

For a town that had faced a disaster of such magnitude and seemed imminently in danger of another should the fissures high on the mountain widen, Frank continued to have a carefree and boisterous existence. Throughout most of its life it was a rip-roaring mining town in the most literal sense. It grew to a booming town of 800, where hotel bars stayed open until the early morning hours and one banker reportedly slept over his bank with four revolvers near the head of his bed, loaded and ready for action. There were murders, too, not the least of which was that of Monte Lewis, one of the

This photograph shows the wall of rock which swept down the mountainside on the tragic morning of April 29, 1903.

many prostitutes who plied their trade in Frank. That story is yet told in the bars throughout the Crowsnest Pass, some 70 years after it happened.

This story, which has become a legend, began one night in November of 1907. Mounted Police Constable Martin was patrolling his beat when he noticed a light streaming from an open door of the house occupied by Monte Lewis. That seemed strange to him for it was late, long past the hour when even ladies of the night like Monte had retired. There was no reply to his knock, so he decided to look inside. Like most policemen, he was not a complete stranger to violent crime, but he certainly was not prepared for this one. The bedroom was splattered from floor to ceiling with blood; on the bed lay the remains of Monte Lewis, who had been fiendishly mutilated by dozens of stab wounds and her skull fractured by what must have been a prolonged and savage beating. Whoever had committed the brutal murder was long gone.

No reason was ever uncovered for the vicious homicide, although it could have started as a robbery, for a set of diamond earrings and a necklace Monte had always worn were missing. Some suspected revenge as the motive and accused a man named Max Pylyczul, who had lived with Monte for a time, with the crime. Pylyczul was apprehended at his home in British Columbia and charged with the murder but, at his trial, held on

May 7-9, 1908, Sam Ching, who claimed he saw someone leave Monte's house on the night of the murder, could not possitively identify Max as the man he had seen and Pylyczul was acquitted. As Frank Anderson noted in *The Dynamic Crow's Nest*: "Today, across the flats of the abandoned village, the ghost of Monte Lewis goes moaning after her beloved earrings and necklace. She will probably haunt the town until Doomsday, for neither her murderer nor her trinkets were ever found."

Today, with approximately 180 residents, Frank is but a shell of its former self. But it seems in little danger of further decline, for it has a couple of stores, service stations and a busy motor inn. Stories are still told of that fateful day when Turtle Mountain moved, and baby Marion Leitch miraculously escaped death when she was flung from her crib to land on a bale of hay nearly a half mile from her home. That story is absolutely true, although some writers have altered the facts to make Marion the sole survivor of the slide. The truth, of course, is that by far the majority of Frank citizens survived.

One fact, however, cannot be changed. Today, for all too see, is the all-too-visible evidence of that disaster of April 29, 1903, when some 90 million tons of limestone came tumbling down from Turtle Mountain and 76 men, women and children lost their lives. ●

Frontier nurse Maude Lucas, far right, with the graduation class at Holy Cross Hospital in 1914.

FRONTIER NURSE

Drastic measures were sometimes called for, improvision often a necessity on the Alberta frontier. During 37 years as a nurse, Maude Lucas proved herself to be more than a match for the thousand and one challenges, far from a modern hospital.

MAUD Lucas could hardly have chosen a more historic spot to be born. As the second daughter of Frank and Margaret Lucas, she entered the world on her father's farm some five miles north of Wetaskiwin. It was later known as the "Peace Hills Agency Farm," for it was near here that a temporary peace treaty between Cree and Blackfoot tribes was agreed upon in 1850. The farm has also been known as the Fort Ethier Farm, for it was here, in 1885, that Captain Joseph Ethier of the 65th Mont Royal Rifles erected a block-house dubbed Fort Ethier as a place of refuge for soldier and civilian alike during the North-West Rebellion. The fort still stands and is visited by hundreds of history-minded tourists each year. This is the same farm that Sam

Lucas, brother of Maud's father Frank, established in 1878, when he was sent from Ottawa by the Department of Indian Affairs to act as Indian Agent and to instruct the Indians in farming. Frank Lucas and his wife Margaret did not arrive from their native Quebec until 1884. By then Sam had erected a house and plowed some land. Maud's father took over the operation, added another quarter section to the holdings and continued to improve the farm.

Maud did not come along until 1886, a year after the North-West Rebellion, but that does not mean she was not influenced by it. It seems the soldiers of the 65th who had built Fort Ethier were adept cussers; in fact, they literally swore like troopers. A neighbor's girl, 10 years Maud's senior, had often heard the troopers and adopted their colorful language. She, in turn, when visiting the Lucas Farm, passed her vocabulary on to Maud. As Daisy Lucas, Maud's sister-in-law who now lives in Wetaskiwin, jokingly wrote, "Before Maud could read or write, she too could cuss like a trooper—a very useful talent on the frontier."

Even had the soldiers of the 65th not passed their colorful vocabulary on to Maud's friend and thus to Maud, it seems quite likely she would have heard considerable colorful language from some of the travellers who passed through after the rebellion. For her father and mother turned their home into a stopping house, one of the most popular on the Calgary-Edmonton Trail. There, a weary traveler travelling by stagecoach could spend the night and eat breakfast for the grand sum of one dollar. Freighters paid more— one dollar and 50 cents— but that included a stall and feed for their horses. With some of the West's most interesting and colorful characters coming and going, it was indeed an exciting place for a little girl to live.

In an interview given to Daisy Lucas in 1960, Maud Lucas remembered that most of her early childhood playmates were Indian children from the nearby Hobbema Reserve. Perhaps, then, it followed logically that Maud, when she became a nurse, should choose a career serving the Indians. When she entered training at Calgary's Holy Cross Hospital in 1911, she renewed an acquaintance of her childhood, Bob Edwards, the noted, or notorious, editor and publisher of the Calgary *Eye Opener.* Maud remembered that while she was a young girl Edwards had published a paper in Wetaskiwin that, like his later *Eye Opener,* had poked fun at local people and events. She remembered being in town one day when Edwards threw a store dummy into the flooded basement of a burnt-out hotel, then began shouting for the doctor. Dr. Walker tore down the street, ripped off his coat and dove into the basement to recover the dummy, while Edwards, quite possibly the worse for having imbibed too much John Barleycorn, stood laughing as though he had perpetrated the greatest joke ever.

While Maud was in training at the Holy Cross, Edwards came to the hospital many times to "dry out" after his extended binges. Once the worst of his great hangovers had dissipated, he would spend the rest of his stay thinking up jokes to play on Maud and the other nursing trainees. Edwards, however, proved to have a thoughtful and generous side to his nature as well, for when Nurse Lucas was serving overseas during the First World War with the Canadian Medical Corps, the first parcel she received from home was a bundle of Calgary *Eye Openers,* courtesy of Bob Edwards.

During her training Maud also met two of the most noted missionaries to serve in Alberta. They were Father Albert Lacombe of the Roman Catholic Church and the Reverend John McDougall of the Methodist church. Both semi-retired, the old gentlemen liked to visit the hospital and talk for hours of their experiences serving the Indians and Metis back when the buffalo roamed in countless thousands across the plains and the Blackfoot and Cree tribes were bitter enemies. Both of these men played a major role in stopping that warfare and in getting the Indians to sign Treaties Six and Seven that made it possible for settlers to open the West.

When Maud Lucas finished her training in 1914, she served for three years at the Wetaskiwin Hospital. She put in her application for overseas duty with the Army Nursing Corps soon after war broke out in 1914, but her application was side-tracked in some military file and she was not asked to report for duty until 1917. As a lieutenant in the Nursing Corps she sailed for England shortly after. In her 1960 interview she told Mrs. Lucas about that trip:

"We embarked aboard a ship at Halifax, the name of which I never knew, but I did know that we were one of a convoy of 20 ships, which for safe passage due to the enemy U-Boat menace, were to be convoyed across the Atlantic to Liverpool. But due to U-Boat activity, when within 300 miles of our destination, orders came to change course and make London our point of disembarkation.

"These orders were received about four o'clock in the afternoon and all soldiers and nurses aboard were ordered to don life belts and stand at attention (as our boats were surrounded by German submarines) at their life boat positions from four to six, and again ordered to don life belts and back again at the life boat stations from seven to nine p.m. when we were ordered to bed with our life belts still on (in case of an emergency arising) to try and obtain a little rest.

"When we arose next morning there wasn't another ship in sight; the whole convoy had scattered — we had been attacked during the night — and the boat carrying our contingent of the Canadian Army Medical Corps was considered a very slow boat and we were left behind. But why we were not attacked remained a mystery until we reached London, then it was discovered that we had a German spy aboard who must have been in communication with the enemy and thus our slow boat to London was unmolested."

Maud had an interesting career overseas, serving mostly in Wales. She returned home to Canada in 1919. Said she, "In order to better equip myself I took a post graduate course in general nursing at Bellevue Hospital in New York City, after which I took a position at Billings, Montana, and returned to Canada in 1925 to nurse an aging mother, laying her to peaceful rest in October of that year..."

Maud was just getting started. "Early in 1926," she told her sister-in-law, "I took a position with the Federal Government at Ottawa with the Department of Indian Affairs. In the discharge of my duties in this department it was necessary for me to travel by primitive modes of transportation via: boat, dog-team, snowshoe, saddle horse, horse and buggy, and car." Much of her work was in Alberta, although she also served in both northern Saskatchewan and Manitoba.

Continued nurse Lucas: "One of my first assignments was requested by a priest of the Anglican Church who wanted me to visit an Indian family at a reservation. "When I arrived at the Indian hut there seemed to be many Indian people inside. When I opened the door the stench almost flattened me; I immediately set about clearing the hut of Indians so I could attend to the sick.

"After getting all the Indians out I discovered seven dead skunks, and one very sick woman. Fresh air was what this woman needed and after a few aspirins and much cleaning up she soon revived."

One of the ingredients Maud needed for her work with the Indians was a keen sense of humor, and that she had in abundance, along with ample good sense. "Cleanliness," she said, "was the hard lesson to teach these people who had lived for generations as nomads. Their uncleanliness made them easy prey and a fertile field for the development of tuberculosis, or 'Coughing Sickness' as the Indians called it… Consequently on request of the government I took a post graduate course for the treatment of T.B. at St. Agathe, Quebec. My duties then consisted of visiting various Indian reservations in the Western provinces, instructing the women in personal hygiene, baby clinics, etc."

On one of her visits to a reservation in 1930 she ran into a full-fledged smallpox epidemic. She was alone and as she stated, "No white people lived near, so I had to pitch my tent and live there, while the Indians brought me wood and stacked it around the base of my tent. Then I requisitioned the school house and converted it into an isolation hospital, doing the cooking, cleaning and nursing myself. After that I vaccinated 165 patients and after six weeks of strenuous work I had the disease fully controlled."

During another outbreak of smallpox on the Ebb and Flow Reservation near Winnipeg, Maud thought she was very fortunate in that she was able to find a boarding place within 12 miles of the reserve. "It being winter I preferred traveling the 12 miles in preference to living in a tent. To travel the 12 miles I hired a man to drive me with horse and cutter, which proved quite satisfactory until the man discovered I was treating smallpox patients, then he refused me transportation. I looked the man squarely in the eye and asked him, 'Do you really refuse me transportation?' to which he replied, 'Yes, ma'am'. 'Then I'll have to find temporary lodging,' I said, and that is what I did until I had the outbreak completely under control."

Until her tenure on the Ebb and Flow Reserva-

tion, Maud made no claims to any veterinary prowess, but treating sick animals just happened to follow as an adjunct to her treatment of sick people. At least it did on one occasion. "In addition to treating sick Indians and acquainting the women of the Reserve with methods of hygiene and treatment of infant diseases," she told Daisy Lucas, "I was asked if I knew anything about animal diseases. Having been raised on a pioneer farm, where each farmer is his own veterinary, I examined the sick animals, mostly cows, and diagnosed the complaint —the cows had lost their cud, i.e., were unable to regurgitate their food and rechew it as is necessary for cattle in their digestion process. I also discovered that due to a very wet period in the previous fall, the rain had penetrated the haystacks, and consequently froze during the winter. This frozen hay had brought about the digestive disturbance that had caused the animals to lose their cuds. I immediately sent for 100 pounds of Epsom Salts and instructed the Indian men in how to drench a cow by the simple operation of taking hold of the animal's head by the nostrils, pulling the head to one side and inserting either a long necked bottle, or a conveniently curved cow horn and giving each animal a dose of at least two pounds of Epsom Salts dissolved in water.

"I am pleased to say that all the 15 cows I so treated completely recovered. My reputation as a veterinary reached other reserves and consequently one night about midnight I heard a plaintive wail of an Indian boy calling, 'Nurse, Nurse!' I got up to find out what the trouble was and found the little Indian boy had walked some miles from another reservation. He very sobbingly asked me if I would come and treat their sick cows. That I did the next day and discovered another outbreak of 'lost cud'." Apparently that was Maud's last act as a veterinarian for the Indian's sick animals, but she was more than amply rewarded for her extra-curricular activities. For when she was leaving the Ebb and Flow Reservation some time later she was pleasantly surprised to be treated to a farewell party. The natives for miles around turned up to wish her 'Bon Voyage' and good health wherever her duties should take her.

Maud used many means of transportation during her duties as a frontier nurse but, as she claimed, "My most novel means of transportation that I can recall was floating ice. It happened one night in early spring when I was called to a reservation across a river where an Indian had suffered a nose bleed for two days. Immediate help was needed and I therefore had to go. But it was at the time of year when the ice in the river was breaking up and no ferry was yet in operation. But if there was any way of getting across the river at a certain point, it would save me many miles of arduous travel. It was late at night, the ice flows were freezing together, so two Indian men piled my bags on a toboggan, placed me on it, and with that each grabbed a side of the toboggan and raced across, dragging me with them." Fortunately for all concerned, the ice held and Maud reached her destination at 6 o'clock in the morning. As she put it, the unnerving shortcut "saved a lot of time, and a man's life."

Undoubtedly most of Maud's patients were grateful to be relieved of their pain, but, as she claimed: "The most grateful patient I ever treated was a little Indian boy who had a fishbone stuck cross-ways in his throat and penetrating his tonsils. It was a simple operation to carefully insert my finger and extract the tortuous bone, but I shall never forget the delightfully happy smile that this little Indian boy gave me after I had accomplished the operation. Indian children have a very sweet way of expressing their appreciation for relief from pain."

Maud became a firm believer in an Indian legend that wolves fear light and will not attack anyone carrying a lantern at night. "I saw that proven one night when I was called to a reservation where a very bad epidemic of measles had broken out and it was necessary to go through heavy bush which was infested with wolves. My driver had a lantern on the tongue of the sleigh and hung another on the back. He had a gun and I drove the horses, and though we could hear the wolves howling in what seemed close proximity to us, we were not molested." Quite possibly the wolves feared the man with his gun as much as the lanterns, but carrying a light has always given people a sense of security, so perhaps Maud was right in attributing their safe passage to the lanterns.

However, Maud attributed her most dangerously exciting experience not to wolves, but to man. She was called to the bedside of a very sick young Indian woman, whose complaint Maud diagnosed as pneumonia. "I stayed with her for 10 days," Maud said, "until the crisis was over, and in order to assist her recovery I administered small doses of brandy.

"One evening the father arrived much the worse for liquor and was determined to relieve me of some of my brandy. After grabbing me and threatening to stab me with my scissors, I was really scared. I finally told him that I could not give him any brandy until he let me go, and as soon as he let go my throat I threw my suitcase out of the window, while I made a hurried exit out of the door. My assailant was too intoxicated to be able to follow me and I walked back to Gleichen, which was about a mile away. I discovered later that chokecherry wine, a very potent brew, was the cause of this disturbance."

Maud had a similar experience some time later at a reservation near Kamsack, Saskatchewan. "I was living in a tent," she recalled, "and treating a man's wife, which also involved the administration of small doses of brandy. The husband returned home one day, smelled the brandy, and demanded some of the same medicine. I managed to satisfy his demands at least temporarily by promising him a

drink when I was ready to leave. I waited until I got outside of the hut, then presented him with a drink I had prepared for him while his back was turned. It consisted of a trace of brandy liberally laced with three tablespoons of castor oil. Needless to say, I hurriedly got into my conveyance and headed back to town, where I reported the incident to the farming instructor, who in turn reported it to the RCMP constable. He drove out the next day to see how my male patient was doing. When the Constable reported back, he informed me that the poor man was having a very rough time."

Maud obviously was not afraid to use drastic measures when drastic measures were called for. She was also seldom reluctant to improvise. For, as she claimed, "Improvisation was always an ally of my profession. Medical supplies were often either non-existent or a long way off. This was so when I called to attend an Indian boy who was suffering from diphtheria. When I visited him he was having great difficulty in breathing due to an accumulation of considerable mucus in his bronchial passages. I realized that something had to be done very quickly, for any orthodox treatment for diphtheria would be too slow. Knowing that coal oil (kerosene) was a drastic remedy but one that might work, I took a 20-to-one chance and poured a small dose of coal oil down his throat. I am very pleased to say that it worked wonderfully, the boy was able to breathe more normally and gradually recovered. I can safely say that the coal oil saved his life."

The time inevitably came when Maud could no longer stand the rigors of the nomadic life of administering to the Indians, and after 19 years of this strenuous life, as she put it, "I felt a desire to settle in a more permanent residential position." If Maud's friends thought she would simply take a matron's position in a hospital, work a few years, then quietly retire on her civil service pension, they did not know her as well as they thought. She had only worked as matron of the Grande Prairie Hospital for a few months when she decided to embark on a brand new career: marriage. In 1945 she met Archie Smart, a civil engineer who had an exciting career in his own right— working as a government engineer. Among his projects were the Bassano Dam in southern Alberta and the designing of the Canadian Exhibit for the 1939 San Francisco World's Fair.

Both Archie and Maud worked as hard at making their marriage work as they had at their engineering and nursing careers. Consequently, they had 15 good years together before Archie passed away in 1960. After spending her final three years in the Good Samaritan Nursing Home in Edmonton, Maud followed her husband into the world beyond on Christmas Eve, 1963.

Altogether Maud Lucas Smart spent 37 years in her chosen profession. Not all of those years were in Alberta, but enough were so that she surely qualifies as an excellent example of Alberta's pioneer nurse. ●

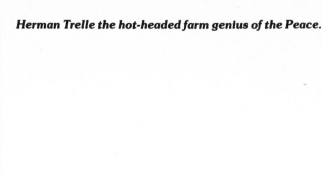

Herman Trelle the hot-headed farm genius of the Peace.

The Wheat King of Wheat Kings, they called Herman Trelle. An undisputed genius when it came to growing wheat, he found it difficult to work with others. But he left a record that likely will not be duplicated.

AN historical scrapbook in the library in Dawson Creek, British Columbia, contains an article clipped from the local newspaper. Written in August of 1960, and entitled "The Peace River Story," it is a story about Herman Trelle, whose name in the 1920s and 1930s was splashed over every farm periodical in the nation. For Herman Trelle of Wembley in the Peace River Country was the wheat king to top all wheat kings. Not only did he win the World Wheat Crown four years running but, according to E.C. Stacey, Superintendent of the Dominion Experimental Station at Beaverlodge from 1947 to 1962, "He collected some 135 champion awards in about 10 years' time and his helpers, the equivalent of today's 4-H youths, Lloyd and Justin Rigby, Peter and Saul Sebastian, and Douglas Clarkson, took almost as many more." It is a record not likely to be duplicated.

Genius he was when it came to displaying seed grain, but not necessarily when it came to dealing with people. Hot-headed, flamboyant and decidedly lacking in tact, he tried to persuade every Wembley farmer to buy and plant his championship Reward wheat. He charged strangers $20.00 a bushel for his seed wheat—neighbors got it for $5.00. He must have been a pretty persuasive salesman, for one ex-Wembley farmer tells of his father going deeply in debt to buy Trelle seed wheat, only to have the bottom drop out of wheat prices in the fall of 1929, the start of the Great Depression. When his father died and the son inherited the farm, it took him well into the years of the Second World

War to pay off his debt for that wheat. "Maybe," says the now-retired farmer, "it was a blessing in disguise. For since then I have never bought anything without paying cash."

Herman Trelle, however, never seemed to worry about such trivial matters as being in debt. His greatest fame came during the early years of the Depression when his neighbors, struggling to keep from going bankrupt, could not help but be envious as Trelle, after a trip to Edmonton, unloaded new equipment, including a new tractor, household furnishings, a fur coat and even a grand piano, from a boxcar. All were gifts from companies wanting to use his name in testimonials, he claimed. A Mediterranean cruise for him and his wife was sponsored by the Canadian Railway Development Company, he said.

The neighbors, however, finally learned the truth when, after Trelle left the Peace River Country, the railway put a lien on his land and finance companies seized some of his prize possessions for non-payment. His gifts, apparently, were nothing more than goods he bought himself, using the now only too familiar instalment plan.

No one ever accused Herman Trelle of being a shrinking violet. On one of his trips to Toronto to collect yet another batch of awards, he stepped down from the train at Wembley, wondering aloud why there was no band to greet him. In his book *Peace Country Heritage* Clifford Stacey wrote: "Trelle once boasted to University of Alberta'a Dean Howes that he could talk in 10 languages. The

Hot~Headed Farm Genius of the Peace

somewhat sardonic dean commented, 'You know, Herman, you should learn to keep quiet in 10 languages.'" Perhaps it is just as well that Herman did not take the dean's advice for, as well as singing the praises of his wheat wherever he went, he also never tired of praising the Peace River Country and he is undoubtedly responsible for persuading many landseekers to homestead there.

Herman Trelle was born in Kendrick, Idaho, in 1894 and emigrated to the Peace River Country with his parents over the old Athabasca Trail in 1910. The land that was to bring him so much fame was adjacent to his father's original homestead near the since vanished town of Lake Saskatoon.

Apparently Herman Trelle was a brilliant student at the University of Alberta where he enrolled as an engineering student about 1912. He won the first oratorical contest ever held there, his topic being "Empire of the Peace." His graduation thesis was on the Peace River Country's geological formation pertaining to water supply. His paper was later proved to be correct in almost every detail by the Federal Government Survey.

After his graduation he farmed with his father and on Christmas Day, 1919, he married Beatrice Irene Burdick, who was to play a prominent role in his success. It seems that Trelle grew one of the finest grains in the world, by exercising the patience of Job—patience he seldom displayed with people. He would pick out his samples seed by seed, usually assisted by Beatrice. His first display at the Chicago International Hay and Grain Show in

1923 won him no more than a modest third place. But it was enough to whet his appetite for more. He captured his first wheat crown in 1926 and from then until 1932 when he was barred from showing any more wheat at Chicago for four years, he established a record not likely to be equalled—135 International awards for Peace River grown grains, including field peas.

For all of his success, some claim that when Trelle left the Peace he was almost broke. He served a hitch during the Second World War with the Royal Canadian Engineers then, in 1945, sold his Peace River Country holdings and moved to California to start a new life. Instead, he met a violent death.

There are at least two versions of what happened on that fateful day of September 1, 1945. One has it that Trelle bought a ranch and that he was having trouble with a ranch hand, whom he fired. A few days later the ranch hand returned with a shotgun, argued with Trelle and shot him. The "Peace River Story" version has Herman and the ranch hand arguing over who was the foreman of the ranch on which both were working. After the argument the ranch hand returned with a shotgun and shot Herman Trelle, who died the following day.

As the article, "The Peace River Story," stated: "The shotgun blast was the final punctuation in the story of a strong-willed, egotistical farming genius who, in life, whipped controversy and, even today, fans the embers of argument to flame among the dwindling band of Peace River residents who knew him." ●

(1) Cairn and grave of Constable Graburn.
(2) Supt. J.M. Walsh, who was in charge of Fort Walsh at the time of Graburn's murder.
(3) Fort Walsh, Saskatchewan, in the 1880s.
(4) "F" troop, NWMP, at Fort Walsh, a year after Graburn's murder.

More than once the Cypress Hills have known murder and massacre. It was here that Constable Marmaduke Graburn became the NWMP's first casualty.

MURDER IN THE CYPRESS HILLS

IT seems ironic that the first member of the North West Mounted Police to be murdered should meet his death in the same hills where occurred a murder—or a massacre, depending upon one's point of view—that was largely responsible for the forming of the force in the first place. On November 17, 1879 Constable Marmaduke Graburn was killed in the Cypress Hills. Six years before, in May of 1873, a group of wolf hunters from Fort Benton, Montana, got into a fire-fight with a band of Assiniboine Indians near Abe Farwell's post and killed a large number of them.

The wolfers had had their horses run off near Fort Benton and had followed their trail north, where apparently they lost it. Since they knew a band of Assiniboines were camped in the Cypress Hills, they headed there and accused the Indians of stealing their horses. Though at this late date no one will ever know for sure whether or not the Indians did steal the horses, what is known is that the wolfers found no stolen animals in the Indian camp. Nevertheless, probably because both wolf-hunters and Indians were drinking, a gunfight broke out and one wolfer and many Indians lost their lives.

The hunters were later tried for their crime in Helena, Montana, but were never convicted. But if the massacre brought little discredit to the wolfers in their home country, when the report of it reached Ottawa it stirred up such a stink that Prime Minister John A. Macdonald and his cabinet quickly passed a bill bringing the NWMP into being. For various reasons, not excluding the Fenian raids into Canada in the 1860s, there were strong anti-American feelings in Canada at the time. American traders had invaded what is now southern Alberta and built their whisky posts such as Fort Whoop-up from which they were decimating the Indian population by selling them potent "firewater." Then came the news of the massacre, with more Indians dying with each telling. It was the last straw. The NWMP formed and marched into the West in 1874 and brought law and order.

Strangely, for all of the violence that had occurred before their arrival, not a single man lost his life to violence during the first years of NWMP takeover. Then, in November of 1879, near Horse Camp, an outpost of Fort Walsh in the Cypress Hills, Constable Graburn (also spelled Graeburn and Grayburn) was shot and killed.

Why he was murdered or by whom is as much an enigma today as when it happened. Some claim the wrong man was accused and tried for murder. It really does not matter now, but since the murder took place in the Alberta sector of the Cypress Hills, the story surely deserves a place in this book.

According to some sources, Constable Marmaduke Graburn was a well-liked veteran of the force, who spoke the Blackfoot tongue fluently. Sam Steele, in his *Forty Years In Canada*, said Graburn could speak Blackfoot fairly well, but he was no veteran. Graburn, about 24 years of age, and his friend George Johnston had both been recruited in Ottawa in the spring of 1879 by Superintendent L.M.F. Crozier and sworn into the force at Fort Walsh in June. Young Graburn, therefore, had been a Mountie for less than six months at the time of his death.

The Cypress Hills, a strange formation that rises in places to 4,000 feet and straddles the Alberta-Saskatchewan border 50 or so miles north of the Canada-United States boundary, was at times the gathering place of hundreds of nomadic Metis, Cree, Assiniboine, Blackfoot, Peigan, Blood and Sioux hunters. Skirmishes between various tribes were by no means rare and, in the spring of 1875, Inspector James Morrow Walsh led "B" Troop of the NWMP to establish Fort Walsh in the Cypress Hills just inside the present Saskatchewan border. To keep the peace the NWMP kept up a constant stream of patrols. This required hundreds of horses, which were pastured at various camps around the fort. Constable Graburn was stationed at the biggest of these, called Horse Camp, which was about 10 miles northwest of Fort Walsh, just inside the present Alberta border.

For some reason the Blood tribe who were camped around Horse Camp were particularly hostile to the camp's being established there. Frank Anderson, in an article he wrote for his now defunct *Sagas Of The Canadian West* magazine thinks it was either because the camp was near a favorite preserve or beside a trail the Bloods used as an escape route after horse stealing sorties into other Indian camps. Anyway, they apparently made a constant nuisance

of themselves, harassing Constable Graburn and the five other men who were stationed at Horse Camp looking after the horses.

There are several versions of what Constable Graburn was doing away from Horse Camp that fateful day of November 17. One has him out on patrol with other members of the camp, then leaving them while returning down the trail to pick up some tools they had forgotten. Another has him leaving the main camp on his own to look for some horses that were foraging to the southeast, then, not finding them as he expected, following their trail to within four miles of Fort Walsh. Whatever he was doing, when he did not return to camp, his fellow officers went looking for him, only to have to abandon their search and return to camp because of darkness.

Early next morning, when Graburn still had not returned, the other men sent word to Fort Walsh. One version has police scout Louis Leveille leading a search party, while another claims Jerry Potts led the search. Either man was abundantly qualified. Jerry Potts was as fine a plainsman as ever lived, and Louis Leveille was one of the original scouts, having joined the force for its westward trek. Whoever led the search soon found the tracks of Graburn's horse, leading off in a southerly direction, and was surprised to find that two other sets of hoof prints joined those of Graburn's pony about a half mile down the trail. The trackers had no difficulty following the trail, but could not be sure if the three riders had travelled together, or if the two unknown riders had simply been following the young constable. They were quite sure, however, that since the two unknown riders were riding unshod ponies, they were probably Indians.

Still farther down the trail was a spot where it looked as though Graburn's horse had lunged forward and near the spot was a large pool of blood. Farther along was another pool of blood, which was revealed when one of the tracker's horses kicked up the snow. (Sam Steele's version of the event claims a Chinook partially obliterated the trail, while others claim the trail was covered by a new fall of snow.) Anyway, not far from the new pool of blood and down over a bank in a clump of bush, one of the trackers found the body of Constable Graburn. An examination revealed he had been shot in the back.

The following day, November 19, scout Jerry Potts led a search party in an attempt to track down the killers. They found Constable Graburn's horse, tied to a tree in some dense timber and shot twice in the head, when the search had to be abandoned because a Chinook or a new fall of snow obliterated the trail. Again there are conflicting reports, one version stating that the constable's personal effects were intact, while another states that his newly-issued Winchester and other items were missing. Sam Steele believed the murder to be an act of vengeance, although it remains a mystery who would bear such a strong grudge against young Graburn.

What is known is that on November 20, 1879, Constable Graburn was buried near the trail where he fell. Jerry Potts again tried to pick up the trail of the killers but had no success. There was one prime suspect, however, a Blood brave named Star Child, one of a number of Indians who had harassed the men at Horse Camp during the previous summer. Inquiries as to his whereabouts only turned up vague answers that he might have gone to Montana. Nothing more developed until the following summer when two Blood braves were incarcerated at Fort Walsh, accused of stealing horses.

After long interrogation the guards learned that the two braves had been camped near Horse Camp at the time of the murder. Major L.M.F. Crozier, who was in charge of Fort Walsh, suspected the two Bloods knew more of the murder than they were telling and decided to hold them for awhile, hoping to get further information from them. The two braves, suspecting they were being held for more than horse stealing, tried to escape. They were abetted by their wives, who passed rifles to the two warriors as they ran from the stockade.

Sam Steele, who was also stationed at Fort Walsh at the time, later wrote: "Crozier, Cotton and Kennedy were playing tennis in front of the fort and, when they saw the escape, followed the fugitives. I sent the first men who turned out after them, mounted. They caught the Indians in about half a mile. Ignoring their levelled rifles, they rode at them and soon had them back in their old quarters in the guard-room. Their attempt to escape having failed, the two asked to see Crozier in his quarters at midnight, and after the windows had been covered with blankets so that no light could be seen from the outside, they gave him the name, description and full particulars of the Indian who had murdered Grayburn...."

Major Crozier sent a message to Commissioner James Macleod, who was in Fort Benton on business, that Star Child was hiding in the Bear Paw Mountains. Commissioner Macleod tried to persuade the U.S. authorities to apprehend and return the fugitive, but the Fort Benton sheriff wanted $5,000 for his trouble. Since Macleod had no such sum at his disposal, Star Child remained free for a while longer. The NWMP bided their time until the fugitive returned to Canada.

Wrote Steele: "This did not present itself until 1881, when Sergeant Patterson at Macleod learned that he (Star Child) was in the Blood camp (about 25 miles south of Fort Macleod) and proceeded there, accompanied by Jerry Potts and two constables. They arrived at dawn and went to the lodge in which the murderer, Star Child by name, was concealed, their intention being to take him without arousing the camp, which, it was believed was hostile. The Indian came out at dawn, fully armed; covering Patterson with his rifle, he told him that he would shoot if he moved a hand or foot; but the sergeant as a ruse, spoke as if addressing someone behind Star Child, causing him to turn his head, whereupon Patterson threw himself upon him. In the struggle the gun went off, rousing the whole camp... In the meantime Patterson had the murderer underneath him half choked, and finally handcuffed him while Jerry Potts, Strangling Wolf, One Spot and Constable Wilson...kept the remainder at bay. The sergeant then took Star Child towards Macleod at the full speed of his horse...followed by the majority of the band as far as the fort, where they were forced to halt and turn back...."

Star Child was charged with murder and locked up at Fort Macleod. According to Sam Steele, he confessed to the murder, although if he gave a reason for doing so, it has never been revealed. Despite the confession and corroborating evidence, at his trial held in Macleod on May 18, 1881, the six-man all-white jury voted for acquittal. There are suggestions that the jury feared Blood reprisals if they found Star Child guilty. Anyway, there was nothing Colonel Macleod, acting as stipendary magistrate, could do but turn the accused man loose.

If Star Child was guilty—some think he only confessed to gain some sort of prestige—he did not escape punishment altogether. Two years later, he ran a herd of stolen horses into Canada from the U.S. and was arrested by Sergeant Ashe of the NWMP. He stood trial on July 5, 1883, and was sentenced to four years in Stony Mountain Penitentiary. Apparently not all Mounties shared Steele's belief that Star Child was the murderer of Constable Graburn. For, after his release from prison, Superintendent R.B. Deane hired him as a police scout. Star Child served in that capacity until his death from tuberculosis in 1889. Superintendent Deane was sufficiently pleased with Star Child's performance to state, "I should be glad to get another scout of similar calibre." Could this be the murderer of Constable Graburn?

As for the murdered policemen, his grave rests on a bench above the creek that bears his name. In recent years the Alberta Historic Sites people erected a cairn and enclosed both cairn and gravesite with a fence made of steel pipe. The cairn reads:

MURDER OF CONSTABLE GRABURN
CONST. MARMADUKE GRABURN, NWMP, WAS SHOT AND KILLED BY UNKNOWN PERSONS IN THE CYPRESS HILLS NOVEMBER 17, 1879. HE WAS THE FIRST MOUNTED POLICE KILLED BY VIOLENCE SINCE THE FORCE WAS FORMED IN 1873. STAR CHILD, A BLOOD INDIAN, WAS ACCUSED OF THE MURDER BUT WAS ACQUITTED IN 1881.

The message on the cairn seems to contain the only substantiated knowledge existing of the baffling murder that took place in the Cypress Hills a century ago. ●

(Left) The enigmatic millionaire Charles Bedaux repairing a rifle. His famous Canadian expedition of 1934 left many questions unanswered upon his death by suicide during the Second World War.
(Below) One of the Bedaux pack trains leaving Fort St. John, British Columbia, in 1934. For many of the horses the eccentric Frenchman's foray into the Canadian North was to be disastrous.

No one ever created a bigger stir in Alberta or in northeastern British Columbia than Charles E. Bedaux. It was 1934 and the heart of the great Depression and scarcely anyone had a five-dollar bill to call their own. Then into the country breezed millionaire industrialist-sportsman Charles Bedaux, flashing more money than most knew existed.

THE BEDAUX EXPEDITION

BEDAUX needed horsemen and was paying $4 a day, twice the going rate. He needed horses, too, and was paying $75 each for them. That was about three times the going rate. It was all very overwhelming.

An additional indication of Bedaux's wealth were five shiny new Citroen half-track trucks, which he claimed could do anything but swim. Loaded aboard them were electrical generators, a lot of newfangled radio gear, asbestos tents, movie cameras, tons of fancy foods and wines, and three inflatable rubber rafts to carry the vehicles over any water barriers encountered.

There had been advance notice that Bedaux planned to take those shiny Citroens all the way from Edmonton to Fort St. John in the British Columbia Peace River Block, then across northern British Columbia some 600 miles to Telegraph Creek on the Stikine River, across a trackless wilderness of rivers, timberland, muskeg and mountains. Why? Mostly for the adventure, said Bedaux, and because no one had done it before. Moreover, he claimed, it would open a route from both the Alberta and British Columbia sections of the Peace River Country to the coast— something that was surely needed if this vast agricultural area was ever to reach its full potential.

To the skeptics who suggested he had rocks in his head for attempting such a foolish journey, Bedaux only smiled. He had been told he could not cross the Sahara Desert using wheeled vehicles, where only camels and tracked machines had previously gone. Yet during the winter of 1929-1930 he had done just that— driven across the great African desert from Mombasa on the Indian Ocean to Casablanca on the Atlantic, traversing some 9,500 miles in standard cars. Now many were doing it. He would, he boasted, cross northern British Columbia and soon others would follow.

It was not for lack of effort or money that his plan

failed. Bedaux spent a cool quarter of a million dollars— a substantial fortune at any time, let alone during the Depression. But a combination of events that included an unusually wet summer, the inability of the Citroens to stand up to Peace River gumbo, the inability of the horses, which took over when the Citroens broke down, to cope with overly-heavy packs, and several other unexpected factors forced Bedaux to turn back in the Sifton Pass with 300 miles to go.

Some likened his retreat to that of Napoleon's from Russia. Dead horses, wrecked vehicles, torn rafts, tents, clothing, saddles and pack gear were strewn along the route. But if the ebullient Bedaux was much perturbed, it was not too evident. "I failed because it was the wettest summer on record," he told an Edmonton *Journal* reporter. "It won't be next summer, but I'll be back and try again. And next time I'll succeed."

So he might had there been a next time, but that was not to be. Nevertheless, his attempt was surely the highlight of the Depression years for citizens of Alberta and northeastern British Columbia.

Charles Eugene Bedaux was born in France, but emigrated to the United States in 1906 when he was 16 years old. In due course he became an American citizen. If ever there was a prime example of the American success story, he was it. When he landed in New York he had scarcely a dime to his name. Yet when the Americans entered the First World War in 1917 he was a multi-millionaire. After spending his first five years or so in America working as a laborer washing dishes in a saloon and later as a sand-hog building the New York Subway, he perfected and patented a method of extracting extra work from factory employees. He called it his B-unit and quickly made his fortune by selling it to enterprising factory owners around the world.

He set up offices throughout the United States and Europe and married vivacious Fern Lombard, daughter of a wealthy Michigan industrialist. He bought lavish homes in both America and Europe, including a palace not far from Paris. His palace was his favorite spot for entertaining the moneyed elite from around the world.

Later he set out to show the world his ability to do things no one else had even thought about. Besides crossing the Sahara in 1929-30, in 1926 and again in 1932 he made exploratory safaris into northern British Columbia on horseback. Something about the region must have intrigued him for, in 1934, he was back, spending more money than he had on either of his previous jaunts.

Preparations for what Bedaux called his "Canadian Sub-Arctic Expedition" got underway in January of 1934 when he hired New York public relations man, Austin Carson, to build up press interest. He also hired Edmonton geologist John Bocock to accompany the expedition as second-in-command.

Bocock journeyed to Victoria to contact the British Columbia Department of Lands to acquire their sanction for the trip. Upon learning that the expedition would pass through some 70 miles of unmapped territory in the northern part of the province, the government saw an opportunity to get the mapping done partially at Bedaux's expense. They pitched in $600 and lent him two geographers, Ernest C.W. Lamarque of Vancouver and Frank Swannell of Victoria. In February Bedaux sailed to France to order five specially-built Citroen tracked vehicles.

While on the coast John Bocock acquired the services of surveyor A.H. Phipps and radio operator Bruce McCallum. Then, on April 4, with a crew of three axemen and a string of pack horses, ex-champion bronc-rider Tommy Wilde set out from Fort St. John to cut a trail for Bedaux to follow. His primary goal was Redfern Lake, some 150 miles to the northwest.

When his equipment arrived in Edmonton in early June, Bedaux created a big stir by staging impromptu parades through town, then took his entourage out to Jasper Park for training. "I suppose it sounds funny training for such a journey, but there's nothing like being fit when tackling something hard," Bedaux told curious reporters. "We'll go up there and climb mountains and chase mountain sheep for a few days and that will take the fat off us." Since Bedaux's idea of training seemed to consist more of banquets and champagne parties than hard work, it is debatable whether his group was in any better shape when it left Jasper at the end of June than when it arrived.

Nevertheless, on July 6, after another series of parties in Edmonton, a full-dress parade down Jasper Avenue and a farewell speech by Alberta's Lieutenant-Governor William Walsh, Bedaux was off for his rendezvous with the Peace River Country and the northern British Columbia wilderness. With him were his wife Fern and her pretty Spanish maid, Josefina Daly; Mme. Alberto Chiesa, wife of a noted European sportsman and an accomplished huntress in her own right; Bedaux's valet, a huge, mustachioed Scotsman by the name of Robert Chisolm; Charles Balourdet, a slim, dark French auto mechanic on loan from the Citroen people; alpine guide J.A. Weiss from Jasper, who was forced to carry a pair of skis he never used; radio-operator Bruce McCallum; movie cameraman F.D. Crosby, who later became famous in Hollywood for such films as "High Noon"; his assistant E.D. Withrow from Toronto; J.B. Bocock; geographer Frank Swannell and his assistant Al Phipps. Geographer Ernest Lamarque had taken a party from Fort St. John on April 30 to clear a trail beyond Redfern Lake.

The Citroens rolled along without trouble until they encountered the first Peace River Country gumbo near Valleyview. Loaded with two tons each

(Above) Pack horses of the Bedaux expedition crossing the Cameron River in British Columbia.
(Below) A river landing on the Finlay River, as members of the historic Bedaux expedition prepare to make camp.
While "roughing it," Bedaux believed in nothing but the finest of foods and wines.

of costly gear, fancy clothing and mounds of exotic foods and wines, they bogged down in the rain-soaked Peace River mud and did not reach the jumping-off spot, Fort St. John, until July 17. They had travelled 550 miles, but there was still 600 to go.

On this first stretch of the safari, Frank Swannell learned just how much Bedaux cared about mapping new territory. In order to lessen the weight of one vehicle bogged in the gumbo, Bedaux jettisoned 100 pounds of Swannell's survey gear rather than some of the excess camping equipment. Then, to add insult to injustice, Bedaux appropriated Swannell's assistant, Al Phipps, for his houseboy. It was shaping into a most unusual journey.

At Fort St. John Bedaux met his two head packers. One was Commander Reginald Geake, a retired navy officer who owned a farm near Pouce Coupe. A flamboyant character, he always had a pack of dogs at his heels, wore a black silk bandana round his head and dressed in shorts regardless of the weather. He was put in charge of an advance party of five men and a pack train of 56 horses carrying gasoline and other supplies. The other head packer was Bob Beattie, Hudson's Hope farmer, game guide and riverman. He was in charge of the pack train travelling with the main party.

In the little British Columbia community Bedaux spent money as if it were counterfeit — some $45,000 in the estimation of Bert Bowes, local garage owner. About $7,500 went to purchase 100 horses and another large sum for 50 steel tanks built by Bowes in which the horses carried gasoline for the fuel-guzzling Citroens. Some went for food,

blankets, saddles, pack gear and bridles. A lot went for wages. Then, just as they were leaving town, Bedaux handed out 10-dollar bills to every man, woman and child taking part in a farewell movie scene filmed by Crosby and company. It was the most money ever seen in the village and to show its appreciation, the Board of Trade threw a banquet for Bedaux.

It was July 22 before the expedition got underway again and only after much speech-making and picture-taking. Recalcitrant ponies, some newly broken, began throwing riders and packs and adding to the general confusion. But finally they were underway and covered a monumental 10 miles before bedding down for the night.

Daily travelling distances did not improve much during the following three weeks. Gumbo, stumps, rocks, sidehills and muskeg proved more than a match for the vaunted Citroens. Much of the time they were being winched out of bogholes or dragged along by the horses they were supposed to replace. Tracks did not stand up and much time was lost while they were repaired. At one time Bedaux wired Paris for four sets of tracks, then increased the order to 10 sets, before sending a countermanding wire cancelling all orders. He had decided to abandon the tractors altogether.

While radio-operator McCallum was with the expedition, daily reports of progress reached the outside. But on July 28 Bedaux decided to fire McCallum and abandon the radio gear. His reason, he claimed, was that the radio did not work well enough to warrant its extra weight and the additional food consumed by the operator. Others

thought that it was because the radio-operator had been too honest in his daily reports. Anyway, from then on reports reaching the outside were conflicting at best.

For instance, in a letter to his New York press agent Bedaux explained how three of the Citroens were lost— two accidentally slipping over a 120-foot cliff and plunging into the Graham River near its confluence with the Halfway. Another, said Bedaux, was lost when the cable broke while it was being rafted across the Graham. According to a diary kept by Frank Swannell, however, those "accidents" were deliberately planned.

When the two Citroens went over the cliff, the sidehill had been undermined deliberately. The drivers, aware of the situation, stood on the sides of the vehicles, ready to jump. Meanwhile, all four movie cameras were focused on the vehicles as they made their spectacular plunge.

Naturally the cameras were also sighted in on car number three as it swept to its apparent doom when, according to Bedaux's report, the cable snapped as it was being rafted across the Graham. What actually happened, wrote Swannell, was that the cable did not let go until given a couple hefty swipes with an axe. Even then things did not work as planned. Downstream a bank had been drilled and packed with dynamite, set to explode as the raft shot by. However, a capricious current steered the raft away from the bank and the explosives did nothing more than blast a cloud of dirt into the air. Consequently the unharmed raft stranded on a gravel bar a few miles downstream and the Citroen was recovered intact the following winter by a couple of grateful trappers.

A fake forest fire scene did not work out much

(Opposite page) Heading north to adventure, the Citroen half-tracks prepared to battle with the Alberta-British Columbia terrain.
(Right) Standing in the foreground, with his back to the camera, Charles Bedaux watches as his men load rafts with equipment on the Halfway River.
(Bottom) Repairing the vaunted Citroen half-track trucks. Although touted as being able to go almost anywhere, they soon proved to be no match for Canadian muskeg.

better. On the evening of August 4, while the movie cameras ground away, flares were set off to simulate fire in camp. Several of the asbestos tents were doused with gasoline and ignited, some of the men tumbled from their tents dragging their gear and Josefina ran screaming into the night. That was the cue for the cowboys to drive the horses toward the cameras in a simulated stampede. Unfortunately, horses fear fire. They spooked in the opposite direction and it took most of two days before they all could be found.

Actually there were enough incidents without having to fabricate them. It rained 32 of the first 37 days on the trail and mosquitoes constantly swarmed round. Cowboy Charlie Blackman got lost when sent back to pick up a coil of rope that was missing. When he did not return men spent a whole night and part of the next day looking for him only to have him drift in on his own about noon. He had been sent 18 miles down the wrong trail by an Indian with a perverse sense of humor.

Another cowboy, Walter Thomlinson of Fort St. John, damaged a knee when bucked from his horse and had to be sent out to an Edmonton hospital. There was tragedy when Thomas Granger was drowned while swimming his horse across the Kwadacha River. Though not one of Bedaux's people, he was attempting to contact one of the advance parties, hoping for possible employment.

When Bedaux made up his mind to abandon the Citroens, he stored the two remaining vehicles on the Wagner ranch and acquired extra horses from the surrounding ranches. He despatched John Bocock and a cowboy named Jack McDougall to intercept Geake and his advance party who were nearly 200 miles ahead. On August 14 Bedaux got underway again, using only horses. The rains had stopped and for two weeks they made good time. Then the rains returned, making travel miserable for horses and humans alike. To their credit the women never complained and professed afterward that they had enjoyed every minute of the trip.

On August 26 Bedaux met the two men he had sent to intercept Geake. Geake had a startling story to tell. He and his men were camped beside the Muskwa River when it rose seven feet overnight. The horses became stranded on a knoll much too small to accommodate them and Geake nearly drowned trying to rescue a fear-maddened pony. He was badly trampled and spent half a day in the water before being rescued. Fortunately, he suffered no lasting harmful effects.

The horses, however, did not fair nearly so well. Unlike Geake, they had no guardian angel looking out for their welfare. They were grossly overloaded and gradually began to weaken. Grass, at first plentiful, became scarce as they progressed into the mountains. Then, on September 19, snow began falling and did not stop until 18 inches lay on the ground. Worse, several of the beleaguered ponies

came down with hoof-rot and had to be destroyed.

Had his trail cutters not been held up by deep snow six miles north of the Sifton Pass, Bedaux claimed he would have pressed on. But with the horses becoming weaker each day and nearly 300 miles to traverse, he decided to turn back lest he be trapped in some remote mountain valley for the winter.

He headed for Ware on the upper Finlay River. It was only 65 miles away, but there were eight rain-swollen rivers to cross. Consequently, it took five days and only 90 of the original 130 horses survived the trip. Bedaux and his somewhat battered legion floated down the Finlay and Peace Rivers to Hudson's Hope in boats hired from the Hudson's Bay Company. They arrived there October 19.

When Bedaux held a press conference at the Hart Hotel in Pouce Coupe three days later, he gave little impression of being a defeated man. Certainly, he admitted to an Edmonton *Journal* reporter, his Citroens had not lived up to expectations. But his idea was sound, for Ernest Lamarque and his guide William Blackman got through to Telegraph Creek. (They arrived there September 14 and rejoined Bedaux October 3 at the Fox Pass on the Upper Finlay River.)

This, maintained Bedaux, proved the route was feasible. Some day soon, he prophesied, a highway would be built following the route he had blazed. His claim proved at least partially true, for when the Alaska Highway was built eight years later, it roughly followed— although farther to the east— some of the route marked out by Charles Bedaux.

Bedaux did not fade quietly from the limelight after his big 1934 splash. In 1937 he again hit the headlines when, after abdicating the British throne, the former King Edward VIII married Wallace Warfield Simpson at Bedaux's French chateau. At that posh celebration Bedaux embarrassed his guest by announcing that he, Bedaux, was an ardent Fascist sympathizer. This became obvious during the Second World War when he openly collaborated with the Nazis and their puppet Vichy government during the German occupation of France.

In 1943 Bedaux was arrested by the American Army in North Africa, where he had been sent to build an oil pipeline across the Sahara Desert to supply the German war machine. Flown back to the United States, Bedaux again created headlines by committing suicide rather than face charges of treason.

In light of his subsequent behavior, many wondered if Bedaux was employed by the Germans when he made his costly sojourn into Alberta and northern British Columbia. If he was, it was a well-kept secret. "I'm making this trip just for the fun of it..." he told reporters in Edmonton.

With his money and insatiable appetite for publicity, it seems entirely possible. ●

William John Tregillus
Aristocrat Pioneer

Times have certainly changed since William Tregillus raised Holstein cows in what was to become the heart of downtown Calgary.

W.J. Tregillus, the aristocratic pioneer who contributed greatly to the birth of Calgary.

HAD William John Tregillus lived a few more years and held onto his property until a propitious time, he could, quite conceivably, have been one of the richest men in Calgary. For, prior to his death in 1914, he owned 4,000 acres, west from 37th Street and south of the Bow River— if not in the heart of Calgary, certainly in what now is considered to be some of the finest residential property in the city.

There he raised a fine herd of Holstein cows, some of the finest hackney horses in the West, and, from his dairy, sold the first bottled and pasteurized milk to the residents of the burgeoning city of Calgary. He was an alderman and deputy mayor and owned a brickyard when building brick was still badly needed during one of Calgary's extended building booms. He was a prominent public speaker, one of the city's most ardent promoters of education, president for a time of the United Farmers of Alberta, and also president of an elevator company that, by 1917, amalgamated into a huge conglomerate that owned something like 200 grain elevators throughout the prairies. With a background such as this, why did he not become rich and famous? Well, that is the story, which should begin at the beginning.

William John Tregillus, or "W.J." as he was known to his friends, was born in Plymouth, England, in 1858, the son of a well-to-do flour mill owner. Not your run-of-the-mill homesteader, W.J. landed in Canada in 1902, accompanied by his wife, two children, Miss Holland, who served as a companion and helper to Mrs. Tregillus, and Hooper, the groom. W.J. must have had considerable financial backing as well, for when he arrived in Calgary he was not looking for a homestead, but a large tract of land to buy or rent. He found land for rent west of Calgary, a large tract complete with house, farm machinery, and house-

Once beautiful "Roscarrock," the mansion of William J. Tregillus, in a state of neglect in 1942.

hold furnishings. A short time later he bought 960 acres adjacent to his leased farm and, in 1903, erected a home that he named 'Roscarrock,' a stately mansion patterned after English homes of the day, and named after a house in Cornwall. Though land then sold for $6 an acre in that area and a fine home could be built for less than $5,000, W.J. sank enough of a fortune into his farmstead that there could be no doubt that he had come to Calgary to stay. Interestingly, today land in the Roscarrock district is worth upwards of $100,000 an acre— one of Calgary's finer residential districts.

According to his daughter, Mrs. Muriel Sanford, wife of Dr. Guthrie Sanford, long-time Professor of Medicine at the University of Alberta, who lives in Edmonton, "The land he bought was unimproved, but W.J. got to work breaking land, erecting stables for horses and cattle and soon had a farm operation going. He was also engaged with Mr. Charles Jackson, a neighbor, in buying horses brought in from British Columbia and selling them to immigrants who had come West to homestead. These were small animals, suited to the price that many with limited incomes could afford. In some cases four men would each buy a horse to make a team to do the breaking on a section (four quarters) of land." Improvisation was the only way some homesteaders could get started on the frontier.

W.J. soon saw the need for another dairy in the area. But no scrub cattle for him. He acquired a herd of pure Holstein stock, great milk producers and relatively easy to handle. W.J. thought the milk he sold should be as pure as his pure-bred cattle. Up until then milk sold in Calgary was delivered in five-gallon cans, from which the milkman poured whatever quantity the homeowner wanted into the buyer's own containers. For Tregillus that system simply would not do. Pasteurization meant nothing

to most people, for they could not conceive of milk coming from a cow as being anything but pure. W.J. knew better. No product he sold was going to be a carrier of typhoid or Lord knows what other disease. He knew of Louis Pasteur's method of sterilizing milk by raising the temperature of the fluid to some 160 degrees Fahrenheit for a period of time long enough to kill all harmful bacteria. He set up a plant that would both sterilize and bottle his product and gave Calgary its first supply of wholesome pasteurized milk.

To keep his dairy going he brought young men from England in a sort of mutual benefit system. He supplied the young fellows with their passage to Canada, employment and valuable training; they supplied him with reliable and affordable help. According to Muriel Sanford, there were usually half a dozen of these young men working on the farm and in the dairy, along with the regular hands.

By the time Alberta became a province in 1905, W.J. Tregillus was well established. He was vitally interested in the province's new Department of Agriculture and lent several of his pure-bred Holsteins to them for demonstration purposes. Mrs. Sanford remembers that he was often away from home, travelling with the cattle and giving lectures to various farm groups on the advantages of owning pure-bred stock. When tours for the Department of Agriculture did not take him from home, often other interests did. He was a strong supporter of the United Farmers of Alberta movement and devoted much of his time to its promotion.

"He was away from the ranch a good deal," Mrs. Sanford remembers, "travelling throughout the settled parts of the province." That was in the era before good roads, where a mile or so from each town, trails in wet weather were next to impassable. W.J., often accompanied by one of his sons, would

The ill-fated Tregillus clay products plant at Brickburn. The outbreak of war and Tregillus' untimely death led to the collapse of his financial empire.

slog through mile after mile of primitive trail behind a team of weary horses, attempting to reach the next farm or town where there was a place to spend the night. Seldom were there "the comforts of home" when he did reach a town. Most hotels, called stopping houses then, were of a decidedly make-do construction, where one large room containing a dozen or more beds provided the sleeping quarters for the weary travellers. Most of the time this room was located above the saloon or dining room and until the revelry died down at the bar, there was usually little sleep for any but the most insensitive traveller.

Soon after arriving in Alberta, Tregillus saw the need for a strong voice for the farmers and became vitally involved in an organization called the Society of Equity, which by 1908 led to the formation of the Farmers' Union of Alberta. By 1910 he was elected vice-president of the union and that same year led a delegation of western farmers to Vancouver to investigate the possibility of shipping prairie grain through that Pacific port. Until then grain for over-seas shipment went east to the grain terminals at Port Arthur and Fort William (present Thunder Bay) to be loaded on ships and moved east via the Great Lakes. Mrs. Sanford remembers that her father's delegation "was given a hearty welcome at Vancouver and generously entertained." They were

taken on a tour of the great harbor on a tugboat and were impressed with the vast grain handling potential of the city. Later great grain elevators were built to handle shippings of prairie wheat to Japan, China and other countries of the Far East.

Mrs. Sanford believes that "The most significant achievement of the UFA in the early days was the launching of the Farmers' Elevator Company." Her father spear-headed that development which grew from an idea into a company that owned 40 grain elevators by 1913. And it did not stop there. By 1917 the Farmers' Co-operative Elevator Company amalgamated with the Grain Growers Grain Company of Manitoba to form the United Grain Growers Limited, a firm which operates some 200 grain elevators throughout the Canadian Prairies.

An interesting sidelight to the W.J. Tregillus story is that after becoming established as a farmer-dairyman, W.J. began looking for more land to expand his holdings and found what he wanted in a 3,000-acre ranch that cornered on his original property. He and Tom Edworthy, another prominent early Calgarian, submitted equal bids of $6 an acre for the parcel. But W.J. apparently submitted a certified cheque for the full amount and he was awarded the property. That property alone, had he been able to keep it long enough, would have made him a millionaire many times over.

By 1910 W.J. was serving his first term as vice-president of the UFA. He was re-elected in 1911 and that year attended an international meeting of agricultural officials in Rome as a private observer. In 1912 he was elected president of the UFA which in itself was probably a full-time job. But it seems that W.J.'s energy was boundless, for that same year he launched his Tregillus Clay Products Company, which his daughter describes as "a ceramic plant that produced a wire-cut tapestry brick that was fired in downdraft kilns that burned gas. The color cf the brick could be varied by changing the fuel from an oxidizing to reducing flame."

W.J. probably got the idea for his brickworks from another plant, the Grandel Brick Yard, which had operated close by. The Tregillus plant, which produced an excellent brick known as Tregil Rough, was located on his property on the south side of the CPR mainline. Wrote Mrs. Sanford: "The plant had just gone into production when World War One broke out, and at the death of the owner, the Tregillus Clay Products plant was closed down. The Arts Building of the University of Alberta and the Holy Trinity Anglican Church in Edmonton were built of the brick, also a few buildings — one an apartment block (Lorraine Apartments, 600 Block, 12th Avenue S.W.) — in Calgary. But other orders were cancelled on account of the war." Here again Tregillus just missed becoming a very rich man. For had he launched his brick yard a couple of years earlier during one of Calgary's greatest building booms, he probably could have sold as much brick as his plant could have produced. For 1912 was a great year in Calgary, when building permits amounting to $50 million were taken out. Not until the 1950s would there be such a year again, and it must be remembered that, in 1912, $50 million was indeed a great deal of money. W.J. did not miss hitting the jackpot by much.

Mrs. Sanford also remembers that horses were always one of her father's great loves. In England he had owned three or four hunters on which he "rode to the hounds." Says Mrs. Sanford: "After a few years at Roscarrock he went seriously into raising registered Hackneys, purchasing a few mares and a stud from Sir Walter Gilbey's stable in England. He drove horses regularly as he went to his office in Calgary, spurning the use of a car." Those trips to Calgary became a daily matter for, in 1913, although he lived outside what were then the city limits, he was elected as an alderman on the city council. For a time he was even acting mayor during the absence of the regular mayor.

W.J. was always interested in public affairs and Mrs. Sanford remembers him bringing home the speaker from various functions so that he could discuss the topic of the day in greater detail. "In his day," she says, "Calgary was fast developing a cultural atmosphere and he took great enjoyment in music. He was president of the choral society when it was awarded a citation as best chorus west of Winnipeg... Mrs. Beatrice Chapman, my aunt, for many years a prominent musician in Calgary, was a sister of W.J. Tregillus."

Not surprisingly, W.J. was associated with some very prominent people, including none other than R.B. Bennett, the well-known Calgary lawyer who went on to become the Prime Minister of Canada from 1930 to 1935. Tregillus and Bennett worked together to found the University of Calgary, with W.J. donating 160 acres of his Roscarrock property for a campus, as well as $50,000 for a faculty "chair." It was not the fault of either man that the Alberta government withheld a charter to grant degrees, or that the University of Calgary was disbanded during the First World War. Not until 1966 did the University of Calgary become a fully accredited university, although it did function as a part of the University of Alberta for some 20 years after 1945, until given its own charter.

The war contributed to more than just the demise of W.J.'s university. Indirectly at least, it contributed to the downfall of his entire empire. As well as being involved in education, music, city council and a thousand and one other things, W.J. was also a member of the Canadian Manufacturers Association. In November, 1914, he went to Winnipeg to attend a meeting as a delegate for that group. He was not feeling well, but attended the meeting and sat on a platform with the other officials. Because of his condition, he did not notice that his chair had not been placed squarely on the platform — that one leg was placed over the edge. When he went to sit down his chair tipped over backward and he was severely injured. Because of his injury and the illness that turned out to be typhoid fever, he was unable to stand and barely survived the train trip back to Calgary. He died in a Calgary hospital on November 12, 1914. He was only 56 years of age. He left a family consisting of his wife and four children. Letters and telegrams paying high tribute to a most worthy citizen streamed in from all over the country.

Although the war dealt his burgeoning empire a devastating blow, most who knew him thought that rather than going bankrupt, with his seemingly boundless energy he would have soon recouped his losses and gone on to greater things. It seems entirely possible.

Many think that because of his great contribution to the farmers' movement and to education there should be a plaque, cairn or some other monument to a man who gave so much of himself to the province. So far, no such monument exists. Then again, perhaps that is not entirely true, for the United Farmers movement still goes on. Moreover, United Grain Growers elevators stand like sentinels throughout the Canadian West.

And lest anyone forget, WILLIAM JOHN TREGILLUS played a great part in establishing both. ●

Home Cures For Pioneer People
GRANNY MEDICINE

Some of Granny's Cures were pure superstition.
Guaranteed to cure all that ails you, many of them
sounded more lethal than the disease. Yet Granny was
often right, too, as modern research has confirmed.

GRANNY medicine, for those not familiar with the term, was the pseudo healing science practised by mothers and grandmothers charged with the chore of keeping their families healthy on our early frontier, when doctors were perhaps hundreds of miles away. Many of the cures really worked, although granny seldom knew why. But many of her cures were downright weird — pure superstition at most.

For instance, a sure granny cure for asthma consisted of a walk around the house at midnight. Convulsions were supposed to be cured by pouring baptismal water over a peony bush. Think that is strange? Then how about the cure for quinsy—infected throat? It required capturing a yellow toad in a neighbor's cellar and placing it on the afflicted throat. If the cure did not work it was because the toad was not the proper hew of yellow, or because someone had cheated and had not actually caught the toad in the neighbor's cellar. Did granny have a cure for epilepsy? Why, certainly. She hung a slice of peony root on the right arm and left leg of the victim. When the last slice fell off, the epileptic was cured!

As a matter of fact, granny cures pretty well ran the gamut of diseases and afflictions. Probably not many will want to try her cure for heartburn, which

consisted of eating fishworms — no specified number. But, presumably, you continued eating them until the heartburn was gone — or until something more drastic occurred to make you forget your original complaint. Have trouble remembering things? Boil the heart of a barn swallow in milk and wear it on a thong tied around the neck for a few days. Presto, the mind should be crystal clear. Backache troubles? No sweat. Turn a somersault the minute the first robin of spring bursts into song. A broken leg or arm might result, but the backache definitely should be gone.

Then, of course, there was the famous, or infamous, granny cure for spring fever — a strong dose of sulphur and molasses guaranteed to purify the blood. Surprisingly, there are people around who still believe in the healing magic of a rabbit's foot. Like the rabbit's foot, three dead mice hung on a string around the neck were supposed to prevent toothache and many other ailments. If toothache occurred despite those delightful charms, one could, according to granny, alleviate the pain by picking the affected tooth with a nail drawn from an occupied coffin or with the splinter from a tree that had been struck by lightning. If that did not work, the ultimate cure was to tie one end of a strong string to a bent sapling and the other end to the ailing tooth. Let the sapling spring back into place and if the string did not break, your troubles were over.

Not many Albertans, especially those living north of the Red Deer River, are bothered by rattlesnake bites. But pioneers living in rattlesnake country — the extreme south of the province — had plenty of granny cures. One sure cure, presumably, was to cut the tail off the snake that did the biting (if you could catch it) and apply the fleshy part to the bite. The victim held it there for a few minutes, then threw that piece away and cut off another two or three inches of snake and again applied the raw flesh to the wound. He or she did this until the entire snake was used up, the theory being that snake toxin had more affinity for snake flesh than for human flesh. Consequently the procedure quickly transferred the poison from the victim back to the snake.

While on the snake topic, one granny cure for sore throat was to catch a snake, kill and skin it and apply the skin to the throat — a couple of wraps should do. Moreover, rattlesnake rattles shaken vigorously were supposed to cure a headache, while to cure deafness the victim simply shook the rattles and strained to hear them.

By no means all of granny's cures were worthless or pure superstition, however. Long before the advent of penicillin many grannies were using the mold from cheese to ward off infection in open sores and wounds. It worked, too, for penicillin comes from a certain type of mold. Granny also treated burns as we do today. She applied wet tea leaves to the burn, while modern medicine has simply substituted tannic acid, an ingredient contained in tea leaves. Some grannies also used cobwebs to stem the flow of blood from severe wounds. She was way ahead of her time for it was not until fairly recently that medical science discovered that cobwebs do indeed have great ability to stem the flow of blood.

An article written sometime around the turn of the century, entitled "For The Pioneer Family," its author unknown, states that food on the pantry shelves and from the fields would provide cures for most every ailment a pioneer family was likely to encounter. Here is a partial list of the items mentioned in that article and the ailments they were supposed to cure:

DANDELION LEAVES: (Picked fresh and cooked as greens or uncooked in salads): To cleanse the skin and blood in springtime; also to fight indigestion of the stomach, kidneys and gall-bladder.

SUMMER SAVORY (fresh leaves): To relieve the pain of bee stings.

FRESH BUTTER (unsalted): For quick relief of burn and skin ruptures; also a balming ointment for tired and aching feet.

THYME (as tea): To use in case of whooping cough, catarrhs and colds; also to serve as a good mouthwash.

SAFFRON (as a tea): To use as a mild (non-habit-forming) sedative.

GINGER ROOT (simmered in water): To ease an ailing stomach.

HONEY: To speed healing of small wounds; also to improve digestion if taken by teaspoonful one hour before meals.

LEEKS: To clear and brighten the voice... not only for singers.

RAW MILK: To rub on hands if housework makes them raw and rough.

CUCUMBER JUICE: To relieve sunburn and brighten skin at all times.

HONEY AND TURPENTINE (a drop of each): To keep hands "dry" rain or shine.

POTATO (cooking water): To bathe frost-bitten limbs...to give relief and healing.

SUGAR (lump or granulated): To rub on insect bites (takes sting out of bite).

RAW POTATO JUICE (fresh): To relieve pain of gout, rheumatism, burns and bruises.

ONION SOUP: To fight colds and bronchitis.

RAW ONIONS (chopped): To remove corns and warts. (Soak onions in vinegar before chopping).

SAUERKRAUT JUICE: To cleanse the intestines.

LEMON JUICE: To sip in drops every three or four hours to relieve colds.

CARAWAY SEEDS (as a tea or soup): To keep bowels free of gas; also to chew as after-dinner miints...and to aid digestion.

CAMOMILE (as a tea): To use as daily mouthwash or gargle; also to make a wet dressing for skin irritations and minor burns.

DILL SEEDS (as a broth): To fight obesity.

FENNEL: To go into soups and drinks for those already grown fat.

SWEET MARJORAM LEAVES (fresh): To chew away a toothache.

DRY MUSTARD: To mix with bear fat and rub on chest for colds; also to use in bath — half teaspoonful to stimulate circulation.

PEPPERMINT LEAVES (tea): To cleanse the stomach; to remove pimples from face.

RED RADISHES: To cleanse the liver and gall-bladder.

ANISE SEEDS: Chew before retiring for a good night's sleep.

BORAGE (the young leaves): To drive away melancholy.

ROSEMARY: To keep young...put in the bath; also drink as tea for colds.

To the above list let me add a recipe many frontier grandpas swore by. For colds: two ounces of rum, one-half teaspoonful butter, a tablespoonful of honey. Place ingredients in a tall glass and fill glass with boiling water. Of course this concoction did not cure a cold. But it sure made having one a lot more pleasant! ●

Boucher's Mysterious Message

MANY a tale has been told in the West of the extra-sensory powers of the native people. No one can quite explain how some Indians have been able to telepathically communicate over hundreds of miles. But communicate they did, for too many forthright pioneers have testified to the phenomenon for scoffers to laugh off. Not all these stories can be true. But many are, and surely the uncanny experience related by Peace River Country pioneer Fred Brick more than a quarter century ago is one of these.

Son of early pioneer Anglican missionary, the Reverend J. Gough Brick, Fred Brick was homeward bound to Peace River town from a trading trip down the Peace River to Fort Vermilion when this strange incident occurred. It was in the spring of 1894 and, helping Mr. Brick to pole his fur-laden canoe upriver, was a rather remarkable Cree Indian named Boucher. Boucher, Mr. Brick claimed, could handle the 25-foot-long birch poles used to propel the canoe better than anyone on the river. Moreover, he was a sincere fellow, one Fred Brick would not have hesitated to trust with his life. Moody at times but very intelligent, Boucher could speak fluently in Cree, Chippewyan, Beaver, French and English.

Brick and Boucher were making good time poling up the long, lonely river, and had seen no one since leaving Vermilion. Brick was dreaming about a home-cooked meal and a good rest— that is, he was daydreaming to the extent one is able to while straining every muscle to the utmost while propelling a canoe against a nine-mile an hour current— when, about 3 o'clock in the afternoon of June 20, Boucher suddenly stopped poling.

"Boss," he said, "I've got to go ashore." No explanation, just that terse message. There was no arguing with him that they could still make many miles before stopping for supper. Boucher was adamant and, reluctantly, Brick allowed him to turn the canoe shoreward and to tie up to a big spruce tree.

On shore Boucher climbed the bank, built a smudge fire to deter swarming mosquitoes, sat down with his back firmly planted against a large spruce and stared vacantly into space. Towards evening, Brick set about preparing supper, frying up a big batch of eggs he had obtained from a lady in Fort Vermilion who owned a small flock of laying hens — a rare luxury in the North at that time. With the meal ready and smoking hot, Brick called to his friend and helper to come and get it before the mosquitoes and flies ate it all.

"Can't eat," said Boucher.

"You sick or something?" asked Brick.

"Nope," said Boucher, "not sick," and gave no further explanation other than, "You wouldn't understand— no white man would."

All that night and most of the next day Boucher sat with his back to the tree, neither sleeping nor eating or giving any explanation for his peculiar behavior. Finally, late in the afternoon, he stood up, stretched, made himself something to eat and said, "Let's travel."

Again, to Brick's inquiry as to what was wrong, Boucher replied, "You wouldn't understand." Then, seeing the consternation on his friend's face he finally explained: "I was getting a message from out there. Last night my wife had a baby, a girl, but it lived for only a couple hours." Naturally Brick was quite certain his companion must have somehow loosened several intercranial screws and was hallucinating. However he was pleased that Boucher was now ready to travel.

Travel they did, Boucher practically lifting the canoe out of the water with every mighty heave on the pole. He even refused to stop for supper till dark, even though he had eaten next to nothing for two days. He continued to work like a man possessed for the next two days, and in that span the two men poled upriver half again the distance they would have ordinarily gone— well over 70 miles. As later Brick explained: "If you think that's not good traveling, try poling a heavily loaded canoe up the Peace River yourself sometime!"

It was not until the evening of the third day that they saw the first other human being since leaving Fort Vermilion a month before. As the Metis trapper came down from his cabin on the riverbank to greet them, Brick asked, "Heard any news from upriver lately?" "Not much," was the non-committal reply.

Looking at his friend with the words, "I told you so," or something to that effect, Brick got the stubborn retort: "Boss, you don't know what you're saying. I told you I got a message and it's true."

Another 10 miles upstream and again the two travellers met some men, this time a logging crew busily working close to the riverbank. Again the query concerning news from upstream brought a negative answer. This time Brick only looked at Boucher with raised eyebrows. Boucher said nothing, but his jaw protruded stubbornly.

They were a few miles from their Peace River town destination and poling their canoe near the steep south bank when they heard a voice hail them from above. It was Allie, Fred Brick's brother, riding his pony toward them. "Boucher," said Allie as he approached, "I've bad news."

"Yes, I know," Boucher replied.

"You know," continued the puzzled Allie, "that three nights ago your wife had a baby girl, but it only lived two hours?"

"Yes, I know. I told Fred but he wouldn't believe me. Now if you don't mind I'll borrow your pony and go see my woman." With that Boucher mounted the pony and rode off, leaving the two dumbfounded brothers staring after him. ●

Bibliography

REMINISCENCES OF THE GREAT NORTH-WEST — S.B. Steele (Don Mead & Co. 1915)
KOOTENAI BROWN — William Rodney
JERRY POTTS: PLAINSMAN — Hugh Dempsey (Glenbow Institute—1966)
PIONEERS OF THE PEACE — Isabelle M. Campbell (Grande Prairie Oldtimers '75)
THE RUM-RUNNERS—Frank Anderson (Frontier Publishing 1968)
BLANKETS AND BEADS — J.G. MacGregor (Inst. of Applied Arts 1949)
ALBERTA FIELD FORCE OF '85 — F.C. Jamieson
CALGARY EDMONTON TRAIL — A. Belanger (Frontier Publishing 1973)
PADDLE WHEELS TO BUCKET WHEELS — J.G. MacGregor
THE CYPRESS HILLS — Tom Primrose (Frontier Publishing 1969)
THE NORTHWEST PASSAGE BY LAND — Milton and Cheadle (Coles Publishing 1970)
PEACE COUNTRY HERITAGE—E.C. Stacey (Western Producer Books 1974)
LAND OF TWELVE FOOT DAVIS—J.G. MacGregor
KLONDIKE RUSH THROUGH EDMONTON—J.G. MacGregor
GRANDE PRAIRIE (CAPITOL OF THE PEACE)—Isabell M. Campbell
BLOOD RED THE SUN—W.B. Cameron
SADDLE, SLED AND SNOWSHOE—John McDougall (Cincinnati, Jennings & Graham '96)
MONKMAN PASS HIGHWAY—E.C. Stacey 1974
JOHNNY CHINOOK—Robert Gard 1945
LOST LEMON MINE—(Frontier Publishing)
BUFFALO DAYS AND NIGHTS—Irene M. Spry (Glenbow-Alberta Institute 1976)
POSSIBILITIES OF CANADA ARE TRULY GREAT—T.D. Regehr
THE FRANK SLIDE STORY—Frank W. Anderson (Frontier Publishing 1968)
MAGAZINES—ALBERTA HISTORICAL REVIEW & ALBERTA HISTORY (Various)
FILES—EDMONTON JOURNAL, CALGARY HERALD, GLENBOW ALBERTA INSTITUTE, ALBERTA LEGISLATIVE LIBRARY, ALBERTA PROVINCIAL MUSEUM & ARCHIVES
CHAPS AND CHINOOKS—Foothills Historical Society
COMMUNITIES SIX—Accounts by Calgary Authors

Credits

I would like to thank Sheilagh S. Jameson, Chief Archivist at the Glenbow-Alberta Institute, through whose help I was able to stay at my typewriter, picking away, while she and her staff located reams of reference material and stacks of photographs for many of the stories. Miss Isabell M. Campbell of Grande Prairie and Mr. E.C. Stacey of Beaverlodge gave invaluable assistance with the sagas of people and events in the Peace River Country. I also owe many thanks to the staffs of the Provincial Museum and Archives and the Alberta Legistative Library for their help with photos and reference material and to volunteer librarian Janice Hopkins for her help with reference books from the Edmonton Public Library.

Special thanks to Mrs. C. Sanford of Edmonton for her contribution to the W.J. Tregillus story; to Dr. A.M. Carlisle for his frontier doctor story, and to Mrs. Daisy Lucas of Wetaskiwin for invaluable assistance with the Maud Lucas biography. Michael Verigin of Cowley supplied the material that made the Doukhobor history possible and I owe him a deep vote of thanks.

Without the writings of dozens of historians and others who were, and are, concerned with recording our rich heritage for posterity, this book could not have been compiled. Hopefully I have mentioned them all, either in the stories or in the bibliography.

I would also like to express my sincere appreciation to all individuals who kindly donated the use of photographs used in this book. Without your help many of the stories would have little or no artwork.

I would also like to thank the following institutions for contributing photographs: Glenbow-Alberta Institute, Alberta Provincial Museum and Archives, Alberta Legistative Library, Victoria Public Archives, Public Archives of Canada and the Saskatchewan Archives.